AMERICAN FAMILY

AMERICAN FAMILY

A NOVEL

CATHERINE MARSHALL-SMITH

SHE WRITES PRESS

Published 2017
Printed in the United States of America
ISBN: 978-1-63152-163-8 pbk
ISBN: 978-1-63152-164-5 ebk
Library of Congress Control Number: 2017934119

Cover design © Julie Metz, Ltd./metzdesign.com
Interior design by Tabitha Lahr

For information, address:
She Writes Press
1563 Solano Ave #546
Berkeley, CA 94707

She Writes Press is a division of SparkPoint Studio, LLC.

To my father, Rod Marshall, who taught me that in writing, less is better.

To my mother, Carol Ritchie Marshall, who was my original story teller and gave me my first library card.

I wish you had both lived long enough to see this book.

To my husband, Chris Smith, who patiently listened to my obsessive talk about Richard and Michael as though they were neighbors and not fictional characters, you are my rock and my foundation. You kept me safe, thank you.

MOVING DAY

Moving in with Michael should have been perfect. It wasn't supposed to feel like this. Richard stood on the honey-colored oak floor of the upstairs study and inhaled the scent of the Pacific Ocean coming through the dormer window. He whistled to convince himself he was happily preoccupied with unpacking, but the sound grated against his ears.

As he stooped to pick up another box, he saw the corner of the letter poking out, demanding attention. He yanked it out and unfolded it, as if somehow this time it would read differently. Brady's picture fell out. It was the standard school-picture pose. She smiled in it because she had been told to do so. He searched for himself in her face. Except for the curly hair, she didn't look like him or what he could remember of Brenda. He touched the picture and leaned closer to the window, but there was no breeze and the sun pressed in on him. Sweat trickled down his back. He closed the window and turned on the AC.

He shelved a box of books on the mahogany bookcases that matched the Civil War–era desk Michael had given him to encourage his writing on the same period. Richard had admired the desk in an antique store but had never mentioned it. Today while Michael was at work, it was delivered. The gesture, so tender, caught him off guard and made him cry. Now he ran his hand over the surface of the desk and then slipped the letter inside a paperback of Lillian Hellman's *Pentimento*. He'd never be able to write until he settled things with Brady.

Desperate to stop thinking, Richard decided to go running. Thinking hurt. Trying not to think hurt more. Maybe going for a run would clear his head. Richard selected running clothes that comforted him, his shirt from the Big Sur Marathon that qualified him for the Boston and the lucky hat he earned running it. He placed his crusty Nikes against the wall and began stretching mostly so he could tell himself he had done so. He pressed chest against thigh, but the image of Brady's face floated up in his mind and a spasm of guilt clenched his stomach. This was the moment to call, and he was letting it pass. But he should call Michael first. He switched legs, clutching his ankle as he pressed forward. He would call Michael, he thought, reaching for the phone. But he called information for Oregon instead, asked for the Nordland's number. His voice echoed through the empty house. He lowered it as if he were doing something sneaky, wrong, or both. The phone was slippery in his sweaty hand as he listened to it ring, half hoping, half dreading they wouldn't be home. He stared around the room and then at his feet.

He wanted to hang up. He *wouldn't* hang up. He'd put this off long enough, and now, safe and sober in Michael's house, he was ready. He was going to hang up after the next ring.

"Hello," a gruff voice answered.

He cleared his throat, "Frank Nordland, please."

"Speaking."

"Mr. Nordland, I'm Richard Lawson. I, well, I was married to your daughter."

"I know who you are, Mr. Lawson."

He could feel his heart pound. It was like those seconds at the top of the first hill of a rollercoaster before the plunge began. There was no getting off the ride now. He had identified himself.

"I wondered if I could talk to Brady." His voice sounded mincing. He hated it. His hand shook, and he fumbled with the phone. He pressed it harder against his ear, trying to steady it.

"She isn't here," Mr. Nordland said.

"Where is she?"

"In school, like most kids her age."

Richard cringed. Of course. Real parents knew when school was. He opened his mouth to apologize but Frank didn't give him the chance.

"Last I heard you were in some rehab in California. You still there?"

"That was a long time ago. I've been sober for three years, four months . . . and something," Richard said.

"You waited three years to call? Why now?"

Richard couldn't remember why. He just knew he desperately needed to talk to Brady. "I'm sorry I left the way I did. But I want to . . . to make amends. Make it up to her." Richard's voice trailed off. He was losing his one chance to do so. He forced himself to continue. "I think it would be good for her to know me too. I'm her father, Frank."

The silence went on so long that Richard wondered if Frank had hung up.

"You're not her father. I am," Frank said.

Richard held the phone away from his face, but he could still hear Frank railing.

"Kathleen and I have raised her and we love her!"

"Exactly," Richard interrupted. "I want a chance to love her too."

Frank talked over him. "We know she's allergic to strawberries and loves peaches. We were the ones the cops called after they pulled her from the wreck. We know she is afraid of the dark, and we know why. We know how to comfort her so she can sleep. You are nothing more than a name on her birth certificate." Frank stopped.

Richard could hear him breathe.

"I can't change the past. But I can make the future better," Richard said.

Frank continued. "It was hard enough losing her mom, but

what made it worse was the fact that after the accident her father didn't even care enough to show up. I know it's just a call, but it's going to make her ask where you've been. Are you ready to answer that question?"

Richard's thumb rested on the end-call button, and he leaned against the wall to steady himself. But he made himself answer. "I know I haven't done anything to make either of you trust me. But I think it would be good for her to know me." He held the phone with both hands to keep it still. "It wasn't easy for me to make this call."

Frank spoke slowly, enunciating every word. "I'll ask her if she wants to call you, but I won't force her. Make sure you know what you're doing is right for her and not just for yourself."

Richard started to say goodbye, but the dial tone stopped him. He held the phone to his chest.

"I am her father," Richard said out loud to himself. "It's just a phone call. I do have a right." But was he kidding himself? Was that really all he wanted?

He dropped the phone on the entry room sideboard and ran out of the door. He bounded down the red tile steps to the sidewalk. The path to the beach was wide, and people were sparse. They were probably at home starting their cocktail hour. An image of a gin and tonic flashed in his mind. A drink would feel good right now. Fear released adrenalin in his brain, and he sped up.

Around the third or fourth mile, his breathing finally became deep and rhythmic. He didn't need to be afraid. Michael loved him and wouldn't mind a phone call with his daughter—not when it meant so much to Richard's recovery. He would be honest with Michael, and the rest would fall into place. He raised his hands over his head as he leapt up the steps and into the house.

A savory smell of roasting beef drew Richard to the kitchen. "Be not afraid, for I bring you tidings of great joy. For unto us a child is born," he called out.

"Ritorna Vincitor" resounded as *Aida* blared from the speakers accompanied by Michael's singing, loud and off-key. "What? I can't hear you. The music is too loud," Michael shouted, turning down the volume.

Richard exhaled deeply, relaxed from the run and relieved to be able to share news of his phone call. Despite having driven the length of the state three times in the process of selling homes to the upwardly mobile from the overly entitled, Michael was in full cooking mode. He had changed from his Armani suit and tasseled loafers and now wore a flour-sack apron over his UCLA T-shirt and jeans. Enclosing Michael in a huge, musky bear hug, Richard ran his fingers through his naturally curly hair, noting that it had just been cut and now stood in tidy furrows.

"I love you," Michael said, "but you're sweaty and you're getting me sweaty. Please tell me you remember that we're having Tom and Vince over."

"Right, Tom and Vince . . ." When had Michael mentioned they were coming over? Richard didn't have a problem with Tom, Michael's ex, whose dot-com had survived the shakedown of the '90s and IPO'd, making him a millionaire overnight. He was a good guy, warm and funny, but Vince, his much-younger boyfriend, had a predatory nature and only Richard seemed to be able to discern it.

"What were you saying when you came in the door?" Michael asked. Testing the sauce, he looked at Richard. "You're all buzzed up about something."

Richard crossed his arms and stepped back, bouncing slightly on his toes. "I called Frank today."

Michael opened the oven and lifted the roasted vegetables, took a deep sniff. He smiled before pivoting and placing them on the dark green granite counter.

"Frank who?"

"Nordland—in Oregon." Richard said. His breath caught and he dug his fingers into his upper arms.

"Oregon? What? You did what?" Michael stepped back from the counter. Richard shot forward and closed the hot oven, straightening up to catch Michael's round-eyed stare.

"Shit! What were you thinking?"

"I'm sorry, I felt I had to. And anyway you said you wanted a child." Richard said, his hands outreached with fingers splayed.

"I do. But now? Jesus, we just moved in together." Michael punctuated his words with open palms. "And tonight we have guests." He exhaled and crossed his arms over his chest.

"It's just a phone call." Richard touched Michael's shoulder, but Michael brushed his hand away.

"Just a phone call? It's so much more than just a phone call." He ran his fingers through his hair. "Go get ready. We'll discuss this later."

He raced up the stairs to shower and then paused at the top. What if the grandparents called during dinner tonight? Should he turn off his phone? He looked down at Michael, still busy cooking, and then at the table in the alcove next to the bay window, which would offer a view of the setting sun. The table was decorated with a centerpiece of pink magnolia blossoms in a glittering cut-crystal bowl. Beneath the flowers was the pink batiste tablecloth embossed with Michael's grandmother's initials. Matching napkins lay beneath silver cutlery that reflected the candlelight.

Maybe they wouldn't call tonight.

He emerged from the shower freshly scrubbed and smelling of lavender, lemon, and mint. All of Michael's soaps came in elaborate bottles with French writing, and Richard was never completely sure if he was putting soap into his hair or washing his body with conditioner. He smelled like Michael now though—which was all that mattered.

The comb moved easily through Richard's frizzy curls made dark by the shower water. He smiled at himself in the mirror. Sobriety became him. As the sober years progressed, his complexion had gone from red to ashen, and now he was tan. He'd lost weight and then gained a little, and now he was healthy and slim. He pulled on a pair of Lucky Brand jeans, topped by a Ralph Lauren striped shirt, and unbuttoned it lower than usual. He looked at himself critically in the mirror. The outfit was worthy of the impending event, he decided. He descended the stairs and rounded the corner into the kitchen, where Michael was bending to test the pastry. He considered snuggling up behind Michael but drew back at the last minute.

Richard cleared his throat. "How do you like me now, cowboy?"

"You'll do." Michael sighed and then smiled. "You look great, as always. Let's enjoy our evening."

The doorbell rang and Richard followed Michael to the door. "If I'm really good, can I be dessert's dessert?"

"Absolutely." Michael pushed Richard against the wall and gave him a deep kiss and then reached for the door.

FUN WITH TOM AND VINCE

⚓ ⚓ ⚓ ⚓ ⚓ ⚓ ⚓

The door sprung open before Michael's fingers could make contact with the knob. Tom held out a potted begonia, and Vince handed Richard a bottle of non-alcoholic wine.

"How thoughtful," Richard said, accepting the bottle and exchanging a look with Michael.

"I'll take it," Michael said. And as he did, Richard whispered, "Non-alcoholic wine is for non-alcoholics."

Michael nodded.

Despite his fifty-seven years, Tom moved with the energy of a twelve-year-old boy. He was slim and naturally tanned, and he bore what seemed to be a permanent smile that caused crinkles to form around his eyes. Richard remembered that Tom once described his hair as black with gray highlights. He wore an unconstructed white silk blazer over a pastel blue oxford cloth shirt. His unbelted slacks matched the jacket. He wore his sleek, brown leather lace-ups, without socks.

Vince, twenty years younger and a foot taller, jingled his keys as he placed them on the oak sideboard. "I don't want them to wear a hole in my pants pocket," he said to Richard, who smiled and gave him fleeting eye contact before he moved to Michael's side.

"Great to see you, Mickey and Dicky!" Tom said. "I hope you like the wine. You should not have to compromise taste to be alcohol free."

Michael ushered them into the living room, where he poured the wine for the guests and brought out sparkling water for himself and Richard.

Tom and Vince settled deeply into the chocolate brown leather couch. Richard pushed himself into the wingback Windsor chair as their guests launched into a travelogue about the lavish vacation in Napa from which they'd just returned.

This might have been interesting, but the conversation centered on their pug, who had contracted food poisoning after eating some improperly refrigerated catfish. They had dashed from their hotel room in the foothills to downtown to find a vet in the middle of the night because the poor dear was erupting from both ends and they desperately feared dehydration.

Richard tried to tune them out and savored the aroma of the appetizers Michael was arranging on a silver tray. Tom had produced his iPad, loaded with two thousand pictures from their trip—but all roads led back to the ailing dog.

Richard feigned an intake of breath to show how anxious he was to find out whether the beleaguered pug pulled through at last. This encouraged Tom, who took hold of Richard's elbow and leaned closer and angled the iPad at him. "Do you want to see?"

Richard drew back, not wanting to see Pugsly lying in a pool of his own vomit. But Tom shifted to another slide show that showed Pugsly in drag, Pugsly dressed as the Easter Bunny, Pugsly as Santa, and Pugsly as a Jack O' Lantern."

"This one is my favorite," Tom said. "It really captures his nobility, don't you think?" He held out a picture of Pugsly in silhouette, staring off into the distance in continental ennui.

Richard gave the picture a passing glance, realized he was rolling his eyes, and blinked instead.

"He slips him his Viagra." Vince tilted his head toward Tom.

"He should have some joy in his life," Tom said. "He's such a good dog."

"I told him it doesn't work that way," Vince said, leaning away from Tom to whisper to Richard. "It increases the blood flow, not the desire."

Richard nodded but couldn't think of anything else to say.

Michael gave him an understanding smile as he set down the tray of savory canapés next to the small stack of delicately flowered Limoges plates.

Richard realized he hadn't eaten all day and lunged for the food. He put an entire pastry in his mouth. He bit down into the crust of one that was filled with steaming spinach and melted cheese and regretted it. While sucking air all around the morsel, he tried to chew and swallow quickly. He could visualize its progress by following the burn all the way to his stomach. What he could taste of it through the seared flesh on his tongue was wonderful.

As Tom and Vince's chatter bounced to other travels and the final remodeling of their faux Versailles in Palos Verdes, Richard emptied the tray.

"Looks like we're done with the first course," Michael said.

Richard looked down at the now-empty tray and saw Michael's arching eyebrows reflected in the silver. "Sorry," he said through a full mouth.

"Let's move to the table, shall we?"

"Oh, this is splendid," Tom said, as Michael led the way. "You're giving us a lovely soiree, like old times."

Michael smiled and lowered his eyes.

Richard felt a stab of jealousy and raised his gaze to Vince, who leaned toward him, nodding. Richard stood and escaped to the dining room table.

Michael placed both couples on the sides of the table facing one another, rather than seating himself and Richard at the heads of the rectangular table. It was more democratic, he said. Richard would have felt safer at the head of the table. He stared at the flowers as Michael retrieved the salad and began tossing it with balsamic vinegar and olive oil infused with lemongrass and garlic.

Richard always found it hard to make small talk because his mind seemed to have a small army of pop-up ads that shot through his consciousness at random. He really was trying to listen, but there was so much interference that he was afraid his response would be illogical. Now, making it all much worse, he was distracted by the possibility of the Nordlands calling. He could feel the weight of his phone in his pocket. He looked up and found both guests staring at him, waiting for him to answer an unheard question. *Oh shit!*

"We haven't really thought about a dog. Have we, Richard?" Michael bustled in from the kitchen giving Richard a knowing smile. He lowered a tray of plates bearing Beef Wellington, asparagus, and parsnips.

"Beef," Richard smiled into his plate. "I knew I smelled it. Have you had some sort of culinary conversion?"

Michael's abstinence from alcohol had morphed into control of food. Richard admired Michael's fierce dedication to a vegan diet but couldn't quite make the change. Michael's serving beef for Richard was a true act of love. Richard jumped up and kissed him.

Michael blushed and smiled, clearly pleased that he'd scored a hit with Richard.

"This is a party to welcome you, so I served what you would want."

"What are you having?" Richard asked.

"The same thing, only with tofu. I don't see the difference."

All eyes focused on his plate, which contained identical pastry with gelatinous goo oozing from it.

"No difference at all," Richard said, picking up his knife and fork.

"Pets are wonderful," Tom continued, as if there had been no interruption. "They really round you out and make you a family. You should definitely consider a pug. They're so smart and loyal."

Richard flicked a look up from his plate and caught Vince staring at him. Vince nodded as though agreeing with Tom. Richard looked back at his plate and cut into the tender meat, such a beautiful red under the pastry. He lifted the forkful to his mouth and savored the mélange of garlic and thyme on the shallots and mushrooms. There was creamy peppercorn sauce on the parsnips, and Richard could hardly wait to get it in his mouth. But since he had been given this wonderful meal, he felt he needed to join the conversation.

"We don't need rounding out, do we, Michael?" Richard said, swallowing beef and pastry that he'd dipped in the peppercorn sauce. "I have a child—a daughter." He looked up from his food and added (possibly, he realized, a little too late), "*We* have a daughter."

The participants at the table fell mute. Slowly. In unison, it seemed.

"Richard, stop," Michael said, his eyes wide and jaw set.

Richard felt his face blaze and looked at the floor. "She's from a previous relationship," he said, shrugging.

"We somehow assumed that," Tom said. Vince smirked. The two exchanged glances and barely suppressed smiles. Vince turned his gaze on Michael, eager to see his reaction.

"We've never even met her," Michael said, staring at Richard. "Neither of us."

Just then Richard's phone rang. All eyes turned in the direction of the sound.

"I have to get this," Richard said, pulling his phone out and bolting for the den.

"Let it go to voicemail," Michael called after him.

Richard slammed the beveled glass doors shut and gasped his greeting. There was silence. He moaned audibly. He'd betrayed his excitement to everyone, and this was probably just some robo-dialing phone bank.

"Hello?" he heard a small voice say just as he went to hit END. "Hello?"

Richard turned away from Michael and their guests and sank into the desk chair.

"Hello," he answered. "Who is this?"

"This is Brady Lawson." She had his name. Of course she did. All these years, she'd only existed in his thoughts. But she was real.

"How are you?" he asked.

"I'm fine," she said. "I thought you were dead."

"Rumors of my death have been greatly exaggerated."

"What?"

"Never mind, I'm not dead. Why did you think so?"

"I asked about you and why you never called or anything. And Grandpa said you were probably dead. When I never heard from you, I figured that must be true."

Richard gritted his teeth. "How's school?"

"Fine."

"What's going on in your life?"

"Nothing."

"Got any hobbies?"

"Not really."

This was worse than talking to Tom and Vince.

"Got any travel plans for the summer?"

"Nope."

Richard sighed.

"I'm going with the marching band to Disneyland for spring break, though."

Richard rested his hand on his chest and felt his heart thump. "I live very close to Disneyland."

They talked about their favorite rides, which forced Richard to reach way back to his childhood. "I remember one ride on a snowy mountain," Richard said.

"The Matterhorn!" Brady said. "That's a good one. But it's not the scariest anymore. There's Space Mountain."

Richard wasn't listening to the words as much as delighting in the soft and gentle rise and fall of Brady's ten-year-old voice. When she laughed, he felt tears rise and ached for all the laughs he had missed. At one point Richard heard conversation in the background. "Is that your grandparents I hear?" he asked.

"No, it's the TV. They're watching *Jeopardy*. They like to see how much money they'd win if they were on the show."

"I would love to get to know you. Do you have an email address?" Richard asked.

"Yeah."

Richard's breathing became shallow as he wrote it down. With email he would be able to talk to Brady without the grandparents knowing.

"This'll be fun," she said. "I've always thought about meeting you. Do you have other kids? A wife?"

"No."

"Why not?"

"Just didn't work out," Richard said.

"Grandma says it's time to hang up now. It's a school night."

Richard wasn't ready to let go of her. He stood, pressing the phone harder into his ear. "I live very near Disneyland. Maybe I could meet you there?"

"I can ask my Grandma."

Richard tried to stop her, but he could hear Brady's breathing change as she moved. He blew air noisily through his lips as he listened to the phone being passed to another hand.

"Hello."

Richard straightened in the chair as he recognized Frank's voice.

"Hello, sir." Richard heard his voice squeak, and then there was silence. "Brady mentioned she's going to Disneyland, which is very close to where I live. I was wondering if I could meet her there." He paused, but there was still silence. "I've never seen her, and you're so far away, and it just seems like this would be a good, easy way for us to get together.

"No."

Had he imagined that? Frank's voice was so quiet. "Excuse me, did you say some—"

"No, you may not visit her at Disneyland."

"I am her father," Richard forced himself to say, "and—"

"Good evening, Richard."

Richard kept the phone pressed to his ear even after he heard the beep signaling the call had been ended. He stared through the French doors at the trio of men silhouetted in the candlelight. Michael laughed at something Tom said. He wished the guests were gone. He needed Michael.

Richard pushed open the French doors and padded across the Turkish rug, clearing his throat. Michael turned to Richard and his smile was replaced by a look of irritation, making Richard want to retreat to the den.

"So, everything okay?" Tom asked.

"Work?" Vince asked.

"Something like that, yeah." Richard sat down at the table and stole a glance at Michael, who gave him cold, passing eye contact. Tom touched Vince's arm and nodded. They stood, thanked Michael, looked sympathetically at Richard, and escaped through the door.

GLASNOST

As the door closed, Richard stared at the floor and wrapped his arms around his chest, each hand holding tight at the elbows. "Was I gone long?"

Michael snorted. "Do you want any dessert? We ate it while you were on the phone." Without waiting for an answer, he scooped up a heaping portion of the chocolate soufflé and sloshed it onto Richard's plate. The puffy dessert was withered like old skin, and the creamy inside had melted and was seeping out. The mess slid across the small dessert plate, barely stopping at the edge.

"I'm sorry," Richard said.

"So am I." Michael began stacking dessert plates haphazardly onto his forearm, and Richard followed him.

"Let me clean up. I want to help," Richard said.

"Your help isn't helpful."

Richard winced as Michael pushed the dishes into the soapy water, drenching his shirt and clattering plates against one another. Michael wouldn't put hand-painted Limoges in the dishwasher, but with the way he was slamming them together, Richard thought they might be safer in the machine.

"I had to take that call," Richard said.

"No you didn't, Richard," Michael said, turning and staring at Richard.

Richard's shoulders caved slightly and he felt his face soften. "Still," he said, "Mickey and Dickey! Come on, Michael, what do you see in those guys?"

"What do you object to, Richard?"

"They're so . . . I don't know." Richard paused.

"Faggy? Or does 'queer' feel better in your mouth? They are openly gay and proud of it. Isn't that what we all want? What you want?"

"No, it's what you want me to want. I don't know what I want. It cannot be healthy to carry around a picture of a pug pumpkin in your wallet and to dote on it as though it were a child. If I had to sit through one more puppy story, I was going to be the one vomiting."

"Maybe you're jealous of what they have. Maybe we should consider getting a dog." Michael had turned back to the dishes, and his face reddened with his vigorous scrubbing of the soufflé pan.

"We don't need a dog to substitute for a child. We do have a daughter. That was her during dinner. That's the call I took." Richard held his breath and looked at Michael. "I know, I know." Richard held his hands palms open in front of him. "I should have talked to you first. I'm sorry. It just seemed right, you know. She's going to be at Disneyland in two weeks." He paused and shrugged, adding, "I can't see her though. Frank, the grandfather, said I can't visit her there." Richard opened his palms. "I don't think he can do that. I may be the world's shittiest father, but I am her father. Do you think he can tell me I can't spend a day with her at Disneyland?"

Michael dried his hands on the dishtowel and walked past Richard into the living room, bumping his shoulder as he stepped around him, and dropped into a Windsor chair.

Richard stopped and looked at Michael, as if willing him to speak. His palms hung open at his side in a silent appeal for Michael's support. He couldn't give up and so he continued. "I am sorry. I should have talked to you before I called."

"You sure as shit should have told me. Jesus, Richard, you've just moved in here. I can't deal with this right now." Michael sat with his shoulders caved and his hands limp on his thighs.

Outside the timer turned on the sprinklers and the porch light. The men remained silent in the dimly lit room. Around the corner, the candlelight barely lit the remaining silver pieces.

"I'm sorry. I felt that if I didn't do it now, I'd never do it." Richard said.

Michael shifted in the chair and gestured toward the kitchen. "I need to go to bed. We'll clean up in the morning." He stood and began to climb the stairs but stopped in the middle to look down at Richard, who stood in the living room staring at the rug.

"Richard?" Michael said.

"Yes?" Richard looked up and noted Michael's drawn face and set mouth.

"Where are we going with this?" Michael asked. "I mean, it was just a phone call, but that phone call became a visit in Disneyland. What is it that you are trying to do?"

Richard shrugged. "I don't know. I know I need her, and I think she needs me. Calling her was the next right thing." Richard looked up at Michael, his eyes pleading. "Or it seemed right at the time." He put his hands in his pockets and stared at the rug.

Michael cleared his throat before he spoke, causing Richard to brace. "Is that why you moved in here? So you could get your daughter?"

"No, no, it's not like that," Richard said, and he realized that was exactly what it looked like. But it couldn't be true. He had loved Michael since they met in the overly air-conditioned room in the basement of the treatment center that smelled of burned coffee and stale doughnuts. Their fingers had touched as Michael passed a clipboard with a sign-in sheet to him, and Richard had felt such a surge of electricity he was surprised he hadn't seen a spark. Since that moment his sole goal had been to be closer to Michael, and that meant moving in with him to share his life.

Michael's voice rose. "You didn't think you'd look as good or as secure in that apartment in Culver City, so you moved into my house?"

"We said we would contact her when we were ready," Richard said. "You said you wanted a family but it wasn't in the cards for you. You said we'd reconnect with her. You were happy to be able to have a family." Richard held out his hands with each phrase, beseeching.

Michael had turned around fully on the stairs but made no move to come down. "I said we'd connect with her when the time was right. Now isn't good."

"Then when, Michael? When is right in your mind? Five, ten years from now? She's ten. She'll be a teenager soon—all emotionally closed off and shut down. I'm sorry, I wish I had called you first, but I felt myself losing courage."

"You felt yourself losing courage so you called the *grandfather*? After all, it is my house you're moving your kid into." Michael jabbed his chest with his finger.

"You said you wouldn't say that," Richard said. "You said it would be *our* house. Not just yours. I knew this would happen and that's why I wanted to buy the other house. So it really would be our house, but the neighborhood wasn't good enough for you."

"It was unsafe, Richard—there was gang graffiti. Is getting caught in a drive-by an experience you need to have? Not to mention that it would be stupid to give up what I have here to move away to a worse place."

"Listen to yourself, 'what *I* have here.' Like I'm what—a renter? I knew this would happen. We haven't even been here a whole day. And you're saying—these are *my* rooms so you can't have your kid visit." Richard threw his hands up in disgust and then clenched his arms around his chest.

"Stop it, Richard. It's not fair. Bringing a kid in here, however briefly, is different from making sure you feel at home," Michael stated, leaning toward Richard before turning away and heading up the stairs. "I'm going to bed. Michael called over his shoulder, "We'll talk in the morning,"

Richard watched as Michael disappeared from where he sat at the base of the stairs. The light went out in the bedroom, leaving him alone in the dark. Was a phone call with Brady enough, or was it custody he had always wanted? Was he using Michael? Was he sabotaging himself? The thoughts chased one another and he could not shut them off.

Richard was rubbing his temples when he felt Michael's hand on his shoulder. He covered Michael's hand with both of his own and waited.

"I can't sleep without you," Michael said. "Come to bed."

Richard stood. Still holding Michael's hand, he followed him up the stairs.

NOW WHAT?

Although Richard and Michael hadn't done much more than drop from exhaustion last night, Richard felt buoyed by hope simply because Michael knew he wanted to contact Brady. Honesty cleanses wounds, and hope heals them. He hurried downstairs, finished cleaning up, and made coffee. He carried the *Los Angeles Times* under one arm and a white ceramic mug of black coffee in each hand.

"Smells good," Michael said, and then he added, "Can he do that?"

Despite the lack of context, Richard knew exactly what Michael was asking. Could Frank stop Richard from visiting Brady on the school trip to Disneyland? Richard knew he needed a lawyer to find out. He didn't have the money for that—but Michael did.

"I don't know what to do," Richard said.

"Okay, before that, let's work out what it is you—we—want," Michael said. Richard felt light with euphoria and squeezed his coffee mug.

"I do want to get to know your child and have her in my life," Michael said. Richard could feel Michael watching him as he spoke.

"I am certain that she is very special," he paused, "and very, very lovable. But let's please go slowly. Understand?"

"Okay," Richard's mouth was a straight line and he nodded slowly.

"Tighten your seatbelts. We're in for a bumpy ride," Michael said, reaching for a pencil and yellow legal pad.

OREGON

⚞ ⚟ ⚞ ⚟ ⚞ ⚟ ⚞

Ever since the phone call from her father, Brady's grandparents had looked at her like she was dying. She really wanted them to stop. She wasn't going anywhere. She would see her father, and then life would go on the way it always had.

So when she heard Grandpa Frank yell up the stairs this morning that she'd better hurry or she'd be late for school, she was actually happy. Finally, he wasn't tiptoeing around her. Finally, he was acting normal again. She lugged the huge cage that housed her class's two hamsters, Bear and Whacko, and started down the stairs.

Wobbling under the weight of the cage, she tried not to scrape the walls, but in the process she knocked a bunch of books off the bookcases built into the stairwell. Finally she handed it off to Grandpa Frank at the base of the stairs.

"You be careful, now!" Grandma shook her finger at Grandpa.

Grandpa had had a heart attack earlier in the year, but he continued working at the ranch. Sometimes Brady worried that he did it to pay for her private school, but she also knew he hated being lazy and never went on a vacation, so what else was he going to do anyway? Grandma talked a lot about healthy eating, and for her that meant switching to decaffeinated coffee and from butter to margarine. Brady heard Grandpa say to Grandma that making these changes made him want to die before God called him, which he was pretty sure was a sin. Brady could tell this made Grandma mad and she never mentioned food again. It seemed to Brady that Grandpa wanted to die working. Brady could tell this scared Grandma, so Brady felt guilty when Grandpa lugged the heavy cage past her fuming grandmother.

Brady watched Grandpa move his arthritic knees stiffly and brace his jaws to keep the pain from showing on his face. She followed him out and shoved her backpack onto the floor in front of her seat as Grandpa lowered the cage into the bed of the weathered white truck. She peaked through the bars of the cage.

"You know, I didn't find a single snail on Nana's lettuce this morning." Grandpa swept his eyes off the rearview mirror and down to Brady. "There were so many yesterday," he continued.

"I collected the snails," Brady said. "I didn't think you'd care, and I wanted them to live because everyone, even snails, is part of God's plan and if they're killed, they can't do what God wants." Brady studied Grandpa from the side.

He stared at her sidelong. "How many snails did you get out of the garden?"

"As many as I could find. I don't know—thirty-seven or something." Brady shrugged. "Are you mad?"

"Why would I be mad? If you're willing to cart them out of the garden, I don't care what you do with them. What in the world *are* you doing with them?"

"I put them behind the school, where they can eat the garbage that the cafeteria ladies throw out. I think this may be God's plan. Nana's lettuce and basil are safe, and so are the snails, who are eating the garbage." Brady waited for Grandpa to say something.

Grandfather laughed and touched the tip of her nose gently.

"You have created the Underground Railroad for snails. You are the Joan of Arc for escargot. The Mollusk Resistance Movement. The Invertebrate Liberation Front. And without doubt the kindest, sweetest soul I know."

"How come you don't want my dad to go to Disneyland with me?" She held her breath.

Grandpa shook his head. "There are things you don't know, Brady."

"Like what?"

Brady so hated the silence that followed. "I know he was drunk a lot," she said quickly. "And I know he was in the hospital for it. But he just wants to see me." She stole a glance at her grandfather. She knew very little about her mother and father because she sensed that the memories were painful for her Grandma and Grandpa. She had stopped praying for her father to come back, but she had never stopped hoping. She wasn't unhappy with her grandparents. But she did want to be like everyone else and have a dad to make a card for on Father's Day or coach her in soccer. She even felt a pang when a kid said to her, "My Dad grounded me for not turning in my work."

We'll see," Grandpa said, and he stared through the bug-spattered windshield. Brady knew better than to push it. This wasn't asking for ice cream after school or having a friend over. There was something big about this that scared them.

GRACE

Frank drove the rest of the thirty-minute trip in brooding silence. His stomach clenched, and he muttered under his breath as though Richard were there to hear.

Thirty minutes later, they pulled up in front of Valley Christian School. Brady climbed out and pulled her backpack on. "I'll carry the cage in, Grandpa."

"Not with that on your back, you won't, Frank said, and hauled the cage out of the truck and started up the cement stairs to the school. With the cage in his hands, he could not use the rail, so he leaned against it with his hip to balance himself. Cars pulled up to the curb behind him, depositing laughing kids who jostled him as they streamed by. His knees hurt with each step and sweat began to roll into his eyes. He was relieved to see the principal Edmund Hammond and headed for him. Without the rail to steady him, Frank staggered.

Mr. Hammond closed the gap between them, his hands reaching ahead to take the cage.

Frank breathed deeply and pulled out a handkerchief to wipe the sweat off his brow.

"Are you okay, Mr. Nordland?" Mr. Hammond asked. "My office is just inside. Go in and have a seat and take a rest. I'll take this to Brady's classroom."

Frank forced himself to say, "I'll be okay. I just need a minute."

"Thanks, Grandpa." Brady looked up at him, and seeing his ashen face, said, "You okay?"

"I'm fine," Frank said, touched by her concern. In that minute she looked so much like her mother, Brenda. Brady was what Brenda could have been without drugs—sweet and loving. Frank breathed deeply and smoothed Brady's hair. He brushed her forehead with a kiss before she joined the throngs of other kids and pounded up the stairs.

The last time he saw Brenda alive, she was visibly pregnant and newly married to a silent young man who stood behind her with his hands in his pockets, Richard Lawson. Frank pictured Brenda as she had looked that night with pink hair and pierced lips. She had shivered in an unseasonable midriff top that did not meet her cotton peasant skirt. Her belly poked out over the skirt with a tawdry little earring in its navel. He remembered wondering what kind of life would be nurtured in such an unseemly pleasure dome. But now he knew—Brady.

The school front fell peacefully silent. A breeze blew over his glistening face as he savored the fragrant April air. Whistling as he returned to the truck, Frank mapped out the day ahead. As he doubled back to the ranch, unwanted memories of Brenda's death played through his mind: being awakened by the police knocking at four in the morning, his long, cold walk to the door, and the certainty that this was going to be the news he had dreaded for most of Brenda's life. He was not surprised to hear that Brenda had died, but he did feel he had failed her. He and Kathleen had spent large portions of their retirement on rehab, counseling, and hospitals, but more than that they had invested hope. This program or that hospital would be different, they told themselves. This one will save her life. All hope died with that knock on the door.

He remembered how Brady looked when he and Kathleen met her. She was seated on a gurney in the hospital after the accident.

Although malnourished and dirty, her eyes were bright, and she looked at them as though they were just the people she had been hoping for her whole life. In the five years that had followed, they had done everything in their power to live up to that hope. Raising Brady gave their lives purpose and atonement for all that had gone wrong with Brenda; but more than that, she was just fun to be around. It made him sick to realize that Richard Lawson, the silent boy who got Brenda pregnant, then married and abandoned her, was back to wreck all of that.

GOING FOR HELP

M ichael went after selecting a lawyer with singleness of purpose.
He logged criteria onto a spreadsheet that included experience, cost, and proximity as well as questions that revealed openness
to gay men becoming parents. The spreadsheet allowed him to rank
every family law attorney within fifty miles of their home.

Michael was jarred from his reverie when Richard snapped
his fingers in the air and said, "I like this guy, and he's even close.
We just hop on the I-10 and off again."

"I don't know," Michael said, "he's only got four years of experience, and we agreed that we wanted someone with six to ten."
Michael was determined to keep control of the lawyer selection.

Richard interrupted, "Yeah, but he can practice law in both
California and Oregon; that's not been easy to find. Plus, what
he lacks in experience he makes up for in enthusiasm. When I
first phoned him, he and his brother—they're partners in the
business—were expecting a call from a friend and answered the
phone, 'The best and the brightest attorneys in America.' When
they heard my voice, they were so embarrassed; they couldn't do

enough for me. I love that." Richard laughed before he added, "And he's cheaper."

Richard held the phone in his hand, sounding threatening. "Okay, this is it, I'm making the appointment. Can I, please?"

Michael waved his hands over the now-marked-up spread-sheet as though making an incantation. He did not want to make a mistake. "Okay, go ahead," he said, watching Richard squint at the phone numbers.

"Your glasses are on your head." Michael said.

Richard lowered them to his eyes and punched in the numbers. After a minute, Richard covered the receiver and whispered to Michael, "He answers his own phone. Is that good or bad? I don't see it on the sheet."

Michael snorted and rolled his eyes.

Turning back to the phone, Richard greeted Ryan and asked for an appointment.

Michael hissed in the background, "Don't tell him he has the job yet. We're not ready."

Richard waved him away, pressing his finger in his open ear. "Today? You're available today?" He looked at Michael and raised his eyebrows, mouthing, *too easy?*

Michael had to think but shrugged his shoulders.

Richard hung up.

Michael stared at him before asking, "Now what?"

"Now we go," Richard said.

The trip to the lawyer's office was so brief that Michael pointed out that the same song that was playing on the radio when they left was still playing when they arrived. After parking, they were a little confused as to how to get into the building and wound up clamoring over some hedges.

"Aha, outside steps," Richard pointed out, adding, "he mentioned these, and the office is at the top." He led the way up the steps to a yellow-and-white painted door with glass paneling on the top half.

Michael looked at the door critically. "Odd choice for a law office."

"I think it was a hair salon in a previous life," Richard answered, grimacing as he stepped inside. Just at that moment a boyish man in a rumpled shirt and slacks with his tie hanging over one shoulder rounded the corner into the reception area. He was weighed down by a box of files, which he half lowered, half dropped on what appeared to be a cherry dining room table. He came toward them with his hand extended, introducing himself and taking their hands in turn. He vigorously squeezed and shook each one.

Five foot ten and blond, Ryan Stephens had the bulky muscular build of an aging high school football player whose current profession precluded regular workouts.

As Ryan turned from Michael to Richard, Michael made a show of shaking out his fingers and smiled at Richard.

"Come on back," Ryan said as he wove a path between the banker's boxes. Michael watched Richard's eyes settle on the young man's butt and then exchanged a look of appreciation with Richard. This might not be all bad. Ryan had made the cut using criteria not on the spreadsheet.

"Are you moving in or out?" Michael asked.

"In. Our last place was a storefront in a scary neighborhood. The door was shot through last month."

Michael raised his eyebrows and noticed that Ryan hurried to explain, "It wasn't intended for us, you understand. It was just random gunfire. We were down there to provide affordable legal help for people who otherwise wouldn't have had any, but I guess stray bullets showed us the line we weren't willing to cross."

"Indeed," Michael said and nodded.

Ryan opened the door to his office and gestured at the chairs. Michael marveled at the décor—or lack of it, since not one chair matched another. The room was filled with furniture that seemed like it had been left behind instead of chosen. It was, however, brightly lit overhead and dominated by a large open window. On either side of the window stood two metal file cabinets, one with a gaping top drawer blocked from closing by a fistful of files.

"Did you bring the birth certificate?" Ryan asked.

Richard handed him the file.

Ryan leafed through the file, extracted the birth certificate, and read it closely. "So you want a visit with your daughter?" Ryan asked, sinking into a scarred oak chair that swayed under his weight.

"I do," Richard said.

"How come just a visit?" Ryan asked.

Michael felt his stomach tighten. He expected the lawyer to slow things down and bring reason into this emotional transaction.

Richard looked up at Ryan.

"You are the biological father, and the only surviving parent," Ryan said, holding up the birth certificate and pointing to Richard's name. "That gives you the right to drive to school and pick her up." He sat back, making the chair creak. The sound grated on Michael's nerves.

"It's that easy?" Richard asked.

"No," Ryan said, shaking his head. "Not by a long shot. The grandparents can raise a ruckus, and that will make it hard, but you have the right. If they had adopted her, and I can't figure out why they didn't," Ryan stared at the birth certificate and scratched his head, "it would be over for you. Since they didn't, you have every right to parent her."

Michael uncrossed his legs, sat straight up, and leaned toward the lawyer. "We just want a visit. We have never seen this child. Richard left before she was born."

"Why now? Brady's ten. You've known how to find her for three years. What's making you look her up now?" Ryan asked Richard.

Here we go. Michael looked over at Richard.

Richard lowered his head and pressed his hands into his thighs. "I'm ready now. I wasn't before. I was a hopeless drunk, and I had no business having a kid." He looked up at Ryan and shrugged. "But I did. Have a kid. I just wasn't a father. But I'm ready now. I want her to know that she has a father. That she's not an orphan." He shrugged again.

"What makes you think you won't be irresponsible now?" Ryan's eyes never wavered from Richard's. They were selling the lawyer on the feasibility of the case, Michael realized. He felt the cold metal of the folding chair seep through his shirt.

Richard said, "I've been clean and sober for three years—we both are. We met in recovery. We're committed to each other. It's different—I'm different inside and out." Richard tapped his chest and gave Michael a long look, begging for reassurance.

Michael felt himself sliding away from his own sensibilities and into Richard's vision of an instant family. Having this child in their house so soon seemed wrong for them. But pleasing Richard was Michael's first priority, and the look on Richard's face made him ache. Michael couldn't protect Richard from what might happen in the future.

"We just want a visit," Michael said to Richard, cuing his next line.

Richard turned to Ryan. "I do—I just want a visit with her, Ryan, and the grandfather won't let me."

"They're afraid you're going to take her, Mr. Lawson. They're defending their family. Why should they let you into her life? It seems like they have been raising her just fine without you. I'm looking at the notes, and she's in private school. Christian."

Oh, perfect. This is getting worse. Michael watched Ryan look up from his notes and stare at Richard, who held his gaze for a full beat before he spoke.

"I'm her biological father. Her real father. Her grandparents have taken care of her, but they aren't her parents. I could love her and let her know she has a real family with me. There's a difference." Richard paused. "I think."

Ryan, who had been taking notes, stopped, looked at Richard, and asked, "So life would be *realer* for her if she knew you because of your DNA? You think her grandparents *don't* love her? They've been with her every day for the last five of her ten years. What's love to a child if not being taken care of? What makes you think you can do a better job of loving her? Especially since you're only asking for a visit?"

Richard shook his head. "I'm not saying they don't love her." He jutted his chin forward and continued, "Brenda knew her own birth had been unplanned. How could she know that unless her parents had told her? She thought she was worthless because of that. These same people are raising my kid. I'm grateful to them, but my daughter needs to know me too. You said that I am her only living, biological parent, and I am now ready to parent. I believe she needs me in the same way I need her."

Ryan sat back in his chair and took his two hands and shaped them in a rectangle around the image of Richard's face, saying, "I wish I had a video tape of what you just said. That is what a judge needs to hear. You need to avoid attacking the grandparents and focus instead on what you can offer that they cannot. You are her one and only father, and you are ready to be in her life. California and Oregon like parents to parent."

Michael shifted in his seat and looked at Ryan.

"Even if it's only for a visit," Ryan said to Michael.

Ryan read from the file and said, "And then there is that one other problem to which I alluded. The grandparents have been paying $15,000-plus for tuition at a private Christian school, and they attend a Baptist church with her. I'm wondering what brand of Christian they are—the 'love others as you would love God' Christians, or the 'Christians of a vengeful God,' who are going to have serious problems letting their recently sober gay son-in-law have anything to do with their granddaughter?" Ryan paused then asked, "Do they even know you're gay?" He spoke with the speed of bullets from a gun.

Richard looked at Michael with squinted eyes and clenched brows.

"We don't understand the question," Michael said.

"Sorry, I'll slow down." Ryan smiled, blushing. "What brand of Christians are your in-laws, loving and inclusive or vengeful and exclusive?"

Richard grimaced. "This is mostly based on what Brenda said. I only met them once. They said grace at dinner and prayed at night. They went to church every Sunday. And when Brenda refused to do any of it, they told her she'd go to hell."

"That sounds vengeful to me," Ryan said.

Richard looked up as though he had just remembered something. "But it's weird, because they wanted Brenda to get an abortion. That doesn't make them sound like true members of the religious Right. They didn't think she could raise the kid, and they didn't trust me."

Ryan made a note and looked at Richard with one eye closed in concentration. "You actually heard them tell Brenda to get an abortion?"

Richard paused and then said, "What did I actually hear? Her dad said she'd be a terrible mother. He said it would be better if the baby were never born—and he gave her money. What conclusion would you reach?"

Ryan tilted his head and pursed his lips. "Did you hear the word *abortion*?"

"No."

"He could just have been giving up—'You'll be lousy parents but here's some money. Don't say I didn't warn you.'" Ryan said.

Michael watched Richard closely. *Don't make shit up.*

Richard shrugged. "Maybe."

"It's your perception that the Nordlands were giving Brenda money to get an abortion because she would be a lousy mother. They just weren't saying it out loud because that would be against their beliefs," Ryan said, tilting his head and looking off in the distance.

Richard nodded.

"Do they know that you are gay?" Ryan asked, and he continued to write without breaking eye contact with Richard.

"I don't see how they could. Brenda didn't even know," Richard said.

"How did you happen to have sex with Brenda?"

Michael looked at Richard, who spoke with his eyes closed. "We were both really drunk and then she added meth, which made me—I don't know—push the limits, sexually."

Michael turned and stared out of the window at the birds on a phone line, counting them.

Richard squeezed the seat of the chair. "It wasn't good, but apparently it was enough, or we wouldn't be here." He snorted. "I thought I could make the marriage work. Brenda loved me. She made me want to try. I wanted to love her back. I just couldn't.

She just wanted so much—too much for me. So I left. I felt like shit—still do." Richard paused as if to summon strength, "And if I give up trying to be in Brady's life, I will still be that irresponsible sack of shit I was when I abandoned them."

Michael stared at the birds on the wire. Had Richard given as much thought to his relationship with Michael as he had to this daughter he had never seen?

"Okay, your rights as I see them," Ryan said. "Since your name is on the birth certificate"—he brandished the document like a prize—"you have what we call 'parental presumption,' or the belief that you are acting in the best interests of your child. Because your in-laws never adopted her, they don't have that presumption, so their job is to show a preponderance of evidence to rebut or over-throw that assumption. We'll talk more about that later.

"Now there are five factors that they have to prove in order to overthrow that presumption and deny you even a visit." He held up his thumb. "The legal parent, that's you"—he pointed to Rich-ard—"is unwilling or unable to care adequately for the child. But you are willing to care for Brady, if only for a visit, right?"

"Absolutely." Richard raised his right hand as though he were being inducted into the Army. Ryan smiled.

Michael shifted in his seat as his stomach clenched. Earlier he was frustrated with Ryan for not holding Richard back, but now he felt jealousy creeping in.

"Two." Ryan held up his index finger. "The petitioners, that are the grandparents, recently have been the child's primary care-givers. And they have, so that one goes to the grandparents. Three, circumstances detrimental to the child exist if relief is denied."

Michael saw Richard's furrowed brow.

Ryan sped up. "Brady is going suffer psychological or emo-tional harm because she is deprived of knowing you." He paused, met Michael's gaze, and added, "and Michael. That one is in your favor.

"Four, the legal parent, you, has fostered, encouraged, or consented to the relationship between the child and the grand-parents. This one affects you, but we can say you didn't consent to it as much as it simply happened while you were out of town, sort of." Ryan grimaced slightly and said, "Don't worry, I'll punch it up. They didn't try hard enough to find you, so you couldn't have consented to anything.

"And five, the legal parent"—he pointed at Richard—"has unreasonably denied or limited contact between the child and the petitioner or intervener. That's the grandparents. This is not an issue in your case because you have never had custody." Ryan paused and mimed being exhausted before continuing. "Now, what do we do with all of this?"

"We just want a visit," Michael interrupted, giving Richard a warning look.

"A visit's fine. You want a week, two weeks, a month?" Ryan asked, squinting one eye at Michael.

Richard shook his head. "The grandparents said I couldn't connect with her while she is in California visiting Disneyland."

Ryan interrupted, "Yeah, they can't do that. You're the father. They didn't adopt her, so she's your kid. What do you want, Mr. Lawson?" Ryan looked at Richard with eyebrows raised and palms open.

Richard looked at Michael.

"A visit, Richard," Michael said.

"A two-week visit?" Richard asked.

"Okay," Michael said.

"A two-week visit sounds smart," Ryan said. Leaning forward and looking right at Michael, he continued, "You two need to be on the same page on this. You are going to see a very real, very vulnerable child who may want to live with her father. You don't want to have to send her packing back to her grandparents. So make sure that you think before you get this thing started." Ryan cleared his throat before he continued.

"There is another factor to consider: the grandparents can and will ask for ten years of back child support. This is based on your income"—he nodded at Richard and pressed his lips together before continuing—"which is limited. So say about two thousand for ten years, and we can work out payments. You do not have to be current in your payments in order to be in contact with Brady. Child support is to protect a child's right to receive support from both parents. They have to prove you unfit to keep you from having contact. That's not true, so that won't happen," Ryan said. "I'll waive my retainer, but my part will be another two thousand." He stopped and took a breath, "One more thing to consider is that if you choose to go for custody and lose, they can ask that you pay their lawyer's fees and whatever costs they incurred—travel, hotels, gas." Ryan cleared his throat.

Richard audibly gasped.

"Yeah, custody is costly," Ryan said. "Kids are expensive, and you've been gone for ten years of her life.

RAPPROCHEMENT

Richard appeared to be thinking but was completely focused on Michael's movements and breathing as they sat inside their car in the law office parking lot, silently staring through the windshield. "I'm sorry. I'm sorry I started this process without talking to you first." He paused, hoping for a response. There wasn't one.

Michael had the keys in his hand but did not start the car.

"I was afraid if I didn't make the call when I did, I would never do it. So I just did. You know how impulsive I can be." He trailed off. "I am sorry."

"I'm sorry too." Michael said, "but I feel like I'm being railroaded into something neither one of us is ready for. My God, that kind of money for a kid we haven't even met. It's too much, Richard. It's too much to ask."

Richard caught Michael's eye briefly, but he looked away as though it stung. "You're right." Richard squeezed his eyes shut as his confidence waned. He would be dead to Brady again. "Now isn't good. It's too soon. It isn't fair to ask you to pay anything. We aren't ready."

He looked out of the window, seeking escape. It hurt to swallow, and he forced his hands under his legs as if to shore himself up. "But I have to do this. Sitting in there, talking to Ryan, I realized how close I was to doing the right thing. Something has switched over in me. Brady's excited and looking forward to seeing me. She emails me daily." He broke off and looked directly at Michael. "I can't—won't—let her down again. I don't want to be that kind of father anymore—or that kind of person. I've missed a lot and I need—not want, but *need*—to make up for lost time."

Richard took a deep breath and listened to his own steady voice. There was lightness, a relief, in his chest as he said the words, as though putting words to it made it possible. He leaned back against the car seat and exhaled.

Michael started the car and shook his head as he backed up. They drove home in silence. A driver in front of them was parking, and Michael tried to get around him, squeezing dangerously close to a car parked on the other side of the road.

Richard winced as he pulled closer. "Just wait until the guy parks and you can get by."

"Goddamnit, don't tell me how to drive!" Michael hit the steering wheel and glared at Richard.

"Okay, I'm sorry, it's okay." Michael ran both hands over his face and groaned.

"Loving you is maddening." The sound of his voice reverberated off the windshield. "How are you going to pay for this by yourself? How?" His face flashed crimson, and spit flew as he spoke. "You have no money and no hope of earning any. You just fucking moved in. So, yeah, that's a perfect time to start a huge financial undertaking—let's just hire a lawyer and get a kid in here so we can share the fucking misery. Shit!"

"I can leave." Richard's shoulders bowed in and his head lowered as a turtle's would when threatened.

"And go where, Richard? How are you going to pay rent?"

"I have some money and I can take a temp job, or substitute teach, just like I did before I moved in."

Michael interrupted with a groan that grew louder. The car

in front of them had slipped into the space. Michael stomped on the accelerator and had to slam on the brakes to turn the corner, causing the tires to squeal. Richard squeezed his eyes closed and braced for impact as Michael swerved around cars and through the last seconds of yellow lights.

When it was safe, Richard said, "I quit the last job because you said I should take my writing more seriously. You told me to quit. Up until a few days ago, I paid my own way."

Michael fell silent temporarily. "And the lawyer? How're you going to pay him?" Michael asked, eyebrows arching.

"Not your problem."

Richard pictured himself teaching to a room of students who barely knew he was present. He wondered how long he could make himself show up for work. It didn't matter; he would do what had to be done.

Michael exhaled nosily and softened his voice. "Richard, I don't want you to go. I want you to be happy with me in our house together. I understand your need to do right by your daughter. I get that. I meant it when I said I wanted to be a father, and I even understand the need to take action now while she's young. I even want to raise a kid of yours. I mean, she'll be yours, so she's got to be pretty special. I want to see her. I said I would help pay for the lawyer, but I will not pay thousands of dollars of back child support. That's your deal. Got it?"

Richard nodded.

Michael pulled into the driveway. "Christ, I'm a boiled frog. I'm going to a meeting." He nodded at the car door. "By myself."

Richard got out just in time for Michael to back out and peel off down the street.

ANOTHER SIDE

"Oh come on, Lou, this is ridiculous!" Frank Nordland gripped the arms of the smooth black leather chair and glared across the desk at his lawyer and long-time friend, Lou Swanson. Frank could feel perspiration dripping off his bald head and wondered just how high this conversation was driving his blood pressure.

"Frank, calm down. You're going to give yourself another heart attack," Kathleen said as she sat perched on the edge of the chair and stared down at her black patent leather pumps.

Frank gave up trying to stay seated and began pacing. "What's causing the idiot to look us up all of a sudden?"

Lou cleared his throat and shifted in his seat. The couple in front of him turned to listen. "There's more, Frank," Lou said. "He's gay."

Frank stopped pacing and gave Lou an uncomprehending stare.

Kathleen spoke first. "You mean to tell me I have to turn my granddaughter over to a drunken father who couldn't even wait to see her born before he took off? Who never bothered to see her in her whole life? And who's a homosexual?"

"That's the way it looks right now." Lou nodded. "He is the father. His name is on the birth certificate. Unless we can prove that he is dangerous to her in some way, you cannot stop him from visiting her."

"He's a drunk. Doesn't that count for something? Besides, aren't homosexuals considered deviants? They're pedophiles, right? I realize she's a girl and all, but doesn't that seem dangerous to you?" Frank asked.

"No, Frank, gays are not pedophiles," Lou said.

"It's against the Bible," Frank muttered.

Lou shook his head. "Frank, you know as well as I do that the Bible has nothing to do with the law. The courts don't care what's written in the Bible."

Frank spun around to face Lou. "Yeah, and that's a problem."

Kathleen spoke up. "I know that he's relapsed several times. He's been in and out of rehab for years. That seems dangerous to me because I can't trust him." She looked at Frank. "Look at all we did for Brenda, and she relapsed over and over. How can we be sure he'll stay sober?" Frank shook his head, and she followed his gaze to Lou.

"Well, he's been sober for the last three years," Lou said, and he added, "And he's been with the same man for all that time. This is considered a good thing because they have a long-term relationship. They are registered as domestic partners even, which gives them rights commensurate with those of married people. My guess is that's why your former son-in-law is filing for custody at this late date. He's with someone who has money or at least a house that can be set up as collateral."

Kathleen grimaced and lowered herself into the chair. "It may be legal, but it's unnatural."

"There's nothing I can do to stop this?" Frank asked, and then, unable to find words, he growled and resumed pacing. Finally he stopped. "How do I know he'll bring her back?"

"It sounds like a good bet. If he's really interested in gaining custody in the future, he won't risk it by trying to kidnap her. He's going to play by the rules and deliver her to her teacher at Disneyland."

Frank dropped into the chair in front of Lou's desk and exhaled loudly.

Lou looked down at their file and said, "You know, this whole thing would have been avoided if you had adopted her. You could have terminated the father's rights." Lou took off his glasses and looked over the file at Frank.

Frank leaned his head against the back of the chair. He could feel Kathleen's eyes on him. "We thought he was dead, or would never show up again." She'd wanted to adopt Brady, but it had seemed to him not only unnecessary, but wrong. To make Brady their daughter had felt, to him, like erasing Brenda. Frank looked at his wife, who sat stiff, staring at the floor, her arms crossed over her chest. He frowned deeply. "We were busy with life and just didn't think . . . couldn't imagine this could happen."

"I understand, Frank," Lou said. "You two were heroic, really. But it leaves you wide open. Since you didn't adopt her, the law is on his side."

"I'll tell you something else we did not do." Frank punctuated the air with his index finger. "We did not walk away from her when her mother died. No, sir, we did what families should do and stepped in and took care of Brady. We made her our own."

Kathleen said, "Lou, you remember Brenda's memorial service? Even there most of our friends said it was a blessing we couldn't find him. How do you terminate the rights of someone who isn't even there?" Kathleen asked.

"You advertise, hire an investigator, and hunt him down," Lou said.

"So now what do we do?" Kathleen's face hardened with her tone.

Lou shifted in his seat and said, "You let him have his visit but you ask for the back child support. That may stop them. Your son-in-law has very little money, so it'll be easy to make him feel he can't afford to fight for her. But in the meantime, these are your copies of the agreement to visitation, and I need both of your signatures." He uncapped the pen.

Frank stared at Lou before he pushed his face close to his friend's and said, "This is a slippery slope, Lou. Now it's a visit, but custody's next. And if he gets custody and relapses, and she's found hungry and dirty, what will the courts do then, Lou? And who's going to pick up the pieces then? Brady was little when Brenda died, and we were there immediately. This time she'll be old enough to understand and feel bitter and angry. And we'll be far away. Who's going to help her, Lou?" Frank's voice broke.

Kathleen remained seated. "What happens if we refuse to sign?"

"Then it goes to court, and a judge will make you do it. They'll send a sheriff to get her. You don't want that."

Kathleen pulled herself to her full height and laced her fingers in front of her as she stood next to her husband. After he signed, he handed her the pen.

"If he's one minute late in dropping her off, I want to be called. Hear that, Lou?"

DRIVING HOME

Kathleen was surprised how dark it was when they got out. She hated driving in the dark. "Maybe it'll be okay," Kathleen said in the car. "Maybe a visit will get it out of his system. It's hard to be a parent, and to do it all of a sudden would be harder."

"He doesn't want a visit," Frank said, pulling onto the interstate. He turned to look at her and swerved into the next lane. A driver laid on his horn until he pulled back.

"Watch the road," she said. "Please."

"He wants to establish himself with her"—Frank's voice rose—"so he can say she wants to live with him."

She watched as his face was sporadically lit by the headlights of the cars going south.

"You don't know that," Kathleen said.

Frank twisted toward her.

She watched the road for him, hands fluttering as the car wavered.

"We're going to find out, aren't we? She's going to go all the way to California and be alone with the alcoholic father? And his . . . friend." He turned his mouth down as though tasting something bitter.

Kathleen hesitated. "Maybe she should at least know her father."

"I'm sick of hearing him called 'her father.' Deadbeat Dad more like." Frank snorted.

She shook her head. "I do wish we had adopted her."

"We all wish that," Frank said. "But you remember what it was like then. Adoption was so expensive. We were living on our savings, and what we hadn't spent on Brenda, we were spending on Brady." He fell silent for several minutes. "I've loved Brady from the moment I laid eyes on her, and so have you, Kathleen. I didn't want to rile him up and make him want to be a father. I wanted to let sleeping dogs lie. Maybe I was wrong, but I was afraid to make things worse. She became our daughter. She looked like Brenda, only happy. It was like God was giving us a second chance. How could I be sure he'd be willing to sign her away? He looked so—" Frank stopped talking.

At first Kathleen thought she'd misunderstood; maybe she had. "You saw him, Frank?" It sounded like an accusation.

Frank uttered a small "Oh." He blushed and moved his lips, but no words came out. He pulled the car to the shoulder of the highway and ground to a stop. Gravel hit the window.

Kathleen sucked in her breath and braced herself, one hand on the door and one on the dash, feet flat. She looked at Frank, openmouthed.

"Look, I hired a private investigator, and he tracked down Richard in California. I wanted him to sign papers so we could adopt her." Frank paused.

Kathleen felt her scalp prickle. Frank's trips to California to settle business with Harry & David had seemed odd at the time, since the company was based in Oregon. She had so blindly accepted his lie. What else didn't she know?

"I tried to talk to him, I really did. He was living under a freeway. He couldn't even speak, Kathleen."

At the sound of her name, she looked at him and then away. Frank was a strong, domineering man, but right now his eyes were downcast in penitence while anger clenched his eyebrows.

"I know," he tapped his breastbone, "I saw him, watched him from my car, muttering to himself." Frank stopped and he scanned the roof of the car. "I didn't want him to drag Brady into his mess," he turned and gave her full eye contact, "and I didn't want him to see us as a cash cow either. I was trying to find the right thing to do when nothing seemed right. You weren't there."

Kathleen straightened in her seat and leaned her face toward him. "I wasn't there because you," she pointed into his face, "didn't tell me what you were doing." Words seemed to dam up in her mouth. She pushed back against the seat and forced herself to exhale.

The two sat in silence, their breath made visible by the cold air.

"Why didn't you tell me?" Kathleen asked. Her own loud words startled her.

"Somehow by not telling you, I felt I was keeping him—his squalor, his misery—away from us. I know it sounds childish, but that's what I was thinking. I was trying to protect Brady and you. Blame me if it makes you feel better. It won't change anything."

Kathleen pulled away from him and looked through the windshield at the dark. How could he have done something so important and not need her help?

"They'll use it against us, Frank. They'll say we didn't try . . . no, it'll be worse—we found him but didn't tell him. We're going to lose her because of what you've done."

"Not if they don't know, Kathleen. Sometimes these things have to be done to protect a family."

Frank looked over his shoulder and gripped the steering wheel, preparing to enter the light but fast-moving traffic.

Kathleen turned toward her window and stared at her reflection highlighted by the dashboard lights. She sighed, fogging the window, and then shivered. "You also wanted her to get an abortion."

Frank steered away from the highway and put the car in park. He fell back into the seat, head tilted and eyes staring at the roof. His hands rested open-palmed in his lap.

Kathleen forced herself to continue. She would never have the courage again. "You gave her money, a lot of it. And you said it would be better if it were never born."

The lights of a southbound truck illuminated half of his face. "How dare you say that? Now, especially." Frank directed the words, low and menacing, at the roof.

Kathleen felt a tremor of uncertainty.

"I gave her money to pay for the birth. That's all," Frank began before he turned and leveled his eyes on his wife. "Don't you ever say otherwise."

LETTING GO

T he alarm jarred Frank but did not wake him. He was already
awake. Kathleen stirred in her sleep. He could tell from the
near-constant movement of her legs throughout the night that her
night had been as fitful as his. Kathleen called his name in her
sleep with such anguish, and he wanted to soothe her. Since he
was the source of her sorrow, he was unable to comfort her. He had
never felt so powerless in his life.

Frank raised his hand to knock on Brady's door and wake
her in time to get to Medford for her early flight, but the door was
already open. She was dressed and had her backpack on. She pulled
an overstuffed suitcase decorated with faded Muppet characters.

"Wasn't Grandma going to give you a new suitcase?" Frank
asked.

"I don't want the old one to feel lonely if I don't take it." She
pushed past him and pulled the suitcase down the stairs.

Frank pressed his lips together. Everything had feelings in
Brady's life—books, backpacks, and now, suitcases. How had she
overlooked theirs? When they'd told her she'd be visiting her father,

she'd been excited. They expected that. But they also thought she might feel a little sorrow about leaving them. Frank would never have said it out loud, but he could see the unhappiness on Kathleen's face as Brady turned exuberantly to talking about and planning and packing for the trip.

He cleared his throat and followed her downstairs to the kitchen, where Kathleen had poured cereal into bowls.

Now that she was minutes from leaving, Brady became silent. They found themselves talking up her visit to her father.

"It's going to be all right, you know?" Kathleen said, drinking her coffee and letting her own cereal go soggy.

"I know," Brady said, without looking at her.

"You'll have fun and then you'll come back," Kathleen said—as though saying it made it true.

Brady nodded without looking up.

Frank pointed at the clock. "It's time to go. You don't want to miss the plane."

Brady carried her bowl to the sink and began rinsing it.

"Don't worry about that. I'll do it when I get back," Kathleen said.

Brady's lack of response seemed to exhaust Kathleen because she fell silent. They climbed into the gray Volvo station wagon and remained silent for the thirty-minute drive to the Medford airport. Frank watched Brady in the rearview mirror although she never looked at him. They went through the checking in and watched the desk clerk put a sign with her last name around her neck.

"Your granddaughter will be fine," the clerk assured him.

He stared at her. *I know she'll be fine. I just want her to stay.* When they called the passengers to board, Brady swung the backpack over her shoulders and put her head down but did not move.

"It'll be fine," both she and Kathleen said simultaneously, and then they laughed. Each was trying to protect the other, and each was trying to help the other do what had to be done. Brady had to leave, and Kathleen had to let her. Frank found himself sidelined in one of the most wrenching moments of his life, and maybe that is how he survived it.

A REUNION FOR THE FIRST TIME

P lanes started landing and deplaning all at once. Richard was afraid he'd miss Brady in the chaos. But there she was with his name dangling from a lanyard around her neck. She seemed short for a ten-year-old and very frail. Her frizzy hair floated in an almost-solid mass above her shoulders. Her heavy mud-brown bangs overwhelmed her blue eyes. She wore an overly large striped polo shirt, and all four of the buttons were closed, giving her a choked look. Below the polo shirt she wore equally large brick red jeans and clunky oxfords that could have protected her feet from an industrial accident. She walked awkwardly in herky-jerky movements that made Richard wonder if she had a physical deformity, but it just turned out to be way she walked.

Richard guided her out of line and was immediately intercepted by a flight attendant who took Brady's hand and asked for his identification. He pulled out his wallet and noticed his hands were shaking. He gave the flight attendant his license and smiled weakly. She did not smile back but studied his license and finally released Brady to him.

Richard pulled Brady off to the side and crouched next to

her. They hadn't exchanged a word yet. "Hi," he said, noticing that under the bushy bangs her eyes were as blue as his own. "I'm Richard Lawson," he said, pointing to the sign around her neck. "Your dad." He ducked his head awkwardly.

But when he raised his head again she was smiling at him, and he *became* that person. A father. *Her* father. He leaned forward to hug her, and she leapt toward him with such enthusiasm that her lower front teeth drove slightly into his shoulder. He pulled back.

"Sorry, they do that sometimes," she said, covering her mouth with her hand.

"Your teeth sometimes bite people?" Richard asked.

Brady shrugged and stared down.

To spare her further discomfort, he hugged her and noted that he could have wrapped his arms twice around her. Her hair, although bushy, was full, healthy, and smelled like apricots.

Richard took her by the hand.

"This is my friend Michael, who is my roommate." Richard's eyes closed as the lie passed his lips.

"How do you do, sir?" Brady extended her hand, and both men smiled at her formality.

"Are you hungry?" Michael asked as he bent to see below her bangs. They turned to walk down the wide halls of the terminal to baggage claim.

"No, they fed us on the plane."

"Really? There isn't much food on planes these days. What did they give you?" Richard asked.

"Something sort of like a cracker." Brady nodded up at him. "And 7 Up."

"I'm starving," Richard said. They had been planning to go to the buffet breakfast at the Hyatt, but it would be awkward if the guest of honor wasn't hungry.

"Maybe you'll work up an appetite on the way home," Michael said.

"There it is!" Brady shouted when she saw her tiny, beat-up suitcase. She acted as though it were an old friend riding toward her on the carousel. "It looks sad."

Richard heard Michael snort softly, but he himself understood. "All the others are black."

Brady nodded. "And big."

"And new," Michael added. "Maybe we'll get you a new suitcase to go with the new clothes we're going to buy you." Leaning into Richard's ear, he said, "As soon as possible. Baby needs new shoes—among other things."

Richard shot him a look. He could tell Brady was listening. He bent to reach for the case, but Brady darted in beneath him, neatly snagging the handle and flinging it to the floor beside the carousel.

"Is that it?" Richard asked.

"No, sir, there's another one. My backpack. It has all of my books in it. They made me check it because it didn't fit anywhere. I couldn't read for the whole flight." Brady frowned at the floor, but a moment later she hopped up and down and yelled, "There it is!"

People stared when she shouted. Richard fought the impulse to tell her not to point.

Rather than waiting for the backpack, she raced around the carousel to greet it. It took her two tries to haul the overstuffed and very-dirty pink backpack off the moving belt. While the suitcase had been small, this piece was gigantic, and Richard couldn't imagine it ever being carried on her back without knocking her over. But Brady took hold of the frayed black shoulder straps and swung it around her body, threading first one arm and then the other through the harnesses and onto her back. There was one shudder of reverse action. Richard lunged forward keep her from falling, but she centered herself like a compass needle finding north. Once stable, she stooped and snatched up the Muppet case.

"Let me help you with that," Richard said. She looked both comical and sad with all of that weight on her skinny frame.

"Thank you, sir, but I've got it. Now, which way?"

Richard pointed vaguely toward the parking lot sign.

She started off like a heavily laden hobbit on her way to the shire.

Left behind, Richard and Michael exchanged looks and wound up laughing.

"What's the 'sir' stuff about?" Michael asked.

"I do not know, but we're going to lose her if we stay here much longer. She doesn't even know where she's going." Richard scrambled to catch up with her.

"She's just like you," Michael said. "Action first; questions later. This promises to be an adventure."

Richard managed to successfully corral and guide her to the car. The pack was very difficult to get off of her back, but when Richard attempted to help free her arm, she moved away from him and continued the struggle on her own.

"What if we take something out it?" Michael suggested.

"No, I've done this before." She tried to jar the contents of the pack by extending both arms back and shaking her shoulders.

Michael looked away and covered his mouth to keep from laughing.

Richard hovered uselessly over her as she dodged his every attempt to help. Finally, the backpack fell to the floor with a loud smack that echoed all over the parking structure, startling the tourists nearby.

"There, I knew I could do it," Brady said.

Richard stooped to lift the bulging pack and was stunned at its weight. "Are you sure there are just books in here?"

"Gold bullion, maybe?" Michael said, unlocking the car.

Brady was in her seat and buckled in before they had opened their doors.

As the men settled in the car, Richard said, "I guess you really meant it when you said you loved reading." Richard and Brady had been emailing regularly and found she was reading some of the books he'd read at her age.

"Brady balances her reading so that when the subject matter gets too sad, she changes to fantasy," Richard said to Michael.

"Self-medicating through fiction," Michael said, adding, "sounds like you." The conversation, which started out contrived and awkward, gradually smoothed out and made them feel closer.

As they pulled up in front of the Manhattan Beach bungalow, Richard thought about the care he had taken in decorating her room because he couldn't bear the image of Brady sleeping on a foldout couch in their den. He had sat surrounded by magazines and catalogues while surfing Pottery Barn and IKEA websites and finally settled on a Laura Ashley design of pink ballet shoes. It worked, he decided. The ballet shoe border, the white metal bed, and the ruffled pink-and-blue plaid pillow shams and bed ruffle all came together in a symphony of femininity as dictated by our Sister of Perpetual Upper Crustiness. In the end, he was so tired of agonizing over it he told Michael that if Brady said anything remotely critical, he'd rip everything from the walls and room with his bare teeth.

"Your room is at the top of the stairs on the right," Richard said, anxious to have her see her room. She stopped in the doorway. Richard held his breath.

"Oh, how pretty!" she said.

Richard breathed a sigh of relief and asked, "Do you like it? It's all Laura Ashley. There were other choices, but I liked the ballet shoes the best."

"It's perfect. I love ballet!" She smiled as she stroked the comforter and moved on to the pillows, lifting the ruffle of the sham. "It all matches!" She pulled back the comforter and looked at the delicate print on the sheets. "Even the rug and the curtains."

Richard watched her glance up and along the border and jumped up to show her the bathroom with its matching towels, rugs, and the piece de resistance, a fluffy terrycloth robe. He had even gotten a personalized toothbrush in the same pink shade.

But before he could complete the tour, Brady stopped in her tracks. "I have a bathroom in my room?"

"Well, not *in* your room, but adjoining, yes," Richard said.

"And only *I* use it?"

Richard, who was impatient to show her the robe, had to stop and wait for her to catch up.

"Yes, only you use it," Michael said from the door of the bedroom. "Do you share a bathroom at home?"

"Oh yeah, with my grandparents, and they take forever," she said, her voice and gaze trailing off.

Richard stood holding the robe and the toothbrush for

Brady to admire. She smiled briefly, but then a shadow passed over her face.

"What is it, Brady?" Richard asked.

She looked him straight in the eye and asked, "When is Laura coming back?"

"What are you talking about?" he stammered out.

"You said it's all Laura Ashley's. Is she coming back to this room?"

Richard stifled a laugh and said, "She's a designer, and she's never, ever coming to this house. This is all for you, Brady."

"Wow, thank you, sir, very, very much!"

* * *

"Put your clothes in the dresser and wash your hands for lunch," Michael called over his shoulder as he walked down the stairs. "It'll be ready very soon."

Minutes later, Michael put lunch on the table and stood back to admire his handiwork. The sandwiches for Richard and Brady were turkey smoked with mesquite in thick slices of his home-made rosemary bread. He added sliced tomatoes, cucumbers, and lettuce. He sprinkled blueberries over cantaloupe and mango and gave it just a dash of nutmeg.

Richard and Brady came down the stairs and took their seats. Richard was starving and began to eat with gusto. Brady stared at hers. Finally she picked up a fork and began scraping the blueberries off the melon. She pushed the cantaloupe away from the watermelon, which she ate. Then she began scraping the bread.

Michael watched her and exchanged a look with Richard, who shrugged. "What are you doing?" Michael asked.

She raised her eyes slightly without quite meeting his. "My bread has sticks and stuff in it."

"That's fresh rosemary," Michael said. This was his bread that people hoped would be served at his parties. He had taken time to kneed it and let it rise. It was meant as an offering to Richard's Brady. But she didn't like it. Michael looked at Richard for reassurance, but Richard was focused on finding something Brady liked to eat.

Michael lowered his eyes and took another bite. Maybe he had put too much rosemary in the bread?

"You could just eat the turkey," Richard said.

Michael monitored Brady's actions as he ate.

She removed bean sprouts, cucumbers, lettuce, and tomato slices, and then picked up the turkey meat with her hand.

Michael looked away.

Richard handed her a fork.

Brady cut the turkey with the side of her fork and lifted it to her mouth. "It has a funny taste," she said with her mouth full.

"Mesquite," Richard said.

Michael glanced at Richard. Was mesquite a problem too? They both loved it.

Michael could see the corners of Brady's mouth turn down, and he wondered if she was going to spit the half-eaten mess on her plate.

Keeping her gaze fixed on her plate, Brady reached for the milk. She took a huge mouthful. She grabbed a napkin and held it to her mouth as she ran to the sink and spit milk and turkey into it.

"What's wrong with your milk?" she asked.

"Nothing," Michael said.

Richard raised his head and then his eyebrows.

Michael softened his tone. "It's soy milk. It doesn't have chemicals or hormones that give you cancer."

"What?" Brady said from where she stood at the sink. She looked like she might throw up.

"It doesn't matter." Richard said. "You're used to whole milk, and there's some in the fridge."

No there isn't, Michael thought, furrowing his brow and shaking his head.

Richard got up to get the milk and said quietly, "I bought it because I thought this might happen. I should have served it to begin with."

Brady sniffed the milk before drinking it.

"Take an apple from the bowl. I can make you a peanut butter and jelly sandwich," Richard said, settling back in his chair.

Richard was working around him, Michael realized. It felt disloyal or dishonest to him somehow.

"I'm not really hungry."

"Just the apple, then?" Richard said, offering her an apple from the centerpiece.

Michael watched Richard offering the apple to Brady. She took it suspiciously, as if it might be poisoned.

"It's just an apple, Brady. Eat it," Richard said, glancing at Michael.

Michael sighed. He was trying too hard. He meant for all the homemade food to be a welcome-to-our-home celebration. *We've done something special for you.* Richard wanted Brady to be comfortable. They all wanted to like each other.

Brady took a bite from the apple and swallowed.

"So, I was thinking we could go to the beach. Do you like the beach?" Richard's voice was edged with brittle enthusiasm that reminded Michael of his mother's. It sounded just as false.

Brady perked up. "Great, I've never been to the beach. But I don't have a swimsuit."

"We could buy one," Michael said. "Shop at Santa Monica first and then go to the beach. That could be fun, right?"

Brady looked up, eyes brightening, and smiled. She bit into the apple with enthusiasm and chewed faster.

"You'll like it. It's a pier and it's got places to shop and eat." Richard stopped. "Do you like pizza? Spaghetti and meatballs?" Richard asked.

Michael looked down the length of the table full of food and sighed. She had to eat.

As Brady's smile broadened, Richard's voice gained volume. "They've got it all. "It's nice. You really will like it," he said before trailing off to glance at Michael.

Michael began to clear the table.

"Sounds fun." Brady looked at him and smiled.

* * *

Brady sat in the backseat of Michael's Acura, with a delicious rumble of excitement in her stomach. Shopping with Grandma had meant a trip to the mall in preparation for school or some event at church. Shopping with her dad and his friend seemed like an activity that was like going to the movies.

As they were backing out of the drive, Richard said, "You know what else might be good?"

Brady looked up and leaned forward.

Richard looked at her from over the back of the car seat. "A trip to a hairstylist. You're a bit hidden under all those bangs. They can be straightened and thinned."

A haircut? She looked away from him and through the window. She pictured Grandma trimming her wet bangs as she sat on a kitchen chair with a towel around her shoulders. "I mean, just a little straightening?" Richard showed with his thumb and finger just how little straightening would be required.

Michael looked at Richard and whispered, "I don't know. What would the grandparents think?"

Richard looked at Brady in the rearview mirror and asked, "Do you think your grandparents would mind if you came back with a new hairstyle?"

When he said the word *hairstyle*, she pictured nothing. What did straightened and thinned mean? She stared back at him and shrugged.

"I don't know Richard," Michael said, still whispering.

But Richard interrupted. "I bet we can get in with Roger if we call right now. It's toward the end of the day, and he might fit us in if we promise dinner afterward."

"Brady, do you want your hair cut?" Michael asked, resting his hand on her shoulder as he spoke to her image in the mirror.

Brady squirmed; up until now, her whole goal was to draw as little attention as possible. With both men looking at her, the easiest way was to say yes.

"Yes," Brady said.

Richard picked up the phone and made the appointment.

In what felt like minutes later, Brady was sitting in a hair salon that smelled like burnt eggs, hairspray, and coffee that had sat too long on a heater. Roger turned out to be a short man with a gentle touch and a lot of earrings, including some that blinked in rainbow colors, and a barbell in his eyebrow. Brady couldn't stop staring.

Roger filled his hands with her hair, while smiling at her in the mirror. "Looks like we need to straighten all of it, taper the bangs into the sides, and blunt cut the back." Brady stared at Roger in the mirror, waiting for that flash of gold.

She looked straight up as the three men discussed her hair and could only see the underneath of their chins.

"That sound good, Little Lady?" Roger asked.

Brady stared at them and said, "I'm sorry?"

"You, young lady, need to pay attention. It is, after all, your hair we are discussing," Roger said, clapping his hands on the sides of her shoulders while his eyebrows rose to his unnaturally black hairline.

Brady opened her mouth to speak but had no idea what to say, so she closed it and nodded.

That was all they needed, and she was shampooed, rinsed, conditioned, rinsed again, dried, straightened, clipped, shaped, tapered, and blunted.

Roger whirled her around in the chair with great flourish, and Brady blinked at the mirror.

Glossy and fragrant, her hair fell in a perfect A-line from the back to her shoulders, and moved moved fluidly when she turned her head. She looked like a model in a shampoo commercial. It was just that she didn't look like herself anymore. "I have Casey's hair," she said to the mirror. What would her friends say?

"Sweetie, I don't know who Casey is," Roger said, "but I can assure you that it's still your hair. For heaven's sakes! Don't you love it?"

Richard leaned forward and whispered into Roger's ear, "What you really want is for her to admit that her entire existence will now be sublime because of your skills with her hair. Forget it," Richard said, "it's not going to happen." He crossed his arms across his chest and added, "She's very guarded, this one."

The three men stood behind her like backup singers and

stared at her. She knew they were disappointed, and she knew she should thank them, but she couldn't.

Michael filled in the gap. "She looks beautiful, Roger. Thank you for seeing us on such short notice," he said as he pulled out his wallet. The money was exchanged just in front of Brady's nose. "Dinner?" Michael asked.

Roger shook his head, sending one last sulky appeal for Brady's approval toward the mirror.

Brady saw it and forced out the words, "Thank you." She climbed out of the chair and took off the smock.

Roger shrugged and began to sweep up her curls.

∗ ∗ ∗

As they left the shop, Richard asked, "Who is Casey?'

"Casey," Brady paused to find words that weren't too mean but told the truth, "is the most popular girl at school. She is not even a senior and she is more popular than the most popular senior. She is the head cheerleader. She's the best at everything. She's smart but not in a school way. She's smart at getting what she wants." Brady stopped herself because she knew she was gossiping.

"Is she nice?" her father asked.

"Do you like her?" Michael asked.

Without hesitation, Brady answered, "No, to both questions. She's mean and she thinks she's better than everyone else. Everyone's nice to her because they're afraid of her, even some of the teachers, and she's mean to everyone. I don't know why she is and I don't know why people put up with it, but they do. I just try to stay away from her."

"Why don't you tell a teacher when she's mean?" Michael asked.

Brady rolled her eyes and snorted. "Grown-ups always say that. Telling makes it worse. I don't want her looking at me. I don't want to deal with her. She breaks all of the rules but never seems to get caught. I hate people like that, and I never want to be one."

Richard leaned between the front seats to have eye contact with her. "Can you ask your grandparents for help?"

Brady sighed before she said, "I have, and my grandmother tells me to pray for her." She paused. "My grandfather stormed in and yelled at the principal. It made things worse. I know God wants us to love each other and all, but I'm pretty sure he doesn't mean Casey." She stopped and covered her lips with her fingers and looked out of the car window.

Richard nodded. "I know what you mean. Sometimes it's best to just stay out of the way."

"Yeah," Brady turned and caught Richard's eye. It felt so good to be understood.

Richard smiled and blushed, causing her to smile back.

* * *

Brady stood holding tightly to the orange-striped fitting room curtain and stared at her bare feet as she moved her toe in and out of the sunlight on the hardwood floor. Her image was reflected all around her, so there was no escaping how she looked in the soft apricot shift that covered a sunset-colored swim suit. She looked beautiful, and a blaze of pleasure and pride coursed through her body but was chased by fear. What would her friends say? Worse, what would Casey and her friends say?

"Okay," Michael said, "Make sure you get that swimsuit with the blue cover up. That was the reason we came, remember? Wear it under the little sundress with the sunflowers. Save that apricot one for later. Hand them out to me when you're ready."

Brady nodded and stepped back, allowing the curtain to drop behind her. She slipped out of the new clothes and, aware that Michael was waiting, handed them out while holding the curtain tightly shut. She turned back to the bench where only her old, faded clothes and clunky shoes remained. They looked sad, splayed out like Goodwill rejects. She pulled them on and looked at herself. Lumpy and oversized, the clothes had communicated a safe message: "I don't matter. Don't notice me." The new clothes were soft and colorful. Did she want to be noticed? She felt a pang of homesickness and pulled out of her pants pocket the cell phone that her grandparents gave her for this trip and turned it on. She looked at the screen and saw she had three messages. She had turned the phone off when they took off and forgot to turn it back on.

As she called her grandparents, the word *Home* flashed on the screen.

Grandma answered.

"Hi, Grandma, I'm here. I made it." Brady's voice sounded young even to herself.

"You were supposed to call when you landed—seven hours ago," Grandma said.

"Sorry," Brady said, grimacing and rolling her feet out to the sides.

Brady heard Grandpa pick up an extension. "The phone only works if you call us. It's very important that you call us when you say you will." Brady heard him exhale loudly. Had he run to the phone? "We worry, Brady."

"I'm here now, and I'm okay. We went shopping and I got my hair cut." Brady looked at herself in the mirror and ran her fingers through her hair. It fell in a synchronized movement.

"They cut your hair?" Grandma asked. It sounded like an accusation.

"Yeah, it's nice, Grandma. You'll like it," Brady said, adding, "I hope," under her breath.

"Glad you're safe," Grandpa said. "Call us when you leave for Disneyland."

"Okay."

"And, Brady, really call," Grandma said.

"Okay, sorry, bye." She hung up so she wouldn't have to hear them hang up. Drawn back out to the sales floor by a teal green dress, she wondered if she should have bought this one too. She looked over at the cashier for her father and Michael. But they weren't there. Brady tried to remember where she had seen them last and headed back to the fitting rooms, but they weren't there. She bolted to the front of the store and back. She went upstairs, which made her heart pound. She ran back down and looked at the face of her phone. She couldn't call them because she didn't have their number. She went out of the door and stood on the sidewalk to look left and right. She went back inside and up to the sales girl who had a gecko tattoo climbing out of the back of her pants.

"Have you seen the two men who were here with me?" Brady asked.

The girl was ringing someone else up and had a line four people deep. She scanned the store and shrugged. "They must have gone out there." She pointed back to the front door and turned to the transaction. Brady stood there. No one was looking at her and no one was helping. She squeezed her eyes shut and tried to think where they could have gone. They wouldn't have left without her, but they could have thought she was with them. Her Girl Scout training told her not to panic and run around and to stay put and be obvious. She felt awkward just standing. She thought people were looking at her funny and worried that she was staring at them. She tried to shop, but none of the clothes looked remotely interesting now. She walked slowly to the door and then out. The doors closed behind her. She stared at her phone and wished she had given them her number. She checked the time and realized she had been waiting for twenty minutes. Her grandparents must have her dad's number. She wanted to talk to someone just so she wasn't adrift. She brought her grandparents' number up and stared at it. Her grandparents were already nervous; her calling in lost would make it worse. She peered inside the store and could see the salesgirl and a line of customers but no Richard or Michael. Where were they? She pushed the button for her grandparents.

Her grandmother answered. "Grandma, this is Brady and I don't know how to call my dad."

"Why do you need to call him? Isn't he with you?"

Brady scratched her nose. "We got separated at the store. Can you give me his number?"

"They've had her for a few hours and already she's lost," Grandma told Grandpa.

Brady lowered her head and stared at her shoes. "Please just give me the number." She sensed the whoosh of the door behind her and looked up to see her dad and Michael heading toward her.

She gasped and wished she hadn't called. "They're here." She couldn't understand what her grandmother was saying, but she sounded worked up. "Grandma, Grandma, I'm okay. They're here."

"Can I talk to them?" her grandpa asked.

Ducking her head and keeping her eyes down, Brady handed Richard the phone. "Sorry."

"Grandparents?" he asked.

Brady nodded.

"Where were you?" Brady asked Michael.

"Bathroom, and when we came back you were gone."

Richard was holding the phone away from himself. Her grandmother's voice could be heard several feet away. "You have a child with you. You need to pay attention. Give her your number. Plan ahead."

"I am truly sorry. Just went to the bathroom. It won't happen again. Sorry that she didn't call. No, it will never happen again. Sorry. Thank you. Goodbye." He blew air out and widened his eyes at Michael before turning to Brady and saying, "Okay now you have my number. Call me," he said to Brady.

"We have to be careful," he said in a lowered voice to Michael. "She's saying it's against the law to cut the hair of a kid who is not legally yours." He turned the corners of his mouth down in a mock grimace. "I need a diversion—trip to the beach, anyone?" He began guiding Brady and Michael through the crowds back to the car.

"Let's go," Brady said, wondering if he was going to hold her hand for the rest of the trip.

* * *

Michael loved the beach because it brought back memories of vacations on Martha's Vineyard. That was why he lived in Manhattan Beach, but work drew him away and the strongest connection he had with the beach was the smell of the water and the sound of sea gulls. Having a child in his midst gave him a perfect reason to go for the whole day. Once at the beach his obsessive nature took over, and he became lead engineer in the building of a massive and magnificent sandcastle, tiled with tiny stones and glass polished by the sea. The whole edifice circled around in a graduated ramp as a conch shell does. This process required that a lot of water be carried up, and since Richard and Brady were rank and file, that job fell to them. Michael was about to cave in to Richard's more modest plan that required less water when a small girl darted in and dumped water from a broken sand bucket. He turned and watched her sprint back to the ocean, where she scooped more water and whirled around to scamper back to the construction site with it.

"What's your name?" Brady asked the girl on her third trip.

"Fiona." The girl squinted into the sun at Brady. "I just turned ten. I'm small for my age. I'll be in fifth grade next year."

"I'm ten and I'll be in fifth grade next year too," Brady said. "Do you want to help us make tunnels?"

"Yeah, that'll let water in when the waves come up," Fiona said. And they did build tunnels that allowed the water to rush in and circle the building with a moat that glistened in the sun. Everything seemed possible with the presence of effervescent Fiona.

The wind blew the sand from their bodies where it had been stuck in gooey sunblock. But still they stood shivering and admired their work.

"Hey, let's take a picture." Michael brought out his iPhone, and the group pulled together behind the castle. Fiona grabbed Brady in a bear hug, and Richard encircled the two with a hand on each of their shoulders. Weary, sandy, and cold, they smiled the smile that comes from a job well done.

Just at that moment the water made its final crash on the structure, blurring the definition of the lines and wiping away whole sections of the stones.

"Oh no," Brady moaned, holding out her hands in a futile attempt to stop the destruction.

"It's okay," Fiona touched her shoulder. "We can build another, better one tomorrow or whenever we want."

Brady looked sadly at the now-shapeless lump of sand. "I liked this one." "Yeah," Fiona said, "but maybe tomorrow's will be better?" Fiona shrugged and held up her hand for a high five.

Brady looked down and then back at Fiona. "Right," she said, smiling and slapping Fiona's outstretched hand.

Michael smiled at Fiona's perseverance and her ability to reassure Brady. Had he said the same thing, it would have sounded reproving and judgmental.

"Hey, Fi," a teenage girl called from the top of the beach near the sidewalk. "Let's go, Miha! We're going for pizza. Come on." The girl waved her arm impatiently and pointed at a large blue cargo van. Fiona didn't dust the sand off and she did not put on a towel because she did not have one. She sprinted past the girl and to the van where the side door was thrown open. She turned and gave Brady a huge smile and waved.

"See you in school," she said, and she climbed in, followed by the bigger girl, and the door slammed shut behind them.

Brady stared at the van as it pulled away. "No, you won't," she said quietly.

Michael could tell she didn't intend for anyone to hear her. But Michael had, and the poignant tone of her voice made his throat catch.

* * *

At the restaurant, Richard ordered crab and shrimp cocktails and a Caesar salad while Michael had a salad made of local greens with gluten-free bread sticks. Brady ordered a grilled cheese sandwich with fries. When the food arrived the men picked up their forks eagerly.

"We need to say grace first!" She leaned forward to whisper this as though protecting the two men from committing a terrible gaff.

Richard looked around at the other patrons and hissed back, "In a restaurant?"

"Shouldn't we be grateful for food no matter where it comes from?" she asked.

Richard grimaced. "I wouldn't know what to say."

She paused slightly. "Well, usually an adult or our pastor does it, but I can say it if you want."

Richard felt he had failed in meeting his first Christian benchmark, but he didn't feel he could pull off any kind of prayer with a straight face in front of Michael.

Brady bowed her head and held her hands out to each of them.

The men gradually realized they were all to hold hands. Michael kept looking at the door as though he might just get up and leave.

Richard took Brady's hand, which made her smile, and she closed her eyes.

Michael follow suit while closing his eyes tightly. Richard could tell Michael wanted this over.

Richard lowered his head so close to the salad that he was at risk for coming up with parmesan on his nose.

Brady began, "Dear Lord, bless this food and the nutrition that it will give us. Bless our visit with one another, and thank you very much for me getting to be with my dad. Thank you for my new friends Michael and Fiona. Please bless Roger and my new hair, and know that I am grateful for all of the clothes I just got." She paused and then added, "and the beautiful room. Help us to be good people every day. In Jesus's name we pray. Amen." She looked at them expectantly.

They looked at one another and Richard reluctantly mumbled, "Amen." Everyone was quiet for several minutes. Richard wondered if this was due to hunger or because they were happy to do something they considered normal.

"That's nice that you prayed for Roger. He'll like that," Michael said between bites, and then he added, "Is there a special prayer to guard against bad haircuts?"

Richard gave Michael a warning glare as Brady shook her head.

Richard said, "Do they teach you what to say at your school? In a prayer, I mean?"

"No, no one teaches anyone how to pray. You just do it. I've heard a lot of prayers in my lifetime, so I guess that helps." Brady shoved a French fry in her already full mouth.

Richard could hear her crunching from across the table. He hoped she would swallow before saying another word. She ate quietly for awhile and Richard gave a private, silent prayer of thanks.

"What is the difference between prayer and wishful thinking?" Michael asked, looking at Brady with the reverence one might give the Dalai Lama.

Richard watched Michael warily. This could be sincere and it could be mocking. Richard sometimes had trouble reading Michael.

"Wishful thinking is like magic." She snapped her fingers. "But when you pray to God you are asking for help, and you know that you may have to just accept what happens. Prayer helps you to sort out your feelings about what you want, so that you know if you're doing things for good reasons or not. Like, you're not supposed to pray to do well on a test or a game at school. We're supposed to pray to accept God's will. But you never stop hoping." Brady seemed to check their responses and then smiled into her salad plate.

"Maybe they tell you not to pray for tests so that you will study instead," Michael said.

Brady nodded. "Kind of like the lord helps those who help themselves thing, you mean?"

Michael nodded.

Brady cocked her head to one side and looked at Michael thoughtfully. "Where do you go to church, sir?"

"Why do you call us 'sir'?" he asked.

"That's what we call all of the teachers at school—sir or ma'am. Why?"

"You don't need to do that here. It feels, well, overly formal, I think," Richard said.

Brady shrugged and lowered her head. "What do you want to be called?"

"*Dad* is good. It works." Even if it was unearned.

Brady nodded.

"I'm Michael. That's what I want to be called. In case anyone's asking," Michael said.

"So where do you go to church?" Brady repeated.

Richard suppressed a smile.

"I'm Jewish." Michael raised his eyebrows at Richard.

"Oh, so you go to temple on Saturday?" Brady asked.

Michael lowered his head. "No, I don't do that either."

"Well, where do you go, Dad?" Brady asked, furrowing her brow and turning to Richard.

"I don't really go to church," Richard said.

Brady stared at the tablecloth.

Richard wanted this moment to pass, but as though driven by some unseen force, he heard himself say, "Would you like me to find a church?"

Brady nodded.

"We run on Sundays," Michael said.

"What kind of church do you want?" Richard asked Brady.

"Christian. What else is there?"

"There are lots of different Christians: Lutherans, Methodists, Presbyterians, Episcopalians, Catholics, and Baptists." Richard knew she went to a Christian school but was unclear on her actual denomination. *Please don't say* Baptist, Richard thought, because of all the homophobic denominations, he felt the Baptists had to be the worst.

"I've been baptized, so I guess Baptist is what I am," Brady said.

Richard forced a smile.

The rest of the food came and the conversation flowed. She did not like sports because she wasn't good at them and hated letting people down when she missed the ball. She had good grades and worked hard for them. She liked her teachers. She paused slightly when Richard asked who her good friends were and then said hesitantly, "Joanne and Jeanie? Sometimes we get along well, and sometimes not. I can never tell how it's going to go."

And finally, Brady laid down her fork and settled back in her chair, running her hand over her stomach. She smiled with eyes half closed and said, "That was wonderful, thanks."

They paid the bill and walked to the car. She was asleep before they pulled onto the freeway. After they pulled into the driveway, Michael ran ahead and unlocked the door. Richard pulled her up out of the car and onto his shoulder. She was so deeply asleep that her head lolled against his as he settled her on his body. She was unusually light, and the trip up the stairs was effortless.

They took pains not to turn on any extra lights and kept their conversation to a minimum. Michael led the way, pushed her bed-room door open, and turned back the covers on her bed.

Using the light that filtered from the room across the hall, Richard lowered her into her bed. He took off her shoes and pulled the comforter up under her chin. With Michael watching from the door, he kissed her on the forehead and couldn't resist whispering, "Good night, little princess."

She stirred slightly in her sleep, rolling to her side and snuggling more deeply under the comforter and into the pillow. She looked so peaceful, content, and, most important of all, well cared for.

* * *

Richard straightened up and walked into the hall, where he could see Michael's outline backlit by the light from their bedroom. He released a sigh of contentment and smiled to himself as he closed the door to Brady's bedroom. He felt like a father.

Michael smiled a different smile and pulled Richard into an embrace, kissing him deeply. Richard felt himself responding and ran his hands down into the back of Michael's jeans. Still locked in a kiss, Michael pulled him along the wall toward their bedroom. They were just about to round the corner and fall onto the sleigh bed when Richard heard Brady snore.

Michael stared too and then whispered, "It's okay. She's asleep."

But Richard shook his head. "It's her first night, Michael."

Michael let a groan of exasperation escape. He paced to their room and stared into the closet as though unable to decide what clothes he needed for tonight and tomorrow. He pulled the clothes in silent jabs. Without looking at Richard, he walked around him, heading for the door.

Richard touched his shoulder as he passed. "It's only for a little while, Michael," Richard said.

Michael ducked his touch. "Right," he said.

Richard could hear each deliberate step he took on his way down the stairs.

CHURCHED

Richard awakened the next morning with the sensation that the day was beginning without him. The smell of coffee wafted up from the kitchen. He saw the grinding and brewing of coffee as his ritual act of love. Michael had made the coffee himself. Richard jumped out of bed and started down stairs barefooted. He smelled oranges and listened with amusement to Michael whistle as he ground the pulp in the juicer. Crossing the living room, Richard could hear sausage sizzling in the skillet in front of Michael. Although Richard knew it was soy, it smelled like pork, and that made his stomach growl.

Coming up behind Michael, Richard encircled his robed shoulders and buried his lips in his neck. But Michael pulled Richard's arms away from his neck and gestured at Brady, who was seated at the round oak table in the breakfast nook. Her head was leaning toward the newspaper, and she was circling items with a black marker.

"Oh, Brady!" Richard gasped.

Brady looked up. "Hi, Dad. I've got the listings for the churches here but I don't know which ones are too far away," she said, and she looked back down at the paper. "Can you help?"

"Right," Richard said, and he hoped his color was settling. She turned back to the paper, and he poured himself some coffee. He rounded the kitchen counter and approached the table. While he admired her pluck, he knew Michael wouldn't approve and he would have to go without him. This would cause Michael to go running alone. Richard needed to go running with Michael.

Brady had the *L.A. Times* opened to church directories and was circling addresses in Manhattan Beach. He looked over her shoulder, surprised to find there were so many, and saw that one was less than a mile away.

"That one's close," Richard said, "if we eat quickly."

Michael set the plates down hard on the table before he sat and began to eat without a word.

Richard tried to gloss over it. "Doesn't that sausage taste good, Brady?" he asked.

"Uh-huh," she said and nodded, biting a sausage she had skewered on her fork. She had already consumed her eggs without comment.

Michael watched Brady eat the sausage off of her fork for several seconds before he returned to eating.

Looking full, Brady pushed back from the table.

"Drink your juice," Michael said.

Brady looked at the glass before she lifted it to her mouth and began straining the juice between her teeth. She swallowed and frowned. "It has pulp in it."

"Never mind," Michael said, taking the glass from her and setting it on the table. They all looked at the glass as it hit the table. He opened *The New York Times* and began reading.

Richard stared at the newspaper between them and chewed the inside of his cheek.

"I'm going to get into church clothes," Brady said, rushing up the stairs. Over her shoulder she puffed out, "Michael, are you coming?"

"No," came Michael's voice from behind the paper.

Richard stood and tapped his fingers against the sides of his legs. Michael lowered the paper barrier, and Richard noted that his eyebrows were raised and his lips pressed in a straight line.

"Just say no to homophobic churches," Michael said.

"It's one day. It makes her happy." Richard gestured up the stairs toward Brady's closed bedroom door. They could hear her singing. Richard tilted his head forward and said, "See?"

"It's dishonest," Michael said. "When are you going to tell her that you are gay? After you sit through the sermon and you have to go head-to-head with everything she sees as powerful and true? You know, like God and the Bible?" Michael's voice was starting to rise, and Richard held out his hands to make him stop.

"You think I'm being dishonest?" Richard asked, but it sounded like a statement.

"Yes," Michael said, "tell her you can't go and you need to talk to her."

"Come on, Dad, let's go. I hate being late to church," Brady said, coming down the stairs.

The two men froze mid sentence.

Brady galloped down the last three steps still singing. She was wearing one of the new dresses, fire-engine red with white flowers.

Noting her glowing smile, Richard looked away from Michael and said to her, "I'll be right there." He dashed up the stairs to his room, changed in record time, and raced back down.

Brady was sitting at the table, and Michael had begun cleaning the dishes.

"Good bye," Richard said to Michael's back. "We won't be long, an hour max."

Michael nodded without raising his head and continued scrubbing.

Richard touched Brady on the shoulder, and they walked to the door. As he opened it to let her out, he could see her staring across the living room at Michael's silent figure.

Richard felt a growing sense of anxiety in his chest as he started the car and backed out of the drive. Brady was subdued during the short drive to the church. Richard wanted to drop her off and go back to Michael. As he parked, he felt perspiration on his upper lip. He pictured Michael whistling as he squeezed the fresh oranges. What was he doing?

"Come on, Dad; what's taking you so long?" Brady pulled at his hand, looking both ways before leading him across the street to church. A large banner hanging over the door of the church proclaimed, "The Journey of Faith Starts Here!" Richard's breathing felt shallow. He looked back at the car. As they went up the stairs, several people smiled at Brady and greeted him. Richard forced a smile, but his stomach tightened.

As he and Brady went inside, Richard stared in awe at the high-tech sanctuary. There were screens on either side of the congregation and three cameras trained on the choir and the two pulpits. With the exception of the two-stories-tall cross that hung at the front of the church, the sanctuary looked more like a movie set than a place of worship.

A handsome young man with blond hair stood and began playing an electric guitar and was accompanied by a drummer who sat behind him. On both sides, crimson-robed choirs stood and began to sing. In response, the congregation not only rose, but came to life. All of those proper people who had shaken his hand and greeted Brady were rocking out to the choir and the electric band that accompanied them.

Richard had been raised Episcopalian and had grown up sensing it was unbecoming to raise your voice in church at all, but these people were dancing and clapping. He looked over at Brady, who was sitting openmouthed, staring around herself at the people and the screens. After that aerobic workout, Richard assumed the congregation would fall into the pews for a little cool down, but they remained standing. The minister, who went by Pastor Paul, according to the order of service, was a short man with a round pink face, white hair, and an omnipresent smile. He stepped to the podium, and his image flickered up on both screens. "Let us pray," he said, raising his hands.

Closing his eyes, Richard folded his hands in his lap. He felt Brady patting the back of his hand and opened his eyes. She laughed and took his hand, while extending her hand to the woman on her right. He glanced apprehensively to his left and took the hand of a smiling older gentleman in a light blue seersucker suit. What was it with modern-day Christians and handholding? He had always thought that prayer was sort of a private moment between God and the supplicant. He was embarrassed by his sweaty palms. And didn't these people know that holding hands passed germs?

The pastor's voice boomed from overhead. "Dear God, be with us during our time of fellowship and later as we take your word into the community. Thank you for the health we enjoy, and be with our brothers and sisters who are not able to be with us today. May the meditations of my heart and words of my mouth be ever pleasing to you. Amen."

The congregation offered a resounding "amen" and dropped to the pews. As the sermon progressed, Richard learned that he was now among "The Children of God" and that it was very good to be one. Being "Children of God" was not easy but also made you children of promise. All of this hard work paid off in the end because apparently these children never died but had eternal life. If that eternal-life thing were really true, how could they explain that when people died they were never seen again? Richard wondered if he could spend his eternity with Michael. He wondered whether anyone in the congregation could answer his questions, and he looked at the man in the seersucker suit. But just at that moment, the man yelled out, "That's right," to encourage the pastor. This startled Richard, so he decided now was not a good time to ask.

The sermon was mercifully short, and as the minister finished, the children's choir filed onto the steps in front of him. They were led by a thick and energetic man in a choir robe who occasionally jumped in place as he sang along with them. This caused a tsunami to move through the man's shiny robe, and Richard found it mesmerizing. These must be the promised children. They looked very promising indeed, these beautiful little boys and girls of all races, remarkably talented and poised.

With an amplified blessing from the back, admonishing the faithful to go forth and spread the word, they were free to go. He had survived. No one accosted him or asked to fix him as put forth by Parents and Friends of Ex-Gays. He had actually liked the music, and Brady was happy. Now all he had to do was go make it up to Michael. He filed into the aisle and up to Brady, who was already talking to the minister.

"Sure, my dad lives right up the street so he can come any time," she said.

Richard's eyes widened as he realized that Brady was giving detailed instructions on how to get to Michael's house. Michael would never forgive him. "I'd rather call you first. I'd hate for you to waste your time," Richard said.

"It's not a problem. I get more out of visiting parishioners than I do listening to myself preach," Pastor Paul said before releasing jarring waves of laughter into Richard's face.

"No, really, I'll call," Richard said, stepping away and taking Brady by the hand. He pulled her into a run once they passed the large oak doors.

"Dad, slow down. Why are you running?" He looked down and saw that Brady was struggling to keep up. Her brows had drawn together in a look of hurt confusion. "Stop," she yelled.

Richard looked over her shoulder and saw parishioners heading in their direction toward the parking lot. He needed to get her into the car. He needed to tell her the truth. He later wouldn't be able to tell if it was the act of running or the fear of having the Christian Right show up at his door that made him want to tell her the truth, but he did.

Richard looked away and said, "You're not going to want to hear what I have to say." He paused, tried to put feelings to words, but he gave up and blurted out, "Brady, I'm gay." He waited and then when there was no response, he looked at her.

She appeared confused, and he thought he was going to have to explain what *gay* meant. But he saw, by the look of disgust on her face, that she'd made the connection.

He wanted to walk away, but he also wanted to be her father. Parishioners drove out of the parking lot in a steady line behind him, forcing him to move closer to Brady and the car to avoid being hit.

Brady's eyes were red and filling with tears; her mouth was turned down. He put his arm around her shoulder and guided her to the other side of the car, where he eased her inside.

By the time he got in the car, she was crying. "I don't want this," she said. "I want to go home."

"Home, where?" He paused. "With Michael?" He lowered his head, bracing.

Brady shook her head hard. "No, I want to go home to Grandma and Grandpa. I don't want this anymore." She looked at him just for a moment, as though reconsidering, and then cried harder.

Richard groaned before finding the words. "I'm sorry. I really am. I know it's not what you want, and I wouldn't choose it either." His hands gestured wildly as words spilled from his lips. "No one would choose to be gay if they had a choice." He stopped talking because he didn't think she could hear him over her sobs. The crowd was very small in front of the church, and he didn't want to be present when the pastor found himself sans sheep. Richard started the car and pulled onto the road. He wanted a little time to let the situation de-escalate and they were only minutes from home, so he drove to Polliwog Park.

He parked and ran his hand over his eyes. Coming to terms with being a gay drunk had offered him multiple opportunities to feel like shit, but this one was the shittiest moment ever. It was so selfish for him to have her here. Her life had been fine without him, and now she was miserable.

He rested his elbows on the steering wheel and ran his fingers through his hair. "I'm sorry," he said. He offered her his handkerchief. She took it wordlessly and without any eye contact.

Looking at her made him feel worse, so he looked forward.

Brady stared out of the car window. When she finally spoke, it sounded like she had Kleenex in her mouth. He had to lean toward her to decipher the words.

"I knew it would be this way." She paused to draw a breath. "Weird. Everything in my life is weird. I'm not like anybody else. My mom's dead and you've been gone. I live with my grandparents for parents, and they aren't like everyone else. They're old." She squeezed her eyes shut. "And that just makes me weirder. We don't do the stuff other kids do. I can't talk about my dad who coaches soccer because I don't have one. I can't even talk about the TV shows other kids talk about because my grandparents go to bed too early and won't let me watch. I thought, with you, things would be different. I was happy for a while but now you're"—she gestured at him and shrugged—"whatever."

She went quiet for what felt like forever. The "whatever" hung in the air between them. When she finally spoke again, her voice was steadier. "You couldn't always have been gay. You were married to my mom. You are my dad, right?"

"Yes, I . . ." He wanted to be understood, but he did not want to explain. He stared at the clouds through the windshield. "I made love to your mother once, and that's where you came from. And then I thought I could make myself be a husband and a father. I wanted to please her. I probably just made her miserable too."

"No, she loved you," Brady said, her voice sounding as if it were bubbling out of a tar pit. "She wanted you to come back. She missed you." She closed her mouth, and he could see her swallow hard. "I wanted you to get married again. I wanted to be a flower girl." She cried harder than ever and buried her face in the skirt of her dress.

Brady raised her head and stared at him. The movement caught his eye, and he felt he could see another idea play across her face. She leveled her now-translucent blue eyes on him. "So, Michael?" Her lips parted and curled in disgust.

Richard felt his back stiffen. "He's enough mother for ten kids, don't you think?"

She laughed and broke the tension. Richard watched Brady think, her brow furrowing, as though she were holding a conversation within herself.

"It's a sin, you know?" she asked finally.

Richard said, "I am the way your God made me. I don't believe he would want me to live a lie. I've done that. It is awful. It feels so dishonest, it has to be sinful." Richard grimaced and then continued. "I mean, Jesus accepted the tax collectors and the prostitutes." He raised his eyebrows.

She stared at him and looked as though she wanted to believe him. She sniffed again, and he handed her a Kleenex. In return she held out the sodden handkerchief. He had seen her blow her nose in it twice, and it was soaked through. He looked at it and stopped himself from pulling back. In an ultimate act of fatherhood, he took the sodden mess in his hand and put it in his pocket.

"I'm tired," Brady said. Sleep was settling in as nature's anesthetic.

"Do you still want to go home—to your grandparents, I mean?" Richard looked straight ahead, afraid of what she was going to say. He could hear her breathing while he waited.

"No, no, let's just go home here," she said.

Richard started the car and they drove in silence. They pulled into the drive and walked to the door. She followed him into the kitchen but stared up at her bedroom door.

Richard read the note from Michael on the counter: *Running, M.*

The brevity reflected Michael's anger; ordinarily he would have left instructions for lunch.

Richard opened the refrigerator door and stared at the contents with little inspiration. His stomach growled. Although the service had been brief, they had been at the park for a long time.

"Hey, Dad?" Brady was standing next to him, staring into the refrigerator.

"Yeah?" He shut the door and turned to her, crossing his arms over his chest.

"Could we could go for a cheeseburger or pizza?"

"I thought you were tired?" Richard said.

"But I'm hungry too. And, since Michael's not here, we can eat anything we want." The look on her face was decidedly comical given her red nose and swollen eyes.

"I know just where to go." Richard was relieved to have the moment pass, and now he wanted to get out of there before Michael showed up and caught them red-handed, colluding to eat red meat.

He pushed her shoulders gently to urge her to walk toward the door, saying, "Go, go, go," in mock urgency. "This is not a drill."

She laughed and broke into a run as soon as she got through the door. They raced each other to the car, but since Richard had the key, he got in first, mouthing, "and I won" to her through the window. She impatiently worked the door handle and he had to try twice to unlock the door before the lock popped up. She jumped in saying, "Let's go, I'm starving!"

The wheels squealed as he pulled away from the house. "Gee, I didn't even know I could do that," he said, smiling. He drove the short distance down Manhattan Beach Boulevard to The Kettle and parked. Brady looked at the restaurant suspiciously. "I was thinking of something more like McDonald's or Burger King."

Richard said, "McDonald's is gross. This place makes the best burgers ever and you can get French fries, onion rings, and huge milk shakes!"

"Okay," she said. There was suspicion in her voice, but she followed him. At the door she asked, "Do I look okay?"

He scanned her quickly. Although people should notice her red and swollen eyes, they probably wouldn't. The redness had subsided, and he handed her his sunglasses with an air of conspiracy, saying, "We'll eat outside and no one will be the wiser."

They both ordered cheeseburgers, his with "the works" and hers with ketchup. She ordered French fries, and they agreed to share his onion rings. They both ordered huge milkshakes, Richard's strawberry and Brady's chocolate. They stared at each food server who carried trays of burgers and fries from the kitchen. When theirs arrived with sizzle and the savory scent of cheeseburgers fresh from the grill, they attacked them like a pack of Pavlov's slobbering dogs.

"Why is Michael so picky about what we eat?" she asked with her mouth full.

"You are too," Richard said, his voice thickened by burger, bun, and ketchup.

She looked at him across the table. "Yeah, but I don't make him eat what I like. He makes us eat what he likes." She started to reach for an onion ring but decided on a French fry instead.

"It's his way of showing that he cares about us." When Brady rolled her eyes, Richard added, "No really, he was fat growing up, and he lost that weight and now he wants to share that with others." Richard shrugged and his voice softened. "His dad died early of heart failure caused by fat, and Michael doesn't want that for himself or anyone he loves."

"Well, I'm not fat, and I don't have a bad heart. Neither do you, so he doesn't need to force us to eat all that healthy stuff." Brady wrinkled her nose and gestured toward the lettuce and tomato that she had removed from her cheeseburger before she began to eat. "You're a grown-up, and he still tells you what to eat."

"I like the food Michael makes. He grows the lettuce and tomatoes himself, and he bakes his own bread." An image of Michael cooking and gardening flashed through his mind. A wave of soft warmth eased through his chest. Richard began to eat faster without meaning to do so. He wondered if he'd have the courage to sleep with Michael now that Brady knew. The thought made him crave Michael's company. "He wants you to live and be healthy. That's why he gives you good, wholesome food."

Brady considered this. "Some of it's okay, but I really hate soy milk, and mostly I just don't need that much food. He thinks I'm being picky, but sometimes I'm just not hungry."

Richard nodded. "Okay, eat less then. But you still need fruits and vegetables."

She rolled her eyes again.

"Just do it. Try a little of everything, and maybe you'll find something new." Richard was done with the topic.

"You know a little about the Bible. Do you believe in God?" Brady stopped eating and was staring at him.

"I do, and I believe in a lot of what the church does. They give food and shelter, and help people when they are sad or struggling with alcohol or drug addiction. I had problems of my own in that regard." He looked at her, and she nodded. "You know about that?" he asked, feeling panicky. What had she been told?

She stared at her plate. "When my mom died, I asked where you were, and Grandpa said you were probably dead drunk in some gutter somewhere. That's why I thought you were dead. Later, somebody told me that *dead drunk* didn't have to mean dead, just drunk. So I thought you might still be alive."

Richard wanted to touch her hands, but they were sticky with ketchup and mayonnaise. He dipped a napkin in a glass of ice water and started cleaning the condiments off. It made him feel better to take care of her, and it allowed him to find words. "I'm sorry for everything you've been through. I'm sorry I wasn't there earlier in your life." Brady stared at the table, but he could tell she was listening. He could feel her eyes on him when he looked away. "Finding Michael has saved my life. Having both of you together is perfect for me. When we're doing ordinary things like shopping or eating together, it makes me happy. It feels like we're a family. I never thought I would live long enough to get you and him together in my life." He looked at her directly before continuing. "Really, it seemed impossible." He dried her hands with a napkin, but they felt cold, so he warmed them by enclosing them with his own.

She looked up at him, her blue eyes wide and fixed on his. "Can I live with you then?"

Richard gasped, and a pulse of alarm shot from his gut to his chest. He felt his heart quicken. "You want to come and live with us?"

He wanted her to live with them. He wanted them to be a family. But he had to be careful. "It's not as easy as you might think."

Her face fell.

"I'd like for you to come live with us . . ." he began, intending to add *but*.

Her face brightened with joy and she interrupted him. "Oh, yes!" She squeezed her hands into fists and raised them. "Yes!"

Richard gritted his teeth in anxiety but it was too late. She behaved as though he were smiling. Alarms exploded in his mind, but words failed to materialize. He stammered.

She pulled her hand out of his and ran around the table, jumping into his arms and pulling herself into his lap. He had to back the chair up very fast to avoid having it tip over. He buried his face in her hair, which smelled like Michael's shampoo. How was he going to tell Michael?

When they arrived at home, he told Brady to go upstairs and change. The slider was open. He could see Michael sitting in the Adirondack chair reading *The New York Times*. He walked into the backyard, but Michael did not look up.

Richard cleared his throat.

Michael raised his head slowly, as though dragging himself away from some fascinating account.

"Hi." Richard bounced self-consciously on his toes.

"Hello," Michael said, and he gave him a cold stare.

"May I join you?" Richard gestured at the other chair.

"Go ahead." Michael shrugged.

Richard sat down and crossed his legs, folding his hands over his stomach. He stared at Michael, who had gone back to reading. "Church was okay, thanks for asking. It was fun, actually. They have these great big screens on either side of the church like at a rock concert. They have three of these services every Sunday, with rock and roll, gospel bands, and this cute little kids' choir. Really, Michael, it's impressive."

Michael gave Richard a fixed smile. "Good to hear," he said, and he returned to reading.

Softly, Richard went on, "And I told Brady—everything."

Michael looked up. "In church? How did that go? You were gone a long time. What did she say?"

"Well, she cried at first." Richard looked down and took a deep breath. He forced the words out. "And she wants to come and live with us."

"Live with us?" Michael stood as he spoke; the newspaper fell to the ground. "Richard, what have you done? What about the grandparents? Do they get any say in your little plan? Do I?" He jabbed at his chest with his balled-up fist that held the newspaper. "This is a visit, goddamnit. You covered all of that in one conversation?"

Richard nodded. "From hell to the rapture in ten easy steps."

"I hope you understand that legally it's not that simple? You told her that, right?" Michael said.

Richard stared at the azaleas. Their plump, pink blossoms seemed comforting. "She was so happy and she had been so, so sad. You weren't there. You didn't see. I needed her to feel okay."

"No, you needed to be a grown-up. She's a little kid, and you need to guide her through this. You've gotten her hopes up that she's moving here for the rest of her life. We don't have that kind of control. We agreed to return her to Disneyland, remember?"

Richard's unusually full stomach now churned with anxiety. He was going to have to tell Brady he made a mistake. He closed his eyes. He always fucked everything up.

"I hate being forced into the position of saying no, Richard. It isn't fair. You have got to learn to think before you do what *feels* good," Michael snapped. "So where is she?"

"Upstairs. She was really tired. It's been an emotional day. And I guess it's going to get worse," Richard said, looking away from Michael toward the house.

"This isn't just me, Richard. It's the law."

Richard sighed and leaned forward, placing his elbows on the glass-topped table with white filigree. He rested his face in his hands and covered his eyes. "And rapture back to hell in five minutes. Life is never dull. I'll give you that."

Richard felt Michael staring at him. "Look, it is not in our power to make promises." Michael's voice had softened. Richard looked up.

"That is what lawyers and judges are for. We have a lawyer. Let's talk to him when we agree on what we want." Michael nodded at Richard, his eyes soft and understanding.

Richard felt hope make his heart speed up.

Michael sat back down opposite Richard. "Just don't go off half-cocked. Talk to me first, please."

"I'm sorry. It will stop," Richard said. He was staring at his shoes when he felt Michael touch his arm.

"I know you mean well. But you get carried away." Michael had leaned forward, and his voice was close to Richard's ear. "But we don't have a lot of power, and she needs us to protect her from disappointment." Michael squeezed Richard's arm.

Richard nodded. He still had to let Brady know that coming here wasn't quite the slam dunk they'd thought, but at least he had Michael on his side.

"So she knows we're gay? How'd that go?" Michael's asked.

Richard looked over Michael's shoulder.

"What did she actually say, Richard?"

Richard's first impulse was to lie and say Brady was fine with it. But as he played the memory through his mind, he knew she had been disgusted and only sort of accepted it. Richard smiled, put his hands in his pockets, and said, "She knows, and that's all. It's a place to start." He added, "Sorry," as he noted Michael's crossed arms and set jaw. Movement behind Michael caught Richard's eye, and he leaned to see around him.

"Hi, Brady," Richard said. "How long have you been there?"

Brady stood inside of the sliding glass door with her arms crossed, rocking her weight from foot to foot. She raised her shoulders slowly and deliberately up and then down.

"We need to talk," Michael said. "Let's all go inside and sit down." He led the way to the leather couches and sat while Richard and Brady followed.

"So, Brady, tell me what you understand about us," Michael asked, pointing at himself and then Richard.

Brady sat on the couch, hands folded in her lap, and stared at her red Converse sneakers newly bought by Michael. "I don't know," she began and then sighed. "You're gay. He says that you're gay." She inclined her head toward Richard. She stared at the floor.

"Yes, and what does that mean to you?" Michael asked.

Brady stared at the floor and shrugged.

Richard let his head fall back against the couch and stared at the ceiling.

Michael waited.

"It means you love each other like a man and wife." Brady's voice was loud, her back was straight, and she looked fiercely at Michael.

"And how do you feel about that?"

Richard released a barely audible moan and smoothed his forehead. Michael sounded like an eighth-grade guidance counselor.

Brady shrugged one shoulder.

"No," Michael said, "you have to say more than that. Richard tells me you want to come live with us."

Brady looked directly at him, eyes appealing, palms open on her lap, and nodded.

Michael surprised Richard by reaching out and squeezing her arm. "I want that too. I've loved shopping and building castles and everything." He crossed his arms over his chest. "But it is going to take a lot of work to get you here. And honestly, your religion—correct me if I'm wrong—teaches that men loving men is a sin—or an abomination or some such thing, right?" Michael said, waving his hand dismissively.

Brady nodded without looking at him, her head slightly bowed as though bracing.

"How are you going to live with us if you believe that?" Michael asked, opening his hands in an appeal.

Brady shrugged.

"Nope, you need to answer in words," Michael said.

Richard sat up as though to interrupt but stayed silent.

"I know," Brady said, "that I have never given up hope that you," she gestured at Richard, "would come get me. I prayed all the time for it even though everybody said you were dead. So when you called, I figured God was answering my prayers." She stopped, looked into the yard, and sighed before adding, "Maybe he still is."

Richard knew Michael had become a fervent nonbeliever while studying for his bar mitzvah. He told Richard he felt that all organized religion was a threat to independent thought. Richard was surprised to see him nodding and following Brady's gaze into the sunlit yard.

"What does that mean?" Michael asked.

Richard studied Michael's face with curiosity. Was that hope?

"I don't really know. I just know I need to be here right now. It feels right to me. I think this is God's plan for me even though you are gay," Brady said, dropping the last word down to a whisper and smoothing the sides of her legs.

"And your grandparents?" Richard asked. "This is going to be a huge disappointment to them."

Here she stopped and stared at the ceiling. Her lips drew together as her eyes filled. She swallowed hard. "I don't know." She forced the words out, and a sob escaped.

Richard slid next to her and pulled her into him. He tucked her head under his chin.

"I'm supposed to call them," she choked out.

"Then do it once you're able to talk," Michael said, looking at Richard and then turning back to Brady. "None of this is easy for them either, so we want to be as cooperative as possible."

Brady cried and then blew her nose and headed off to the study to make the call.

"And Brady," Richard said, "Don't mention anything about living here until we meet with the lawyer and know what our rights are."

Brady nodded and started to walk away.

"Oh, and Brady," Richard said, holding up his hand.

She stopped again, pivoted on the balls of her feet, and raised her eyebrows.

"Don't mention the gay thing. Not right yet. You know?" Richard said.

"Right, be cooperative but don't mention anything we just talked about for the last fifteen minutes. Got it," Brady said, and she walked away faster than before.

WHAT NEXT?

～～～～～～～

Richard awakened the next morning curled around Michael, both naked. Richard could hardly wait to start the day. After putting on pajama bottoms, Richard lingered at Brady's door and listened to her snore before he went downstairs to get coffee for Michael.

"Hey, sailor, new in town?" Richard said to Michael as he slid back under the covers with two steaming white mugs.

"Show me a good time?" Michael asked, taking the coffee and kissing him.

They sipped and mapped out the next step.

"Let's just call the lawyer," Richard groaned, churning his legs under the covers.

"Lawyers charge for everything—a twenty-minute phone call is going to cost $350. So before we put ourselves on the meter, we need to have questions written down.

"I'm hungry," Brady said, standing in the doorway of their bedroom. She rubbed her eyes. "What's for breakfast?"

Michael pulled Richard's robe from the end of the bed and put it on. "What about waffles?" he asked, snatching up clothes and heading toward the bathroom.

"I like waffles"—Brady eyed their bed sleepily—"and bacon and sausage." She tossed herself onto the bed, burying her head in her father's chest.

Michael stopped in his tracks and watched Richard close his arms around her head and tickle her ribs. She giggled and rolled over on her back, her head still resting on his chest. Richard tickled her again, relishing the sound of her laugh and the softness of her hair against his chest. He felt warm, affectionate, and playful; he liked that Michael was watching.

"Again? We had sausage yesterday," Michael said.

"I want it every day," Brady said.

"Uh-huh," Michael muttered, giving Richard a knowing look as he took his clothes to the bathroom. He reemerged wearing his soft black Hugo Boss pants and a running shirt. "Breakfast, coming up," he said.

Very quickly Richard and Brady were drawn down the stairs by the tantalizing smell of waffles and sausage. Michael was pouring fresh orange juice in glasses.

"This looks wonderful," Richard said as he admired his plate of blueberry waffles and mango and papaya on the side.

"Thanks," Michael smiled; clearly pleased until he noticed Brady was excising blueberries from her waffles.

Richard stifled a moan. Not again.

"I don't like blueberries," Brady said, lowering her head.

Michael sighed and reached for her plate. "I'm sorry. Next time I'll leave them out."

"No, it's okay. I'll just cut them out." Brady held onto her plate. She seemed determined to make this work. Michael let go of it.

"We need to talk about what you do like to eat. Believe it or not, I am actually trying to please you, but I don't know what you want," Michael said, glancing at Richard, who reached forward and stroked his hand.

"I know. I'm sorry," Brady said.

Richard furrowed his brow as he watched Michael rush off to the den. Where was he going?

Michael returned flourishing a printed grocery list that Richard recognized. Michael had been using this list as long as they'd been together.

Michael settled next to her. "You need to have the food you

are used to eating—you know, for future visits." Michael handed her a pen. She added to the list regular milk, white bread, Kraft macaroni and cheese, and Oreos.

Oreos. Oh no.

"I'm not buying Oreos. I make my own cookies," Michael said.

"They have nuts. I don't like nuts," Brady said.

Even Richard wished Brady would knock it off. Michael's father had been a baker, and Michael had adapted his recipes so that they were healthy but tasty. The smell of these cookies had some sort of transformative effect on Michael, making him peaceful and content. How Michael had managed to make the cookies without butter or flour was a mystery, but Richard knew the cookies were a sacred cow and had to stay.

"I'll make them without nuts for you."

"They don't taste sweet."

"I'll put sugar in yours. And butter and flour." Michael curled his lip.

Richard stared at Michael and raised his eyebrows. "White Death?" Richard asked.

"It's better than Oreos," Michael said, rolling his eyes.

"Okay," Brady said.

"Can you say thank you?" Richard asked.

"Thank you," Brady said. She muttered "Sorry" under her breath and finished removing the blueberries from the waffles, isolating them to one quadrant of her plate.

"How did your conversation with your grandparents go?" Michael asked.

"Okay," Brady half shrugged. She looked at Michael and added, "It was a little weird."

"How so?" Richard asked, pouring himself more coffee.

"I know stuff they don't about you and us. I'm excited about it, but I can't talk about it. I had trouble thinking of stuff to talk about. I talked mostly about the beach. They didn't say much." Her voice sounded shaky. He stared at her for a while, but she picked up her fork and began to eat.

The three ate hungrily, the only sound the clatter of cutlery on the ceramic plates. Brady broke the silence with a loud sniff followed by a whimper. Richard and Michael turned to look at her.

"What is it?" Richard asked. When she didn't answer, he pulled her into his lap, bowing his head over hers as she choked down sobs. She smelled like maple syrup.

"I don't know what I want anymore. I don't want to choose. I like living with my grandparents and I don't want them to be alone, and I like you too, both of you. But if I choose to live with you, then I'll miss my grandparents, and if I go with them, I won't have you." She trailed off and dipped her head lower. Richard swept her hair away from the syrup.

"Brady, I'm so sorry. You are such a brave kid and it's so, so complicated. I wish it could be easier, but it can't. All I can say is that we love you and we will work to make us a family," Richard said.

Brady looked up. "I like it here with you. I like living in a family where people do fun things together." She was staring at Michael, not him. The stab of jealousy took him by surprise. He *wanted* Brady to like Michael—love him. He wanted to share his daughter. But the truth was it was hard for him to share her. He had to be a grown-up now. He *would* be, for her.

"But you miss your grandparents. I understand," Richard said. He *could* be a grown-up.

"Especially at night when I go to bed. They must be lonely without me." She looked up at him, her lips pursed. "But when I'm with you guys, I feel like I have what all the other kids have. With my grandparents, I read books but I don't know about TV shows or sports. And that just makes me not fit in." She paused to catch her breath, and when she began to speak, it was as though she were talking to herself. "This morning I woke up and I could hear your music, and you guys were laughing. I couldn't wait to get in there with you. But it made it hard to talk to my grandparents—they seem so far away. Like they don't know me anymore." She pushed herself out of Richard's lap. "I'm full. I'm tired. I'm going back to bed."

Richard stared at her retreating back, a frail form with hunched shoulders. He looked at Michael. "Now what?"

* * *

"Can I please call the lawyer now? I don't know what to say to her because I don't have the information," Richard asked.

Michael pictured the list of questions. They were organized enough to make good use of time with their lawyer. *Here goes.* "It's risky because we don't even know what we're up against. What if it's bad news?"

"God! What if we don't win?" Richard interrupted. "What if they give her to the grandparents and we can't even see her anymore." Richard looked at him with round eyes.

"Exactly, it could happen, and we need to be prepared for that," Michael said, nodding.

Richard spread his palms out in front of him on the dark green granite counter. "We'll win. We have to, that's all. Let's go talk to her," Richard said, skipping every other step as he sprinted upstairs.

"Richard, you're going too fast. Let's call first and then wake her up," Michael said, reaching for his phone and pressing the numbers.

As the call was answered, he heard Richard knock on Brady's door. "Brady, open the door. We need to talk to you."

Michael heard Richard's gasp and hung up the phone to run upstairs. Over Richard's shoulder he was shocked by Brady's red and swollen eyes against the ashen color of her face. Brady walked back to her unmade bed and sat on it, staring at them bleary-eyed.

Richard began, "Please, don't give up. We want you to come with us to see the lawyer. I'm going to call Ryan and find out if he can see us today," Richard said as he left the room.

Michael stared at Richard's back as he left. He'd never been alone with Brady. He cleared his throat. "What's making you so sad, Brady?"

"I don't know," Brady answered. "I've been thinking. When my mom died, nobody came to help except Grandma and Grandpa. Maybe I'm supposed to stay with them."

"Supposed to—like someone's telling to you to do this?" Michael shoved his hands deeply into his pants pockets.

"Maybe that's God's plan for me." She looked at him, and he could not hold her gaze.

He sat down next to her on the bed, stared at the ceiling, and clenched the change in his pockets. He wanted to be respectful of her faith, but he couldn't. Her faith labeled his love for Richard as an abomination. Still silence hung heavy between them, and he could sense her waiting. He had to say something.

"Do you really believe that, Brady?" he asked, looking in her direction but not at her.

Brady lay back on the bed and stared at the ceiling. "I don't know what I believe anymore. I know I don't want to hope things are going to be okay and have them fall apart. I'm so tired of feeling sad."

He pulled one leg onto the bed and rested on his elbow. The idea of a prescriptive god seemed childish. But the legal issue made sense. "I'd like to tell you we're guaranteed to win, but I can't. What I can tell you is that if we don't try, it's certain we'll never win."

Lying on her back on the bed, she raised her hands above her head and clasped them together, staring at them as she traced a continuous figure eight in the air above her. "Do you think there's a possibility we could win?" she asked, turning her gaze to him.

He hesitated a second. "I do."

"Why?" she asked.

He sat up and chewed the inside of his cheek. "Because your dad is your biological father," he said, "and because the judges are looking favorably on families like ours. I think we stand a good chance."

Richard's footsteps resonated against the hardwood floors as he entered the room and said loudly, "I'm starting to lose respect for that lawyer. He's always available."

"We're right here. You don't have to shout," Michael said.

Richard shrugged and tilted his head. "Sorry," he said, ducking slightly. "But I've got the answers." His voice was just above a whisper.

Michael waved his hand to tell him to speak a little louder and hoped he wouldn't regret it.

Richard began again, eyes fixed on Michael. "Some good and

some not so good." He looked apologetically at Brady and then Michael. "Ready?"

"Ready as we'll ever be." He raised his eyebrows at Brady, who nodded.

Richard took a deep breath, pulled out a desk chair, and sat down. He read from a bedraggled piece of paper covered with his scrawl. "You can't just stay with us because you're legally in their custody, which they had to do to enroll you in school."

"Forever?" Brady asked, drawing her head into her shoulders and clutching her upper arms.

Michael put an arm around her and drew her close. He tried to catch Richard's eye. *Slow down. Be sensitive.*

She pulled away.

Richard's eyes followed his finger along the jagged line of his writing. "No, but in order for us to become your legal parents, we have to end your grandparents' rights to parent. We have a good chance of this because they never adopted you and they never ended my parental rights." Richard looked up.

Michael could tell from Richard's quick nod, smile, and raised eyebrows that he expected them to be cheered by this news. Michael watched his smile fade and be replaced by knitted brows and an opened mouth.

"Why didn't they adopt me?" Brady asked without eye contact in a voice as tender as a bruise.

Michael watched Richard close his mouth, soften his eyes, and push back in his chair. If the grandparents had adopted Brady, there would have been no custody battle. Game over. But to Brady this just meant nobody wanted her. Michael searched for words. "People do things or don't do things in the heat of the moment for reasons that were real then. I'm sure they wish they had, and if they had, you never would have found your way to us."

Brady turned and looked at him. He knew he had hit home. "So how do we end rights?" The words sounded awful to Michael, as though they'd be dragging the grandparents in front of a firing squad. Why did one have to lose so the other could gain?

"Parental rights of the grandparents?" Richard asked, turning the paper to find the answer. Finding it, he held up his index finger as he read. "This should not be hard to do because since I am bio dad, I have 'parental presumption,' which means the judge will assume I am operating in Brady's best interests. So that means the grandparents really have to work harder to prove their case. And since they live in Oregon, the case will be heard by a judge in Salem." Richard looked at Michael, who grimaced. When he wasn't there, no houses were sold and no money was made. Michael's money paid legal fees. If he didn't make any money, there was no case.

"We'll be interviewed by a social worker. Ryan says it's important to be honest with her about everything." He hooked eye contact with Michael.

Richard's voice slowed. He was choosing words, sanitizing as he read. "It's actually a good thing I never had custody. They can't prove neglect because she was never here."

"Good," Michael said.

Richard's eyes scanned from Michael to Brady as he folded the paper in half and fell silent.

Michael looked at Brady, who seemed to be in her own world. "So," he leaned toward her, "what do you think?"

Brady kept her head lowered, and her voice came through a veil of hair. "I just want to stay here. I know I can't, but that's what I want."

"We're going to fight to get you back." Richard said. "And the law is on our side. Did you understand that?"

"Yeah, I understand that, but I still have to go." She raised her head and splayed her fingers in front of her.

Michael noticed her eyes were dull and unfocused before she retreated behind the veil of hair.

Richard sat, hands limp and palms open on the notes that lay on his crossed legs.

The rules of the fight were laid out. Michael doubted that there had ever been fighters less prepared.

* * *

Brady knew she had four days left but never said it out loud. No one did. Saying it out loud made it real. Instead she needed contact, affection, and attention from Richard and Michael. It felt right for her to demand it. She pushed the limits. Instead of talking to her dad or Michael through the newspaper, she threw herself in their laps, knocking it out of their hands. She could see the frustration in their faces, especially Michael's, but even that was attention. Besides, after he got over it, he'd smile and pull her in close and let her talk and talk and talk. Every day life became more important as the time ran out, as the clock wound down.

She wanted to please them more than ever. She went to the Getty Museum dressed in her navy blue Lilly Pulitzer shift. She could see the pride on their faces reflected in the glass as she moved from one painting to the next. She was actually bored but would have stayed for hours just to please them. She looked like she belonged with them, grown up and pretty like the women on the covers of the magazines Grandma would read while waiting for appointments and then shove back in the rack. Brady even began eating raw broccoli and tofu as long as it was served with Ranch dressing. She basked in Michael's approval and that in turn pleased Richard. He once thanked her for eating the broccoli and described their family as a balanced ecosystem of admiration. She actually liked the crunch of the broccoli.

Still when they went on their outings, she always noticed they were different. She felt jealous of the mom-and-dad couples walking hand in hand, or with arms around one another. It seemed sad that Richard and Michael never did that. But they did hold hands with her. Since she didn't want to choose one over the other, she held both their hands. It was at *The Flower Drum Song* that she crossed a line without knowing it and carried them with her as she did so. She walked between them holding hands as she walked down the main aisle. But this time she didn't let go—couldn't let go. After they'd sat down, she held on and placed their fingers into one another in her lap, covering their clasped hands with hers. Their fingers curled around one another but were hidden by hers. She looked first at Richard, who smiled back, then at Michael, who pretended to look annoyed but smiled anyway. His smile grew, and he gave their hands three distinct squeezes and mouthed, "I love you."

The music began, and lights went down. She settled back snug and happy. They'd sort of held hands in public. She'd seen to it.

INTERCESSION

A t first Frank thought it was a prank phone call and hung up. The woman's low whisper of a voice was hard to understand. On the second call, though, he heard her distinctly: "I understand no one cares if you save your little girl or not. I can help you find a lawyer who will help you protect your family."

"Who is this?" he asked.

"I'm Angie Wells. I am an aid at Brady's school, Valley Christian. I know Brady, and I care about her. I've worked closely with PFOX for years now since we saved my brother. They have lawyers who can help you."

"How did you get this number? What is PFOX?" Frank asked, fighting down his own excitement. Not only hadn't he found anyone to help him, but no one seemed to understand his outrage at losing Brady to a couple of gay recovering alcoholics.

"I'm sorry, Mr. Nordland. I did have to break some rules to get your phone number. I know I'm breaking some privacy laws, but I also know I'm doing God's work in helping you hang onto Brady. Was I wrong to call?"

"It depends," Frank said.

"On what?" she asked.

"How are you going to help me? I don't want to be involved with something I don't understand."

"PFOX stands for Parents and Families of Ex Gays. We support each other and our confused family members who are being led by homosexuals into sin. We don't force anyone to do anything. They just come to our meetings and usually change on their own."

"Who's they, and how do they change?" His shoulders felt so tight; he lowered his head and squeezed the back of his neck.

"Some are lost before they get to us. I always think we were too late to help, and I pray for them. The change, of course, comes when they decide to join us and live as God intended in a family."

She paused, but Frank didn't know what to say, so he didn't say anything.

She continued. "We have lawyers, Mr. Nordland, who will help you. I care about Brady, and I want to stop her from being led to the gay lifestyle. Surely you don't want this to happen to your granddaughter? I thought I understood that was what you wanted."

Frank wasn't sure he wanted this woman's help, but it was the only positive response he had gotten since he started. It felt good not to be alone.

"Our organization is based in Maryland, and I'll give you the phone number." Frank noticed it hadn't bothered her that he wasn't saying anything. "We have our own lawyer, Evan Cory, and I want you to call him. He will help you protect your granddaughter. God bless you, Mr. Nordland. You really are doing God's work on this one. I like working at this school, and I'm afraid I'd lose my job if anyone knew I'd gotten involved. I hope you can understand that, Mr. Nordland. It seems cowardly to teach children the truth but not be willing to fight for it when they most need you to. It's hypocritical, and cowardly, that's all. So the true Christians are back in the catacombs still singing the praises of Jesus and quietly doing his bidding. Don't you feel that way, Mr. Nordland—that you're in a catacomb of sorts?"

The back of Frank's neck prickled. This seemed far-fetched. He wrote down the phone number and hung up.

Should he trust the woman on the phone? He was so weary of being alone with the fear of losing his granddaughter that he was willing to ignore his instincts. Even Kathleen had patted his hand and said to trust the judge even after that weird phone conversation with Brady in which she barely spoke and hung up as they were saying good-bye. Maybe Brady was trying to tell them something? Maybe she needed help? Maybe she was being turned against them? He could feel his heart beat faster. Staring at the phone, Frank wished that he had asked the woman exactly who or what Evan Cory was and if he expected Frank's call. But he hadn't asked, and now Frank knew that if he didn't call right this minute, he never would.

He dialed the Maryland phone number and, listening to it ring, fought the desire to hang up. "Armstrong and Ballantine," a voice answered. He explained that he had been referred to a lawyer named Evan Cory and was put right through. He described his case. He was fighting to retain custody of his granddaughter and stop adoption by his son-in-law because he was an alcoholic and, he had to pause here, gay.

"I see," Mr. Cory seemed to be taking notes.

"What is it that you see, Mr. Cory?"

"If we don't stand and fight for the families of decent Americans, there aren't going to be any families to defend. It's one thing for an adult to make a personal decision to live a certain way, but to involve little children and try to play house is wrong. I admire you for being willing to take the time and money to fight for your family, and I want to help."

"How much do you expect this to cost, Mr. Cory?" Frank asked.

"In cases like these, we bill by the job, not by the hour, and there are organizations who will help subsidize your efforts, so I think you can end this matter for less than $5,000." Frank gasped and heard Mr. Cory scramble to bring down the price. Frank felt he was being hustled, but he was desperate for help.

"You are the still, small voice in the desert, Mr. Nordland. If you give up, who will carry on the fight not just for Brady but for other children like her? This is a small price to pay to keep your family intact."

Frank's instincts were telling him to be careful and say as little as possible, but he embarrassed himself by warming easily to the man's trite rhetoric.

"I know it's hard," Mr. Cory agreed. "People see the law as inspired by God, but it is only a manmade interpretation of what some people with a political agenda think is right. We will join you in your struggle, Mr. Nordland. You don't have to be alone anymore."

"Brady's father is fresh out of rehab." Having found an ally, Frank's anxieties flooded to the surface. "What's going to happen if he relapses? I saw him at his worst. Brady should not see that. She should not be around it." He was working himself up, he realized, and made himself stop. "What happens next, Mr. Cory?"

Mr. Cory's voice seemed warm and soothing to Frank now. "What happens next, Mr. Nordland, is we fight, you and I. It is not in the best interests of the child to be with that father. He is a bad risk, for the reasons you have given. If he is as insecure as you are describing, my guess is he's very dependent on the man he's with, financially and emotionally. Statistically, homosexual relationships don't last. If they break up, the girl's father will fall apart, and he won't be able to take care of her all over again. How long have you taken care of the girl?"

"Five years since her mother died in a car accident, which was drug and alcohol related. Kathleen and I tried every program we could find, and Brenda would get better for a while and then relapse. That's why I don't believe he can stay sober. I've never seen it done."

"I can bring in expert witnesses with facts about the instability of recovery and homosexual relationships. Kids who are raised in a house with a mother and a father do better, while the kids of same-sex partners are more prone to depression, suicide, and substance abuse, as are their parents. And relapses—well, they happen more often than not. You're doing the right thing, Mr. Nordland. You are saving your granddaughter's life."

SEPARATION

Brady took off the sequined "Flowers for Zoe" T-shirt and shoved it in the suitcase side pocket. Yesterday, when Michael had brought it home for her, she'd loved it. It had seemed like the exact thing to wear to Disneyland. But this morning, like everything she'd tried on, it felt wrong. She pulled on the striped polo shirt and the red brick jeans she'd been wearing the day she got here and stared at herself in the mirror. She looked like herself—her old self—again. Except for her hair. Hopefully, people from school wouldn't notice it and think she was trying to be like Casey.

She smoothed the sheets and the comforter. She tried to smell everything to hang on to her memories. She didn't want Dad and Michael to see how sad she was. She learned when her mom died that it made it harder if her grandparents saw her crying or acting sad. They would act like it was their job to make her feel better. But being comforted made her feel worse somehow. Like they were okay but she was broken or weaker than they were. She had always wondered why her grandparents weren't sadder when her mother died, since she was their daughter. Maybe they were being like Dad and Michael were now—not talking about the bad so they could feel the good.

She started down the steps with the new luggage filled with the clothes Dad and Michael had bought. Would she ever have the courage to wear them? She fixed her eyes on her feet to avoid Richard's and Michael's looks of disappointment at her outfit.

Brady took her place at the breakfast table and ate silently. She struggled to get a piece of waffle down her throat and found tears welling in her eyes. She flattened both hands on the sides of her plate and felt her father's hand, smooth and warm, covering her own. She wanted to turn and bury her face in his shoulder. Instead she hunched her shoulders and held tightly to the seat of the chair.

"The only reason we are letting you go is so that we can have you join us later, forever," Richard said.

"Yes, if we try to violate a court order and keep you, we stand a very good chance of never seeing you again," Michael said.

Brady nodded, picked up her barely touched plate, carried it to the kitchen, and placed it in the sink. She walked to the door and gathered her luggage. She heard chairs scraping as they rushed to join her.

By the time they walked out of the door, she was buckled into the front passenger seat. She stared out of the window, not at them but over them. Michael opened the door and crouched beside it to give her an awkward hug. It didn't comfort her. She wanted this over.

* * *

As Richard drove south on the 405, memories of tortured conversations with his mother flashed through his mind. "I'm sorry," he said, stealing sideways glances at Brady as he steered through the speeding traffic.

She returned his gaze. "Stay with me in Disneyland," she said in a beseeching tone.

An image of himself making awkward conversations with the Christians flashed through his forebrain. "I," he hesitated, "can stay. I haven't been to Disneyland in ages." Her face brightened immediately, and he was able to draw a deep breath for the first time in what felt like days.

Richard navigated Michael's Acura into the line of cars while sweeping his eyes over the clock. They must not be late. He counted backward from their meet-up spot at the first-aid station on Main Street. He'd meant to study the map so they could get there right away, but packing and organizing had seemed so difficult that he'd run out of time, and now he'd added buying a ticket. "What's the teacher's name we're meeting?"

Brady shrugged. "I don't know. My teacher's Mrs. Pons, or it could be her aid, Angie, Miss Wells."

"Neither of those sounds familiar. I think she was an administrator."

Brady shrugged.

Richard's stomach lurched and churned. "Main Street's that big shopping area when you first come in, right?" His lower jaw jutted forward, tightening the cords of his neck.

"Uh-huh," Brady was staring at the Monorail.

"Do you know where the first-aid station is?"

"To the left at the entrance, I think." She waved in the direction of the gate.

Anxiety pumped Richard's heart. "You think?" he asked.

"You'll get a map."

"We can't be late."

"You can ask." She shrugged.

Richard rolled down the window to scan for a parking place. "It's going to be hot," Richard said. The theme music of the Mickey Mouse Club grated and made it hard for him to think. He parked in the section named after the character Goofy. *Perfect.*

Although there was a breeze, the sun bore down on them. He looked at the large tube of sunblock Michael had given him. "Sunblock?" he offered it to Brady.

"It smells funny and feels sticky," Brady said.

"Yeah, we don't have time." Richard threw the tube in the car and locked the door before bolting ahead of her to the main gate.

"Dad, my luggage."

Richard heard Brady yell and ground his teeth as he turned on his heel and fumbled with his keys to unlock the car. He swung the backpack to her before grabbing the suitcase and running past her with it.

The music became louder, and lines of families in garish shades of lumpy shorts were forming despite its being seven forty-five in the morning. The giant floral rendering of Mickey in front of the Swiss train station for the monorail was exactly as it had been when he was nine. The thrill he had felt just being there as a kid was worth the long boring ride from Oregon. Everyone, down to the popcorn seller and street sweeper, was pleasant. How'd they do that? The smells of sugar from taffy, cotton candy, and colorful suckers seemed to be part of the oxygen here. This place was a drug with gates. He noticed their steps quickened as they got closer. Richard cut off a family headed for the ticket booth. They looked complicated. He'd be quick; Brady already had her ticket.

"$96!" Richard said before the cheerful young woman could greet him.

"It's cheaper if you get a two-day pass and combine it with Disney California Adventure Park."

Richard shook his head. "Just one day, thanks." He had hoped to pay in cash but knew he didn't have that much. Michael didn't know he was staying all day, but he'd find out when the purchase went on his card. His joy dampened, Richard took the ticket and followed Brady to another line.

The crowd had swelled, and he was pressed against the family in front of him. He could feel the breath of the man behind him on his neck and turned sideways to avoid it. The couple in front of him was arguing about where to go first and seemed oblivious to the antics of their children, who ran over Richard's feet twice while playing tag.

Richard gritted his teeth and kept his eyes on the clock tower. They had twenty minutes, but the line didn't seem to move. Richard kept counting the people between him and the ticket taker. There was a huge multi-generational family at the front of the line.

Richard looked from side to side. Every other line seemed to move faster. "Go," Richard snarled under his breath. Just then the bulbous boy who'd been outrunning his brother stubbed his toe and flailed into Richard and Brady, dousing them with a gigantic grape slushy.

"Goddamnit!" Richard stood shocked as the frozen drink ran from his hands and seeped into his shirt.

"Sorry, sir," the wife said. "They're very excited."

Richard hated grape soda as a child. The sweet smell made his already-churning stomach rise, and he felt acid burn at the back of his throat. Removing his handkerchief, he began daubing at Brady's polo shirt now marred by a six-inch purple swath. He was relieved she wasn't in any of the new clothes. He looked down at himself. His stain was a dark spot in his jeans that ran from two inches below his belt in a triangular shape. It pointed to his crotch. Perfect.

"Do you want to soak it with water so it doesn't set?" The mother of Thing One and Thing Two held out a bottle of water apologetically. Her husband was turned away to suppress a laugh. Richard could hear him and repressed the impulse to spin him around and pummel his face.

Richard poured water onto his handkerchief and diluted Brady's stain.

Brady frowned at the wet spot that grew with each dab.

"It'll dry. It's a hot day." Richard assured her and stared at the stain on his pants. "I'll take care of it later," he said to the woman and noted that her boys stood with lowered heads and looked at him sidelong.

"What do you say, boys?" the father said, mirth barely contained.

"We're sorry," they chorused as though prompted a multitude of times in the past.

Richard exhaled noisily and looked at Brady's soaked shirt. It stuck to her skin.

"It's okay. Things happen." Brady forced her chin forward and looked at Richard.

Richard glanced away and turned without a word.

Fuck no. This is so far from okay. Keep your kids under control, goddamnit! He cleared his throat.

The multi-generational family finished their elaborate transaction and burst through the turnstiles like trapped gas.

Thing One and Thing Two led their parents forward eagerly, and they were gone.

Brady thanked the ticket taker for the glow-in-the-dark stamp and smiled up at him as she two-stepped through the turnstile. Richard laced his way through the crowd and guided Brady to the clearly marked first-aid station.

A bell tinkled as they entered the bright white room, and the music softened when the door shut. Richard moved quickly to the counter to cover the stain. "We're trying to connect with a teacher from Valley Christian," Richard said, standing back and covering his mouth. *Please don't ask for a name.*

He felt someone poke, not tap, his shoulder and turned to see Mrs. McMillan. He remembered her name as soon as he read the tag on her jacket. She was tall and broad with shoulder-length blond hair caught up in barrettes at the sides of her head. She wore no makeup except fuchsia lipstick that made her teeth seem like a flash of white. She was dressed in jeans and a fleece hoodie that seemed intended for a student and bore the Rogue River Christian logo. She extended her hand to Richard. Her nail polish matched her lipstick.

"I'm glad to see you. Now we can join the others," she said, shooting a glance at Richard's grape stain and quickly reaching for Brady's luggage. She paused at Brady's wet shirtfront but shook her head and said nothing. She placed the luggage in a pile of boxes and backpacks.

Her clipped tone made him feel he was late. Richard's stomach twisted, and he checked his watch. They were right on time.

"Are you going to be joining us?" she asked Richard over her shoulder as she opened the door and exited.

Heat and noise rushed in her wake as Richard followed her out. Her smile endured, but she looked uneasy.

Richard had just paid more to get in the park than he had spent on any single purchase in the last three years. Without a steady income, he bought clothes and books at second-hand stores. Michael paid for food and dinners out. Brady had asked him to come. He needed to do the right thing.

"That was the plan. Is there a problem?" Richard asked, focusing on his feet as her threaded his way through the crowd.

"We just didn't know. We thought you might have taken her already—another time, for instance, instead. The point of a school trip, after all, is to bond with one's peers." Mrs. McMillan smiled but tilted her head back and looked down her nose at Richard as one might down the barrel of a gun.

Richard stared back at her.

Brady stared at her feet.

Mrs. McMillan held his gaze for a few seconds before opening the door and starting out of it with Brady in tow. "But of course," she began slowly, eyes darting to the grape stain and back to lock on his, "you can join your—daughter—Brady. As long as the two of you don't go off by yourselves." Her smile never faltered, but her tone was commanding.

Richard looked at Brady, who was staring at the toes of her shoes. "Why can't we go off on our own?" he asked. His voice shook. A train filled with screaming tourists swept behind him along tracks. The vibration rattled him.

"Brady's grandfather was very specific." Mrs. McMillan said. "He wants someone with Brady at all times."

"I'd be with her," Richard said, and he stopped walking.

"Well, one of *us*, I mean," Mrs. McMillan said. She stood still and stared at him.

Brady pulled away from Mrs. McMillan and took Richard's hand.

"Does it make sense to you, Mrs. McMillan," he called after her, "that I would drive my daughter here and meet you only to whisk her away after having made contact with you? If I were going to take her, I wouldn't have shown up."

"This whole situation is highly irregular, and I am going to do what I have been told to do, Mr. Lawson."

The woman walking by looked up at the sound of Mrs. McMillan's tone. Mrs. McMillan pivoted and strode away.

Richard and Brady had to rush to catch up with her.

"What rides do you want to go on?" Richard bent his six-foot frame as close to Brady as he could and strained to hear her soft voice amid the blare of the music and the screech of brakes and the screams of people plummeting down tracks around the park. The smell of popcorn was so strong that it seemed to be piped in.

"I don't like Star Tours. It makes me sick to my stomach, but I really like Space Mountain. They're both in Tomorrowland," Brady said.

"Can we go there, then—to Tomorrowland?" Richard called in the direction of Mrs. McMillan, closing his eyes and feeling heat rise in his face.

"We'll have to check and see what the group wants to do," Mrs. McMillan said.

As they drew closer to the small band of kids at the opening of Star Tours, Brady's speed slackened further. She scanned their faces. When two little girls popped out of the group, she brightened. The girls hugged in a way with arms rounded as if to encircle a barrel. There was no contact. Why pretend to hug if you're not going to touch?

"This is Joanne," Brady said to Richard, gesturing at a heavy-set girl with thick brown hair, heavy bangs, and bad acne.

"Your hair looks good," Joanne said, touching Brady's hair.

The short blond girl, whom he learned was Jeanie, came complete with green eyes, and she looked suspiciously at Brady's hair and said, "It looks like Casey's."

Brady grimaced and looked away.

Richard started forward, realized he didn't know why he was doing so, and stepped back. His eyes never left Brady. Why was she so embarrassed?

A man in the group reached over the heads of the children to shake Richard's hand. "I'm Dick Reynolds," he said.

"This is my dad," Brady said to the circle of girls.

Richard squared his shoulders and bounced on his toes. He gave Dick Reynolds's hand a vigorous shake. Unlike Mrs. McMillan, the girls were happy to put Space Mountain at the top of the list.

They joined the long lines alleviated by shop windows filled with repetitive recorded warnings about turbulent rides and flashing lights. Richard eased into the heavily padded black leather seat of the sleek rocket-looking car with a bright orange stripe. Brady settled in front of him, and the padded bar lowered in front of her. Although panic raced through his chest, he sat tight and delivered his soul to his higher power or the engineers at Disneyland. He felt queasy, and the car had not yet moved. The car appeared to spin with incredible force, and he found himself clutching the bar in front of him.

"The car isn't actually rolling," Brady shouted to him.

"Really?" Richard tried to look around himself. They certainly seemed to be twisting, and there had been repeated warnings that they would be.

"It's a trick with the lights," she shouted and gestured, but her hand was forced down by the gravity.

The combination of velocity that pressed him into the seat and Brady into him, the bright lights, and being jerked from side to side made his stomach roil. Suddenly all of the speed stopped, and with it went the pressure. He could hear Brady speaking and realized that she had been talking through the whole ride, but her words had been whipped into the void by the speed.

"This must be what astronauts feel like in space," Brady said, and he nodded. There was a brief moment of peace as they floated in among the celestial bodies. Richard's hands rested on Brady's shoulders as she pointed out planets, and then she said, "Here it comes." Richard tried to ask what was coming, but the words were sucked away unheard. As he felt his shoulders pinned to the back of the seat, and realized what "it" was. They plummeted violently through the dark, and he let go of Brady and grabbed hold of the safety bar, pulling it tightly toward them. The car's nose pointed down, and as they twisted from side to side, he felt the bar give just slightly and panic rose in his chest. Just as he was certain they were to be catapulted out of the car and smashed at the floor of the ride, they broke into the bright lights of the station. The workers applauded for them, and Richard gasped for air as he struggled to stand.

Wasn't that great?" Brady exclaimed. Richard nodded wordlessly and prayed that the ride had not sent his heart into some bizarre form of arrhythmia. His reaction went unnoticed by the girls, who wanted to line up again, but there were so many more rides, each with its own long line, so they had to move on, and they did, over and over.

He did enjoy watching Brady with her sweet little friends. The girls seemed content and safe together within the larger group. Brady included him when she wanted, or when she felt he needed it, but mostly he was happy watching her be happy. He tried not to admit it to himself, but he knew it was true that her threesome was a little more lumpy and unkempt than their fashionable peers. He chided himself for wishing that she had worn her new clothes. Would he love her more if she were prettier? Would he be a better father because she looked more chic? Would she have more worth as a human being?

Very soon it was time to convene for dinner, for which they had reserved a table at Blue Bayou in the Pirates of the Caribbean ride. Richard asked Dick, whose name he could not bring himself to use for fear of bursting into laughter, if he had been included in the five o'clock reservation. Dick assured him that he had.

As they entered the Blue Bayou Restaurant, it felt to Richard as though someone had switched off the sun. It became immediately cool and dark, lit overhead by a series of paper lanterns. It took awhile for their eyes to adjust to the dark. It was rustically romantic, with a moonshiner's cabin and banjo music in the background. There were occasional screams and splashes as tourists were delivered to the Pirates down the waterway.

The servers were dressed in post-colonial and pre–Civil War attire. When all the little Christians were assembled, Richard was not surprised, having been consistently prodded to say grace at dinner by Brady, that Dick had the group bow their heads for prayer. They all held hands. He had Brady on one side, Joanne on the other, and he bowed his head as fervently as he could, considering that they were around the corner from a mechanized pirate's den where violent acts of theft, torture, and debauchery were being acted out just a few minutes down the waterway.

The Christians, led by Dick, appeared nonplussed by having an audience. "Dear Lord, we thank you for this day of joy and fellowship. Please bless this food that we are about to eat. Help us to be good missionaries of your word, and protect us from any temptations to stray from your teachings. Thank you for the presence of Brady's father in our company, and please bless her reunion with him. Keep us ever mindful of the needs of others. In Jesus's name we pray. Amen."

Richard noted that even the servers with their heavy trays of drinks had paused for the prayer. He looked around to see if anyone was staring at them, and no one was. Perhaps this only seemed like obsessive behavior to him.

Richard opened his menu, and his eyes widened. He could do with a salad but was supposed to pay for Brady. He hadn't planned to be here today.

"All chaperones are paid for," Dick leaned over and whispered in his ear.

Richard felt warm affection for Dick. "Excellent," he said, seriously considering the filet mignon. Christians were well funded it seemed.

"And we've already ordered the jambalaya for the whole group. Got a discount. Hope that's okay."

"Jambalaya it is."

"It's really good."

And it was. And Richard enjoyed watching Brady chattering with her friends even better. Richard looked around the gigantic table and noticed what a good-looking, albeit homogeneous, group this was. One girl immediately stood out. She was older than the others and made him uneasy. Although she was talking to the students around her, every time he looked up, she fixed him with an unbroken gaze while smiling and tossing her luxurious blonde hair. Her gold cross caught and radiated light beams over the table, drawing attention to her incongruously low neckline. Richard had experienced unwanted sexual attention from women before, and usually a straightforward "I'm gay" stopped them in their tracks. He felt that action might backfire in this particular setting. He increased his attention on Brady and planned a rapid evacuation at dinner's end.

"Is your original name Richard?" Richard asked Dick, eager to be focused away from the young woman.

"No, I was named Dick after Dick Nixon. Apparently my parents didn't know he had another name," Dick said, slapping Richard on the back with such enthusiasm that he coughed. Dick laughed more.

Richard finished dinner quickly.

Brady's little threesome, their thirst for roller coasters not yet satisfied, was making plans to go to Big Thunder Mountain Railroad, but they needed an adult. He didn't know how to tell Brady that he didn't think he fit the bill for this group when Dick offered to go and invited him to come along.

"Yeah, come on, Dad, one last ride! The crowds will have died down because people are going to the get in place for the parade. It'll be great!" Brady looked so happy and, taking him by the hand, she whisked him along the path. The lines had lessened. Minutes later, they were rumbling down the tracks at breakneck speed as fireworks began. One minute they were out and overlooking the park and dazzled by the shimmering lights of the fireworks, and the next minute they were plunging through darkness in a chaotic plummet toward the ground. Richard hoped that would be the last roller coaster he would ride in this lifetime.

Brady, sparkly eyed and red faced with excitement, ran to get in line for the parade, and it seemed to Richard the right time to go. She would still have events to look forward to, so it wouldn't be as lonely. He swallowed deeply, offering a prayer for strength and courage, something he would not have thought to do before getting to know Brady.

Pulling her away from the group, he squatted next to her, gathered her in his arms, and whispered, "I'm going to go now." He paused to let her absorb the information. She nodded. He continued, "This has been a wonderful day for me. I like your friends, and I'm glad I got to meet them. I love you very much, and I want you to have fun for the rest of the evening and call me when you get home in a few days. Okay, sweetheart, can you do that?" Brady nodded, and over her shoulder Richard could see the lighted creatures of the parade dancing merrily, each following its specific theme music.

Brady's eyes drifted from Richard's face to the parade and back. She looked sad, and he held his breath. Then she lifted her chin and shouted over the music, "I love you and I love Michael and I will call you tomorrow." She hugged him like she was trying to consume him, burying her face in his shoulder. Then with a smile, she let go, waved, and moved back to her friends, turning away from him to face the parade. Her silhouette stood still and black against the bright lights and movement.

He bumped into Dick as he turned and explained that he was leaving and pointed to where Brady stood with her friends. Dick nodded and yelled, "God bless you. Have a safe trip home." Richard was caught off guard by the blessing and smiled back at Dick, and then he turned and wove his way through the crowd and out of the gigantic park.

RICHARD

R ichard opened his front door to the soothing smell of Michael's acorn squash soup, a time-tested comfort food. This was usually accompanied by pumpkin ginger muffins, and as Richard rounded the corner, he saw them cooling on the deep green granite counter. He watched Michael moving from stove to counter and back singing to his iPod, and he felt a rush of longing. He waved his hand to get Michael's attention without startling him. Catching Michael's eye set him free, and he aggressively grabbed hold of him. Kissing him fully and deeply, he moved him against the wall of the kitchen. He slid his hand between Michael's legs and ran it gently up his thigh. Leaning against Michael's chest and sliding his hands down into the back of his jeans, he whispered hoarsely into his ear, "I need you and I want you."

Michael laughed. "You're so subtle. Let me turn off the stove." He moved around Richard, flipping switches on the oven and moving saucepans from the heat. Michael grabbed Richard by the hand, and they raced each other up the stairs and into the bed for unfinished business.

Finally, exhausted, sweaty, and satisfied, they rolled apart. "Thank you, kind sir. I'm ever so grateful," Richard chirped in his best Blanche DuBois imitation.

"That did feel good. It's been a while," Michael said, settling against the plumped pillows and drawing his fingers through Richard's hair. He traced the lines in Richard's face.

Richard closed his eyes.

"So, how'd it go?" Michael asked.

"I enjoyed it in spite of myself," Richard said. "Brady obviously enjoyed herself. And you know, the Christians weren't so bad after all. I mean, once you get past saying grace in public, everything else seems normal."

"What are her friends like?"

"They're okay, sweet, a little homely, but nice and really loyal to her, which was reassuring. They liked her hair." He opened one eye. "She loved them loving it—obviously proud."

"Good, being envied is right behind good nutrition for any growing girl," Michael said.

"They prayed for me," Richard said in a thick voice.

"Why?" Michael sounded wary.

"They gave thanks for our reunion—mine and Brady's," Richard covered his eyes with his hand and corrected himself, "—our family's. It was nice. I can use all of the help I can get." Richard continued, "And Brady said she loved you." He could feel the corners of his mouth turning down.

"Yeah?" Michael looked at Richard.

Richard nodded. "By name, 'I love Michael.'"

"I love her too. I walked in after work and there were no shoes or clothes all over the living room." He glanced sideways at Richard and then straight ahead. "You'd think I'd be relieved. I complained about it so much, but it just shows she's gone. I can hardly look in her room. I expect her to be there reading. Sometimes I think I actually hear her singing and have to remind myself that she's gone. We were good for a while—we were a family."

Richard heard him swallow hard. They sat silent.

"I've been thinking a lot about it, Richard."

Richard felt like a butterfly had landed on his hand and he didn't want to scare it off. He looked at Michael.

"I'm willing to pay the back child support." Michael paused.

Richard held his breath.

"I want to adopt her. I do." He seemed to be trying to convince himself. "The house seems so lonely and empty. However briefly, we had something real. I never imagined I'd have a family, but I can and I want to." Michael stopped and swallowed hard. "Or am I being too rash?" He stared at Richard with soft, open eyes.

Richard felt his heart speed, and he reached for Michael, kissing him deeply. When he came up for air, he said, "Not too rash, not too rash at all."

"Okay, so now what?" Michael asked.

"We call Ryan and ask him what to do next."

"Okay," Michael said, and then he grabbed Richard's hand. "And if we don't win?"

Richard felt invincible. Losing seemed impossible. "We'll win." *We won't stop until we win.* "And I've got nothing but time to work on it and no greater priority."

Michael sucked in his breath. "Go for it, guy. Home isn't home without her in it."

* * *

Richard was prepared to fight, but waiting ate away his courage. When Michael went to work for a ten-hour day, it left Richard alone with Richard. It had been the equivalent of a month and still no word beyond "be patient" from Ryan. The pain of Brady's absence grew sharper as time passed and left the house graveyard quiet. Richard stopped jumping out of bed to get coffee for Michael. Today Richard lay under the covers, ebbing in and out of sleep. He imagined himself on a raft in a huge body of water, drifting aimlessly. He kept trying to wake himself up, but if he lifted his head, he'd just roll over and fall asleep again. *Wake up. Go get coffee, walk in the sunshine, and go for a run.*

The harsh ring of the doorbell made that decision for him.

He threw on a robe and walked to the door, annoyed at being interrupted for what he suspected would be a couple of Jehovah's Witnesses.

He opened the door to a grinning young man with untrimmed hair who wore an ill-fitting suit. He held out a manila envelope to Richard. "Are you Richard Lawson?"

Richard nodded and reached for the envelope.

"You have been served. Have a nice day," the young man said before turning on his heel and sprinted down the red clay steps to the street.

Richard stared at the envelope as though unable to understand what had happened. Opening it, he read, "a notice to appear." He gasped as he read that the grandparents were trying to adopt Brady and they were trying to terminate his rights as her father.

He'd been warned about this. He shouldn't panic, but his fingers trembled as he pressed on Ryan's number.

"What's up, Richard?"

"They are contesting the adoption." Richard gulped air.

"Okay," Ryan said.

"Okay?" Richard said, shaking his head. "But you said, 'That was then; this is now.' That all that mattered was what I was doing now." He sounded whiney even to himself.

"They're trying to hang on to her, so this is what they have to say. What they want is to get before a judge so they can say you're not a good risk for her," Ryan said.

"I'm not a good risk?" Richard repeated rather than asked.

"It's our job to prove them wrong. So we'll meet with the judge and show that person that your relationship is solid as a rock and you are not at risk for relapse," Ryan said.

Richard dropped down on the bed.

"Are you there, Richard?" Ryan asked.

"Yes, I am here," Richard said.

"This is just the beginning. You're going to have to be brave. You're doing this for Brady. I know the words sound bad, and it may get worse," Ryan said and then asked, "Are you okay, Richard?"

"It's a shock, and that's all. I'm okay," Richard said.

"There you go. That's the spirit. Talk to you later," Ryan said, hanging up.

But Richard wasn't okay. He pressed Michael's name and held his breath, listening to it ring. "Answer, answer, please be there." It went to voice mail. Richard tried to steady his voice and organize his thoughts. "I—Michael, this is Richard, and I just need you to know that the grandparents are adopting Brady." It sounded so final. "Well, they're trying to, and they're ending my rights for 'willful failure to communicate or support her.'" His vision blurred. This was the humiliation he had feared. He had been a selfish, useless sack of salt. And now people were going to sit around and discuss just how irresponsible he had been in front of Brady. And the worst part was that it was all true. He looked at the phone and realized it was still recording his muttering. What had he said? He hung up and pulled out his dresser drawer for running clothes.

He ran to the beach path, going hard and fast. His heart, lungs, and legs seemed unable to coordinate. He hadn't warmed up gradually and was pushing himself too hard, too soon. He needed to slow down, calm down, and get into a rhythm. He couldn't. If he stopped, the shame would catch up with him. He needed endorphins to dilute the guilt, but they weren't flowing. He was hit with a wave of nausea and stepped to the side of the path, retching violently. He doubled over as spasms rolled through his stomach and he threw up coffee, the only thing he'd consumed all morning. The revolting smell of stomach acid hit his nose, causing his stomach to surge again. He swayed over the stinking mess as his now-empty stomach settled. A viscous string of spit dangled from his mouth. He waited, afraid it wasn't over. A couple running by looked at him with some concern, but he looked away.

Walking off the path, he lowered himself onto a rock and let humiliation explode in his chest. This was what he had feared— what had kept him drinking for all these years—not that he wouldn't succeed, but how he would feel facing his shitty self. He wanted to blame the jerks who described him with such sadistic objectivity, but they were right. Memories surged through his mind of drinking to pass out so he could sleep under freeways in the frozen cold and stifling heat. He put his head between his knees, crossed his hands over his head, and allowed fear to take over.

"Hey, buddy, you okay?" There was a persistent tapping on his shoulder. Richard raised his head and found himself eye to eye with a red-faced cop. Was his sobriety a dream? "I'm sorry, what is the problem?"

The cop straightened up and stood back. "A couple said they saw you on the path and they were worried."

"Oh yeah, I was a little dehydrated and I got sick, but I'm okay now," Richard said.

The officer stared critically at his face. "Do you have any ID?"

Richard realized how bad he must look. *Just answer the man's question.* "No, I live right up the hill, and I don't run with a drivers' license." Afraid that he sounded sarcastic, he softened his tone. "I'm okay, now. Thank you for your concern." Richard pushed off from the rock to a standing position and walked toward Manhattan Beach Boulevard, but the officer followed.

Richard turned to face him with his hands tightening at his sides. "I'm walking to my house. I'm okay. It's just up the hill." He jerked his thumb in the direction of the house.

"My car's right here." The cop pointed to a squad car parked at the end of the boulevard at the trail head. "I'll give you a ride."

Richard thought about running to the house but felt that would escalate the situation, so he walked to the squad car. As they reached the house, Richard squeezed his eyes shut and dropped his jaw. The door was locked, and he had left the key. Adrenaline coursed into his bloodstream, causing his heart to jump. His hands shook and he pressed them into his legs. Hoping the back door was open, he headed through the back gate, trying to act as though this was how he always entered the house.

"Why don't you go through the front door?" the cop asked from behind him.

"I don't have a key because I ran out without it," Richard said, struggling to control his tone.

"That presents a problem, sir."

"Yes, it certainly does," Richard said. He threw a hostile look over his shoulder at the officer. *Don't lose control. People talk themselves into being arrested.*

"No, I mean, maybe you're just having a bad day, but you've thrown up and been crying, it looks like. Now you have no ID and no key to your house. Like I said, maybe you're having a bad day, but you seem a little disoriented to me. I can't just leave you here. How do I know this is really your house? How do I know you are really okay?"

Richard blew air out of his cheeks to try to quell the panic in his chest. He felt dizzy and wanted to sit down but didn't want to show any signs of weakness to the officer.

"Can I call my partner? He'll be able to let me in, and I can get my identification." Richard's eyes were pleading.

"Partner?" The man's eyebrows rose, and Richard closed his hands rather than hit the man.

"Yes, just one phone call will take care of it," Richard said, and then he muttered under his breath, "If Michael picks up and I don't get voicemail."

"I'm sorry, what was that?" the officer asked. His eyebrows knitted in concern.

"I need to make a phone call. I need your phone to make a phone call," Richard said too loudly and slowly as though talking to a child.

"Phone calls are made from the station, sir." The officer rested his hands with his thumbs in his belt, making a creaking sound as the leather stretched.

"I could talk to my lawyer; he's sure to pick up."

"All calls are made from the station, sir."

Wondering what a trip to the police station would look like to the grandparents, Richard heard the blessed sound of Michael's car pulling into the drive.

"That's him!" he said gleefully. He started around to the gate.

"Hold on there, just a minute, let me check this out."

It took all of the self-restraint Richard had to keep from shoving the officer out of his way. As the officer rounded the corner of the house with Richard right behind him, Richard could see Michael standing with the car door open and his jacket in his hands. He was staring at the squad car, and his brow was furrowed. He saw the cop and Richard at the same time and waited, staring from one to the other.

"What seems to be the problem, sir?" Michael finally asked, shutting the car door.

"Your partner, here," he said, and gestured with his head at Richard, "says he lives here, but he has no ID and apparently no key." The officer made it sound like a question.

Richard stood, jaw clenched, eyes deliberately unfocused, and felt Michael scan his body.

"He does live here, Officer. I'll vouch for him. Do you need to see my ID?" Michael asked, but he did not move.

"Yes, I need to know that you live here. He was vomiting and seemed really upset." The officer looked conspiratorially at Michael, who nodded knowingly.

Richard ground his jaws together, sending pain to his temple.

As the officer climbed back into his car, he pointed at Richard and said, "Carry water with you when you run, maybe."

Richard jerked his head in the form of a nod. *Go, for God's sake.*

"Thank you, Officer. Will there be any record of this?" Michael asked.

"No arrest, no citation, no." The officer shut the car door.

Michael led the way silently to the door. Unlocking the door, he turned to Richard and raised his eyebrows.

Richard stood with his arms crossed over his chest. "I got a little bad news, Michael. I freaked out. Sorry." Richard stared over Michael's shoulder.

"I couldn't understand your message, and I called here and left a message," Michael said. "You know, when you leave inflammatory, emotional messages, you could hang around for a few minutes to explain them. Richard? I was really frightened. I finally called Ryan and got the story. I wasn't that surprised. You are going to have to pull yourself together and get ready for this kind of stuff. They're fighting for their kid. It's bound to get rocky." Michael turned and headed into the kitchen, and he added, "Have you eaten today?"

Richard pretended not to remember as he joined Michael in the kitchen.

Michael sighed, "Let's have lunch."

Michael began to pull out and wash spinach leaves, black beans, onions, and tomatoes. "Ryan suggested that we check out the schools, private and public. It will be something constructive for you to do," Michael said, adding, "Running doesn't seem to have its healing effect right now. Maybe you should wait and run with me."

RICHARD

⁓⁓⁓⁓⁓⁓⁓

"Hi, Daddy." Brady's voice sounded so young and very far away. Richard had raced in from the backyard where he and Michael were cooling off from a run and having lunch. Running together had given them more time together.

He walked back into the yard toward Michael. His voice was still breathy from running. "What's up?"

"I miss you, Daddy," she said.

Richard felt his insides go soft and warm. "I miss you too, Brady, but hang in there, and it will be over soon."

Michael had run past him to the extension in the den. "Put it on speaker." Richard commanded.

"Hi, Brady," Michael shouted even though it was on speaker.

"Hi, Michael." Richard sensed that she smiled as she spoke.

Richard prepared to launch into all that he had learned about schools in the area when he heard a small gasp. She was crying.

"Brady?" Richard started to ask what was wrong, but she interrupted.

"Everyone at school knows you're gay. No one will talk to me. I want to come home now," Brady said, "back to California."

Richard felt his heart speed up. He sat down heavily as though hit in the stomach. He wanted to protect her from mean kids. He saw himself calmly explaining to the little bullies that what they were doing was against their own religion. He wanted to be that kind of magnificent father who would lower a protective shield over Brady and cause everyone to love her. But she couldn't come to California just yet. How could he protect her when she was still in Oregon? He said, "Do you feel that you can talk to your grandparents about this?"

"No," Brady's answered.

"Why not?" Richard asked. It was the only idea he had.

"I don't want to. I can't. They probably feel the same way the kids do. I don't want to talk to them about it," she said.

"Is there someone you can trust? Someone you've talked to before? If the kids won't talk to you, what about a teacher or a counselor or Dick whatever his name is. He seemed nice."

She sniffed, "I don't really know him. He mostly works with older kids."

"May I please talk to your grandmother or grandfather?" Richard asked.

"No, they aren't here. I wouldn't be calling if they were," Brady said.

"Have you talked to the principal already? Because that is what I am going to do," Richard said. "This is the same as racism, and they can't tease you about something that is part of your family. Brady, do you understand me?"

"It's not what they're saying. It's what they're not saying. When I walk into the cafeteria, they all stop talking. I eat all by myself. This is worse than before. Please come and get me."

"Brady, we can't." Richard set his jaw. If Michael hadn't been there he would have jumped in the car and driven to her. Admitting he couldn't do anything was torture. He had to do something, "What about Jeanie and Joanne?"

"They won't talk to me either. They said . . . never mind."

"What did they say, Brady?" Michael asked.

"They said you were going to hell," the phone seemed to jump, "and that I would too if I lived with you. Casey's making them do it. I've seen her. She never talks to them and now suddenly they're best friends. That's why Jeanie and Joanne won't eat lunch with me. I hate it. Without them I have no one. I thought they were my real friends but I guess they're not. They can't stand up to Casey to be friends with me." She sobbed. "Why are they like this? What did I do to them? So you're gay. What difference does that make to them—and Casey, why should she care? I'm afraid to look at anybody. I don't even answer questions unless the teacher calls on me because when I do, they all look at each other and smile. Like, there she goes, nerdy Brady, thinks she's so smart."

Richard winced and forced himself to take a deep breath. He'd been bullied every day of his life. Was this his legacy for her?

"Who supervises the cafeteria?" Michael asked.

"Mrs. McMillan," Brady said.

Richard shivered. They did not have ally in her. "Anyone else?" he asked.

"Angie Wells. She's an aid. She's been nice to me when I was lonely."

"Try her. Please be brave and call whenever you need. And know that we're calling the principal as soon as we can," Richard said. There was silence. "Okay, Brady?"

"Send me an email," Brady said after a pause.

"Okay, we will. We love you, Brady, and we are proud of you," Michael said.

But all they heard was dial tone.

RICHARD

Richard left a message for Principal Hammond right after Brady's call. When Principal Hammond returned the call at seven thirty on Monday morning, Richard, jittery from lack of sleep, startled at the sound of the phone.

With adrenalin pumping, Richard summarized his relationship to Brady, explained that she was being bullied, and revealed who the perpetrator was (Casey) in such loud, passionate rhetoric that Michael left the room. Richard never lost a beat, ending with Casey's threat, that Brady had been told she would go to hell if she lived with him.

Mr. Hammond cleared his throat. "I'm sorry to hear that that was said to your daughter. I can assure you that that kind of talk is not allowed at this school, and it did not come from any of the faculty or administrators. Kids can be so cruel."

Richard's eyes narrowed at the principal's tone of acceptance. "How do you handle it when kids make ethnic slurs? You wouldn't let them call her a nigger, or a wet back, if one of those applied?" The shock of his ethnic slurs empowered him.

"We have zero tolerance for that kind of talk, Mr. Lawson."

"But what do you *do* to stop it?" Richard asked.

There was a pause. "Depending on the severity of the situation, we would talk to the parents, and the offending student."

"You'd *talk* to them? That's it?"

"Most kids stop once we point out the damage they are doing and that it violates our code of ethics. Our goal is to raise good ambassadors of Christ's message. Racism is contrary to Christ's message."

"How about homophobia?"

"Not that either, Mr. Lawson, although it is a bit different."

"How is it different, Mr. Hammond?" Richard had risen from bed, and he paced back and forth.

"The Bible teaches that we are all made in God's form, so learning to get along with people who are different from us and see the spirit of Jesus in everyone is part of our teaching."

"So how would this be different for a gay student?"

"No one can choose the color of their skin," Mr. Hammond said.

Richard stood openmouthed, and then he swallowed hard. He felt that he was choking down bile.

"What are you saying? Being gay is a choice? That gay students don't have the spirit of Jesus in them because Jesus wasn't gay?"

"That is not what I am saying, and it is not what we teach. We have zero tolerance for harassment of any kind for any reason. I will talk to the students whom you say are harassing your daughter."

"Mr. Hammond, do you believe that being gay is a choice?"

"It doesn't matter what I believe. We do not tolerate harassment."

"It does matter. You're the principal. And if you believe that being gay is a choice and that it is wrong in the eyes of God, students will pick that up. That gives mean kids the God-given right to bully gay kids or the children of gay parents." Richard punctuated the last words by poking the air with his finger.

Richard heard Mr. Hammond exhale loudly into the phone. "Mr. Lawson, I am not going to argue with you. I will speak to the students and their families. I will call you back."

But Richard wasn't done, "The law is on Brady's side, and if you can not bring those students under control, we will sue for harassment."

"That's not going to be necessary. Let's not have this thing get out of control. Any one besides Casey? Any witnesses?"

"Joanne and Jeanie, Brady's friends, they played a part but they'd also be witnesses," Richard said.

"I'll take care of it, Mr. Lawson, and I will make sure that Brady is okay."

MR. HAMMOND

M r. Hammond sat at his desk for a long time after he hung up with Brady Lawson's father. His hands were folded, though not in prayer. He was stewing in earthbound fear and anger. He dreaded dealing with Casey Davis. A frequent flyer to his office for dress-code violations and disrupting class, her discipline record read like a rap sheet. She never changed. Her parents were divorced. Her father paid the tuition, Mr. Hammond suspected, to keep Casey away from himself. Her mother, a fierce and ferocious defender of Casey, refused to enforce rules. Twice she'd accused him of working with teachers to pick on Casey, a ridiculous accusation that over time made him question himself.

He remembered when Brady first came, the odd little girl whose mother had died. She had a flat affect to her voice and held her head and shoulders bowed. She looked and sounded like a little old woman. It had been hard finding friends for her. So everyone was relieved when Jeanie and Joanne overlooked her habit of talking to herself. The three appeared to gain strength from belonging together, and that relieved everyone around them. Only Casey would be mean enough to crush a friendship so pure.

Mr. Hammond decided to talk to Brady first. He often found that when parents saw their kids as victims, the kids did not. Instead, they accepted a certain amount of torment as a rite of passage and took pride in handling it. The trick was being in the right place to stop the harassment when it became too much. He sent a summons for Brady to her classroom.

Brady walked into his office weighed down by an enormous backpack. She struggled to meet his eyes as she handed him the summons.

"I hardly know you, Brady, because you have straight As and are never in trouble." This was his time-honored compliment for shy, good kids, and it usually broke the ice. Brady stared at the desk and shrank more deeply into the gray upholstery. "What are your favorite subjects?"

Brady shrugged and said, "All of them, I guess."

"I'm told you've been in all of the plays that had have taken place since you've been here."

She nodded and smiled at the desk.

Principal Hammond sighed and wished he could remember a character she played but couldn't. He changed the topic.

"How was Disneyland?" That got him fleeting eye contact and a one-shoulder shrug from Brady.

"Good," Brady said.

There'd be no ice breaking. "Is everything going okay at school?" he asked.

She remained silent and motionless. He thought she hadn't heard him.

"I got a call from your father in California. He says you're having some problems. Is that true?"

She gave a shoulder shrug. "Some kids are teasing me." She stared down at her backpack on the floor next to her chair, as though she might climb into it.

"What about?"

Another shrug.

Mr. Hammond sighed and shot a glance at the clock over Brady's head. "I can't help you if you won't tell me what is going on.

Do you want me to call your dad back and say, 'She says everything is fine'? 'Hunky-dory'?" He settled back hard into his chair, causing it to roll away from the desk. He straightened up to push it back.

"They're saying that since my dad is gay, he's going to hell," Brady said, meeting his eyes full on.

"Who is?" Mr. Hammond leaned forward.

"Joanne and Jeanie and others. They've stuck notes in my binder when I'm away from my desk. And they've filled my email." She shook her head as if to clear it, and tears scattered in the air.

Mr. Hammond gave her a sad look even though she was looking away from him, eyes squeezed closed. "I'm sorry," he said, handing her a tissue. "This is not okay. I will talk to them."

"Okay," Brady said, daubing eyes and nose.

Mr. Hammond felt overwhelmed. What was he going to do? Have Casey drawn and quartered? Shot at dawn? He was the principal, and he'd talk to them. But could he really control them when no one was watching?

Still, she sat expectantly.

"I'm calling their families," Mr. Hammond said, watching her reaction.

There wasn't one.

"And the conversation will be marked on their permanent record," Mr. Hammond said. He leaned forward, eyes unblinking, and waited.

"Will Joanne and Jeanie eat with me again?" Brady asked.

"Yes," he said.

"Okay." She stood, settled the backpack on her shoulders, and left, allowing him to summon Joanne and Jeanie.

He called in the girls one at a time. Jeanie was the first. A diminutive girl, she walked around looking like she had just finished the most joyful experience of her life. As she walked in now, though, her brow was furrowed and her eyes were already filling. *This won't be hard.*

"Did you say Brady Lawson's father was going to hell because he was gay? Jeanie's jaw dropped open. Her eyes widened, and her mouth trembled. "No," she said, shaking her head.

"What if I said that I have witnesses who heard you say it?" Mr. Hammond loved that question because it wasn't a lie—Brady had heard her say it—but it was scary enough to get a confession out of most kids.

"Casey makes us do it. She says being gay is a sin and against the Ten Commandments. We don't want people to think we don't care about the Ten Commandments."

"You do understand that the Ten Commandments never included anything about homosexuality, right?"

Jeanie stared at him and blinked.

"What would happen if you refused to say these mean things to Brady?"

Jeanie shrugged. "Casey just says bad things will happen to us." Jeanie looked at him as though pleading not to be asked to say more.

"Send in Joanne, please."

Jeanie stood but didn't move. "Are you going to call my parents?" She swallowed hard.

"Can you find it your heart to eat with Brady and go back to being her friend?"

Jeanie nodded emphatically.

"Then no, I will not call your parents."

Jeanie sighed as if exhaling fully for the first time in days.

"Go ahead." Mr. Hammond motioned toward the door.

Joanne, a tall, heavy-set girl with long brown hair, brushed past Jeanie on her way into the office. Like Jeanie, she had a reputation among the faculty for being eager to please, always the first to help. He played out a similar scene with her, letting her go only after she assured him that she could hardly wait to break bread with her old friend.

That left Casey. What leverage did he have with her? Whatever deal he struck had to be between himself and Casey. He needed something she wanted that he could take away.

She opened the door of his office and stood waiting for him to look up, her head cocked slightly to the left, eyebrows raised, assessing him.

"Come in, Katherine Constance." He stood at his desk. "Sit down," he told her, but he kept standing himself. Casey arranged herself in the chair, legs crossed so that the upper one was exposed to mid thigh. He noticed and she knew it. She swept her eyes up to his with a hint of a smile.

"Do you know why you are here?" he asked.

She shook her head to say no, but her smile widened.

His stomach tightened. "Did you tell Brady Lawson her father was going to hell because he was gay?"

"Shall I quote Romans, Judges, or Leviticus to you?" She straightened in the chair. "I'll begin with Romans, then: 'For the wrath of God is revealed from heaven against all ungodliness,'"

Mr. Hammond raised his hand to cut her off.

But she had her eyes closed and continued, "I'll cut to the end; 'men leaving the natural use burned in their lust for one another. Men with men committing what is shameful and . . .'"

"Stop!" Mr. Hammond hit the arm of her chair with a resounding smack. He looked through the window and exchanged looks with Miss Nelson, his secretary.

"No, Katherine, I do not need you to quote anything to me. It is God's job to judge; it is your job to love."

"Yeah, well, what's that mean then?" Casey smiled up at him.

He lost his train of thought and looked down at the floor.

She giggled.

His face felt warm. He took a deep breath and exhaled noisily. "I'm done dealing with you, Katherine Constance. If I hear one word of you stirring up trouble for that Lawson girl, you're going to be out on your ear. You hear that? You'll be expelled. You seem to live to cause trouble, and you are not doing the Lord's work when you say mean things to hurt people. You have one year until you graduate. You want to make it out of here with a good record. Picking on a kid almost half your age is unforgivable, and it is going to cost you your graduation. You understand? You will not walk across that stage and represent this school if I hear one more thing about you teasing Brady Lawson.

"And you know something else?" He stood up behind his

desk, and she raised her head to look at him. He continued, "It seems to me that "Judge not lest ye be judged" applies pretty well to you, Miss K.C.," Mr. Hammond said, his eyes flitting to her face.

She stared back at him, no longer smiling, daring him to continue.

Mr. Hammond became flustered. "I mean, is anybody watching you when you leave for school?" His eyes bounced from her low-cut sweater to her short skirt. He meant to admonish her, but he just sounded shamed by his own attraction to her.

"What do you mean?" she asked, eyes wide, but her smile returned. She got the message, but not the one he was intending to send.

"No more trouble, Casey, I mean it. Okay, you may go," he said, flicking his hand at the door.

Casey walked out with shoulders squared and a discernible swish of her skirt. Mr. Hammond stared at the floor and shook his head at the irony of Casey blaming Brady for being a sinner, when Casey engendered sinful thoughts just by walking through the room.

BRADY

⚘ ⚘ ⚘ ⚘ ⚘ ⚘ ⚘

Brady dragged herself home and off the bus. Walking home, she was numb to the cold around her. Her shoulders caved under the weight of her backpack, and her arms crossed over her stomach, bouncing awkwardly against her body with each step. She did not cry because she had no energy for it.

She opened and shut the door soundlessly to avoid invitations to eat and talk with her grandmother as she normally did and headed directly to her room. Closing her bedroom door, she dropped her pack on the floor and fell onto the bed. Finally alone and shielded from stares, she was able to cry quietly. She wanted to talk to her grandmother and tell her all that was going on, but the thought of talking about her gay father humiliated her. Brady didn't think her grandmother would understand, or she might judge her father, and that would make it even harder for her to let Brady go back to California.

She wanted her dad to come get her. She'd already asked, and it hadn't happened. Asking for help and not getting it was worse than not asking at all. She tightened her arms over her stomach and pulled her knees closer to her chest. Tears squeezed out from under her clenched lids and slid down her cheeks. Even behind her closed eyes she could see the jeering faces. She couldn't bear it anymore.

The email indicator pinged on her laptop. She stared at the computer, not sure that she wanted to connect with anyone. Yesterday she'd gotten a quote from Judges about the concubine who was cut into twelve pieces. It had been sent repeatedly, filling her whole screen, with the subject: "When is sex perverted?" It was like the screen was yelling at her. It wouldn't be a friendly message because she didn't have any friends. If it was her dad, it would be useless. She was afraid to look but she was so very lonely.

"Hi," the message read. She could see it was from her dad. She rushed to the computer. "What's up?" she typed back.

Her father answered by instant message. "Are things still getting better since Mr. Hammond talked to the girls?"

"No."

"Last week it sounded better. Jeanie and Joanne were eating lunch with you, right?"

"That was last week. And they were just pretending to like me."

"What do you mean?"

"This week they won't talk to me at all. They talk to each other but not to me. They hate me—can't do this tomorrow."

"Do what?"

"School."

"What will you do instead?"

She did not respond.

"Where will you go?"

Again, she didn't respond.

"Brady, where'd you go? Please answer. You're scaring me."

Finally she typed back. "I'm nowhere. I'm dead."

* * *

Richard pressed against Brady's number to call her. She hadn't answered his repeated texts. He listened to it ring and then go to voice mail. God, was he too late? He stood and punched the Nordland's number. Would they be there? Had she planned ahead for the house to be empty? *Please answer, please, please answer.*

"Hello?" Kathleen answered.

Richard paced as he shouted into the phone, "Is Brady there?"

There was a pause. "Who is this—Richard? Yes, I heard her come in."

"Can you see her?"

Another pause.

Richard groaned. "Please, Kathleen, go and see if she's okay."

"Why wouldn't she be?"

"Because she isn't. Please, I was emailing her and she just stopped—it worried me. Could you just . . ." Richard could hear Kathleen knocking on the door. He held his breath and listened for Brady's voice. He heard Kathleen knock harder and raise her voice, yelling for Brady to open the door.

"She's gone and locked the door. I'm unlocking it. Hold on."

Richard heard the phone hit the table. He waited and prayed and squeezed the phone like a lifeline.

"Well, Brady, why didn't you open the door? Are you asleep? What is this?"

"I'm tired—I'm just tired."

Richard's heart surged when he heard Brady's voice. She was okay.

"Can I talk to her?" Richard shouted into the phone again and again. But Kathleen returned.

"I need to go now. I'll take care of it from here," she said.

"No, please let me talk to her, Kathleen. Please, I've been so worried."

"She just needs to sleep, Richard. But okay."

"Hi," Brady's voice seemed stiff and flat.

"What happened? You stopped talking."

"Oh, that."

"Brady, it seemed liked you were threatening to hurt yourself. You said you couldn't go back to school. Why did you say that?"

Richard felt he could hear air moving in the silence on the line. "Brady, I need you to answer—now."

"What did you ask?"

"Is something wrong at school?"

Brady snorted, "Just the usual. We're damned to hell and everyone, including God, wants me to die. Other than that things are just fine and dandy!" She laughed, but it was delayed and it sounded low and slow.

"Brady, your voice sounds different. Have you taken something—medicine of some type?"

"Yeah, yeah I have."

"What?"

"I had a headache."

"Okay, so you took—what?"

"Aspirin stuff."

"How much?"

"Um, I don't know. A handful."

"Put your grandmother on the phone."

Richard heard the phone being handed over.

"Hello," he heard Kathleen's voice. "Can you see the bottle? Do you know how much was in it and how much there is now?"

"I'm holding it, and it held one hundred. It's half gone but I don't know how much was taken before she got it."

"You need to take her to the hospital."

"Won't it just pass through her?" Kathleen asked.

"No, she could bleed internally. She could die. I've had experience with this. She needs a doctor. Please, Kathleen." The last came out as a whispered fervent prayer.

"I understand. I will."

And then the line went dead.

* * *

Brady opened her eyes the next morning and heard a low groan. Realizing the sound had been her own voice, she closed her eyes over tears. In rapid succession she knew she was alive, that she was in a hospital, and that her stomach hurt. And she desperately needed to go to the bathroom. She did, and outside the door she heard her grandmother's voice.

"They put charcoal in your stomach to soak up the aspirin. So that's why everything's so dark—" she paused—"coming out of you."

Her stomach felt sour and she was afraid to leave the bathroom, so she stood in the doorway and steadied herself against the doorjamb. She surveyed the room. How had she gotten here? Curtains formed the walls of the room, and between them a patient in a rolling bed was whisked by, led by a woman and a man dressed in smock-like clothes Brady remembered from hospital shows. She could hear competing TVs. The bed was ringed by equipment with blank monitors not in use. Her grandmother was watching her, and Brady stared back. Grandma looked as though she'd like to hug her, but Brady looked away from her and around the room while emotions swirled in her mind—shame being the strongest. She didn't want to touch anyone. She still wasn't sure she wanted to be alive.

Her grandfather leaned against the sink facing her, his feet crossed at the ankles and arms closed over his chest as though holding himself in or together. She tried to gauge his feelings but couldn't read his face.

Her grandfather cleared his throat but didn't speak at first.

She and her grandmother turned to him and waited.

"You're unhappy at the school?" Grandpa asked.

It hit her like an accusation. She squeezed back tears and wished to disappear.

"Why didn't you tell me?" he asked. "I know those kids' parents. I could have gotten to them much faster than any principal, lawyer, or whoever from California." He paused and looked at her sadly. His arms cut through the air in a gesture of futility. "I was right here. Why didn't you tell me . . . anything? This . . ." He waved his arm to encompass the room and gave her an expression so sad that her knees weakened and she thrust her hand out to grab a chair. She fell to the floor just behind it.

"Oh, Brady," Grandma said, rushing to help her up.

Brady shook her head and waved away the help. Still it took three tries to struggle to her feet. Hanging onto the back of the chair, she said, "I didn't think that you would understand."

Grandma gasped as though stung, and her eyes glistened with tears. Brady didn't dare look at Grandpa.

"What would make you think we wouldn't understand, Brady?" Frank asked.

Brady remembered back to when she first met them after the car accident that killed her mother. Her grandparents hardly talked about her mother. She wondered why, since her mother was their daughter, her death wasn't sad for them. She picked up from pieces of conversations that her mother was a problem. Brady found it easier not to talk to them about her unhappiness. Now her grandparents were fighting her father to get her to live with them. So why would she talk to them about problems mixed up with her father? It would make things harder for him.

"Do you know why kids are making fun of me?" Brady's voice came out hoarse but calm.

Kathleen turned to look at her from the sink.

Frank shook his head, but Kathleen just waited.

"Because they know," Brady said and then stopped.

"They know what?" Frank asked. His shoulders caved, and his eyes pleaded with Brady to make him understand.

"They know he's gay," Kathleen said. While Frank's grief seemed angry to Brady, Kathleen's shoulders caved as though this was one more disappointment she had been expecting.

Brady watched as a complete look of understanding registered on her grandfather's face.

"So you thought, because they were making fun of that, that I would, what? Think you *deserved* it?" Frank's mouth was open.

"Don't you hate him because he is gay?" Brady asked.

"No," he said.

"Then why do you hate him?" she asked, looking from one to the other.

"I don't," he said, pausing, "hate him."

"Then why are you fighting this?" Brady asked, eyebrows furrowed.

"Because we love you." Grandpa's eyes were wide and round, his hands extended. "And we want you to be safe. I don't think he can take care of you every day, day after day. I don't think he realizes that raising a child is not just a trip to Disneyland." Grandpa had been staring past her but now focused his gaze directly on her.

Brady stared at the tops of her feet, bare against the cold linoleum. "We didn't just go to Disneyland."

"Raising a child is not what happens in two weeks either," Kathleen said. "Are you really that unhappy here?"

She had never seen her grandmother cry. Not even when her cat was hit by a car and died. Brady fell into the chair and arched her back, forcing her gaze up at the ceiling, but tears squeezed out of her eyes and down onto her neck. She couldn't say what she didn't understand. Feelings roared in her ears.

The first time she felt that she fit in was during that two-week stay at her father's house. Being happy with her dad meant her grandparents had failed, at least to them. She swallowed hard and said, "My dad wants to raise me, and I want him to try. And I don't want to go back to school with those people."

"Well, you've got it," Grandpa said. "You're flying down on Friday to meet with a social worker, and we're all preparing to meet with a judge to decide if your school is an appropriate setting for you."

"For how—" Brady's voice was hoarse. She cleared her throat "—long?"

"Until we can prove that we have fixed the problem at school," Grandpa said, shaking his head.

Brady was shocked to see his eyes were red.

Grandpa looked away.

"Now how are we going to prove that?" Kathleen asked, mouth open.

"I guess a judge will tell us. At any rate, you're going to go home with us, so get ready." He walked out of the room, and she wanted to run after him and tell him she'd never wanted to hurt him or grandma. She loved them. She looked at her grandmother, who was laying out her clothes on the bed.

Grandma smoothed out the sleeves of her top and spoke without looking at her. "The worst of this is you not telling me, Brady. Judges and lawyers have a job to do, but you and I . . ." Kathleen trailed off, head shaking. "We are family, and I thought—" she paused and blinked rapidly—"I guess I thought we were closer than we were. I thought we had trust." She walked between the curtains and toward the waiting room.

Brady watched as each deliberate step took her grandmother farther from her. She had never felt lonelier.

BACK TO CALIFORNIA

A s Brady was boarding the plane, she had the feeling she would never be at home with her grandparents again. She turned to call out to them, but they were already walking away, two bent old people lost in the crowd.

Unable to concentrate enough to read, Brady felt an unease grow in her stomach. Strapped in her seat, she stared out of the window at nothing. The engine droned but they never seemed to move.

When they did land, Brady wanted to be happy, so she tried by forcing her mouth into a smile. It became easier when she saw her dad and Michael waiting for her.

Michael was holding a huge bouquet of sunflowers, and her dad had a set of sand toys in bold primary colors with a giant red bow on it. They had reservations for a restaurant on the beach and big plans for possible sand castle designs. Brady buried her head in her father's shoulder and closed her eyes against the memory of her grandparents' faces.

They drove along the freeway and she recognized Santa Monica Place, where both her fathers had chosen beautiful clothes for her at Barney's. She saw Tender Greens where Michael had shown her there were healthy foods she could eat. She passed the sign for Santa Monica Beach, where they had helped her build the first sand castle of her life with Fiona. Would she see Fiona again? Maybe go to school with her? Her mood lightened. As they pulled into the drive, Brady was so glad to see both her fathers' safe little home that it almost hurt. Did she love her dad and Michael, or was she just escaping the bullies? Was she losing her grandparents? To avoid being homesick, Brady focused on the work Grandma had gathered from her teachers and clicked away on the computer or read. She wasn't sure if she was ever going back to Valley Christian, but if she did, she would not be behind. Thoughts grated against each other all day.

Michael had arranged for the social worker to visit. Brady found she liked Mrs. Fisher's Midwestern twang and musical laugh. She was of mixed race and had smooth brown skin, high cheekbones, and a trim figure. Brady took Mrs. Fisher to see her room and talked about the schools she had visited with Richard. She watched Mrs. Fisher make a note when she mentioned the schools. Brady talked about missing her fathers when she was at her grandparents', and she touched briefly on the teasing at school.

Michael walked Mrs. Fisher through the vegetable garden, and Brady heard her offer some tips on pruning. He and Richard left the house as a good-faith gesture while Brady and Mrs. Fisher chatted on in the living room. Mrs. Fisher asked Brady what the biggest difference was between life with her grandparents and life in California. "My grandparents love me in their own way." Brady stopped and gazed around the room before continuing. "But I feel important here. My grandparents always took good care of me, but it's different—better—here somehow. I feel like my dad and Michael understand me more." Brady scanned Mrs. Fisher's face to see if she had been understood before adding, "They love me."

"I see, dear." Mrs. Fisher nodded sympathetically. "How do you know when you are loved?"

Brady tried not to cry. Her hands flapped as she struggled for control. "People who love you stop what they're doing and listen to you. They cook foods you like, watch movies with you, and listen to music that you like. They want to make you happy. They give their time and sometimes give up what they want to do so that you can do what you want. They make you want to do that back for them. At my grandparents I'm okay, but it's not the same. It's better for me in California."

"You feel more understood, better loved?" Mrs. Fisher leaned forward and looked carefully at Brady, who nodded. "They're like that with each other too. Michael worries—actually worries—about what Dad and I eat. How can people who care so much for one another be bad for each other the way my church says? They aren't any different from my grandparents." A memory of jeering kids blasted in her mind, and she felt her breathing speed up. In a final gasp of desperation, she drew her hands together, one hand squeezing the other hand's fingers, and said, "I really want to get back here. I want to live here now." Brady implored the social worker with her eyes.

"I understand, dear," Mrs. Fisher responded, making more notes in her book.

"No, I mean *now*," Brady interrupted. "I don't want to ever go back. I want to stay here *now*."

"That's not a decision for me to make. I make recommendations, and I can recommend that the change in custody goes ahead, but the time frame is up to the courts. Things are really bad at school, I take it?" Mrs. Fisher said.

"Please don't tell anyone unless you can get me out of there," Brady said. She wasn't sure she wanted to go on. So far asking grown-ups for help had only made things worse.

"What is happening, Brady?" Mrs. Fisher asked.

Brady gagged back sobs as she searched for words. The only way Brady could see her situation getting better was by not ever going back to Oregon. So maybe, just this once, going for help would actually help.

Should she start by telling Mrs. Fisher about the notes with Bible verses left in the pages of her math book for her to find? She had long since stopped reading them but had begun slipping them into a shoe box to keep them out of sight. She didn't want them found in the trash either. The thought of her grandparents reading those awful things made her shudder.

"No one will sit with me at lunch," Brady said. It sounded whiney to her, and she ducked her head.

"I see," Mrs. Fisher said.

Just at that moment her two fathers walked in, buzzed up and flushed from their run, talking loudly to each other.

"I fit in here better, and I want to stay," Brady rushed to say.

Mrs. Fisher looked at Brady quizzically and made some notes. She assured her and Richard and Michael of a very positive report.

Michael offered Mrs. Fisher a gift basket of his vegetables that clearly pleased her but that she had to decline. They all shook hands, and she was gone.

Richard and Michael recorded the hearing date in their phone calendars. Brady mentioned in grace that evening that she felt their little family was blessed but that they needed to be open to God's will. Her voice caught, and Richard and Michael exchanged looks. Brady ate rapidly and chattered about the visit with Mrs. Fisher.

After dinner Richard's phone rang. It was Ryan. Casey had been suspended and had been threatened with expulsion if she harassed Brady any further. He said that Frank said it was safe to come home. Ryan gave Richard flight times, which he wrote down. Richard looked sadly at Brady as he talked. He lowered his head as he hung up and sat back, exhaling loudly. He turned to Brady. "You're going back tomorrow but not forever, and Casey's gone so it's going to be okay."

So they had one more day to spend together. Dad told Brady he wanted to take her to the church in which he had been raised, the Episcopal Church. Brady wanted to please him and so she went eagerly. As they entered the church, she thought it was as elegant as the churches in history books. It was full of stained glass windows through which the sun poured warmly. There was a large choir in a loft at the back, and they sang something beautiful that reminded Brady of the music Michael played at dinner. People made the sign of the cross, bowed before entering a pew, and knelt on red velvet cushions when they prayed. Brady thought the ritual was dramatic and tried it out self-consciously.

Brady sensed that Dad was peaceful here because he really prayed and didn't glance around at other people. This made her smile. The sermon began, and she could not believe that it was all about how they had a gay bishop and how some churches were really having a problem with it. The minister quoted another man who said that God was love and that it was not our place to exclude anyone from God's love. Finally, finally someone was seeing what she'd been struggling with since her father had come back into her life. Her father and Michael could not be an abomination to anyone who was love. They were so good to her and for each other.

They ended with a hymn and a rousing, "Alleluia, Alleluia," which she shouted at the top of her lungs. Richard winced and ducked his head but smiled. She didn't care; in fact she hadn't felt this carefree in months.

Richard introduced himself and then her to the minister. She became aware that her father was talking about the sermon. Her father summed it up by saying, "She very much enjoyed your sermon. I am gay and my daughter has been trying to reconcile her faith with my life, and you just helped. A lot. Thank you."

Brady froze. Her father had just told the minister he was gay. She waited for a response. Did he really mean all of those nice things he just said, or was this just another case of, "God loves all of the children of God as long as they like a member of the opposite sex?" Was he going to throw them out or tell them they were sinners and sure to go straight to hell?

The minister smiled and leaned down, and the sleeve of his robe fell softly against her hand. "Welcome. We are pleased to have you in our church, and we hope to see you again very soon."

She stared back at him, not believing what had just taken place. Sensing the absence of fear, she breathed deeply and felt light inside. "Me too," she said, pumping his hand and grinning. "Me too!"

As they walked away from the church, she took her father by the hand, turned to him, and said clearly and confidently, "Dad, I don't want to go back to my school in Oregon because they are mean to me because you are gay. And I do mean super mean."

All of the memories came bubbling out, some so fast that she struggled to make words keep up. She told of the notes, of the constant sidelong glances and giggling of other students whenever she walked by. She described how her friends had been forced to leave her out and that even if she ate alone, kids stared at her. So she ate her lunch alone in the bathroom, only to find the bullies stood outside the stall and smirked at her when she opened it. "I went to that aide I mentioned, Angie Wells," she told him as they got in the car. "She was all nice at first, and I told her everything. I thought she understood. But she came back and told me God wanted me to stay with my grandparents and that's why he sent me to them. She made it seem like I was breaking God's plan by going to live with you." She looked at Dad, hoping for understanding, but she didn't cry. She talked until she was done.

Dad pulled out his cell phone, and she gasped because she thought he was going to try to solve the problem on the phone and send her back. But when he said to Michael, "I'm calling Ryan. No way are we sending our daughter back to that godforsaken school. Somebody should have noticed the harassment that's been going on." He paused and seemed to be listening.

She sat squeezing her hands open and shut with fear. Why was this taking so long?

When Dad hung up, she felt Michael was still talking. He started the car and said, "We're not out of the woods yet. We need to call the lawyer."

Her stomach growled, but lunch would have to wait. What had Michael said? Didn't he want her?

GETTING HELP

"So what is it that couldn't wait until tomorrow?" Ryan said. Five minutes earlier, he had been enjoying a much-needed session of shooting hoops with his brother. He frowned watching his brother now playing alone. He was going to need to set boundaries with Richard.

"You said to call before breaking the law," Richard said.

"What?" Ryan asked. "Now what happened?" He grunted as he pulled himself upright and extended his legs through the open car door. "Is this something I need to record?"

"I think so."

"Okay, and go." Ryan smiled at his phone. His mother had bought it for him when they moved to the new office. It made him feel rich, successful, and much more experienced than he actually was. Ryan squinted as he listened to Richard.

"Brady is being systematically harassed and shunned because I am gay," Richard began, giving Ryan ten minutes worth of examples of why the school was no longer a safe place for her. "I won't send her back to it," Richard concluded. His voice lowered an octave as he added, "And I want to do it legally."

"Okay, when is she due back?"

"That's the thing." Richard paused. "She's missing her flight right now."

Ryan stood up, hitting his head on the top of the door. "Goddamnit," he said, rubbing his head. "This is not good, Richard. You needed to call me or them *before* this point. They would be within their rights to send a sheriff to pick her up. When you violate the court order on picking a kid up and dropping her off, you are non-compliant, and legally it's kidnap. This can backfire terribly. You could lose her because you are keeping her from seeing the grandparents, who currently have the child-parent relationship. This action violates the premise that you are acting in her best interests, which is one of the few things in your favor. We talked about this." Ryan's shoulders dropped; the damage was done.

"Those kids are spiritual sadists. How can this not be acting in Brady's best interests?" Richard asked.

Ryan rolled his eyes. "Because it violates the custody agreement, which everyone said—from the judge on down—was in her best interests." Ryan controlled his tone. He didn't want to argue, so he changed the topic. "Have you complained to the school?" Ryan asked.

"Yes."

"What happened?"

The principal talked to the kids and the families, and it got better and then worse," Richard said.

"Did you complain again, and is there documentation of it?" Ryan asked.

"I didn't know it was still going on," Richard said.

"Why not?" Ryan asked.

"Telling the principal had backfired. She didn't want to make it even worse. So no, she did not complain again."

"How could admin know? Did Brady talk to anyone about the fact that the harassment was continuing?" Ryan asked.

"This is a ten-year-old kid we're talking about. Harrassment that doesn't let up, even for a week or two, seems like forever." Richard paused. "There was someone, an aid named Angie. But she turned out to be worse than no one. She got Brady to confide in her and then told her God wanted her to stay in Oregon." Richard described the rest of the harassment.

Ryan moved on and asked, "Who is picking her up from the airport?"

"Her grandparents."

"I'll call them and handle the damage. Fax me a list of everything—*everything* about the harassment. Give me dates, names, actions taken."

"Even if the actions didn't work?" Richard asked.

"Yes, even then. The intervention did work; it just didn't last. And then when it started up again, Brady needed to call you, and you needed to call the grandparents and the school. As long as they are making a good-faith effort, you have to continue to work with them. The school is in compliance, Richard. You are not," Ryan said.

"She's ten years old. She's a long plane ride, or a day's drive, away. She isn't sleeping, her grades are dropping, and she feels completely alone. She's already attempted suicide. I couldn't send her back," Richard said.

"You could have. You didn't want to. It's interesting that you managed to call me *after* she missed the flight. It's important for adults to be adults when kids need them the most. I'm not saying you were expected to send her back to her oppressors, shrieking and crying. You simply needed to call first." He emphasized each of the last two syllables. "I will handle it, Richard. But you've set us back." He waved to his brother, Paul, and yelled, "Gotta go."

Paul nodded just before bouncing the ball off the backboard and sending it careening around the court.

"No control," Ryan muttered to himself as he slid behind the wheel and drove to the office for his twelfth consecutive day of work.

PUSHING BACK

R yan was not looking forward to telling Mr. Nordland that
Brady was not on the plane. Ryan paced and spoke aloud different ways to present the information. *Bottom line: we got her,
you don't, sorry. My client is completely non-compliant and has the
self-control of a two-year-old. But I'm making this call because I'm a
dumb-ass codependant who feels best when he's being used.*

"Hello?" Mr. Nordland answered the phone.

Ryan hoped he hadn't been heard ranting. "Hello, Mr. Nordland, this is Ryan Stephens. I represent your granddaughter, Brady
Lawson."

"You represent her father. I don't think she's had much to do
with it."

Perfect, he's already pissed off and I haven't even started, Ryan
thought.

"Mr. Nordland, it seems that Brady has been suffering through
systematic harassment at her school, Valley Christian, because the
students know that her father is gay," Ryan said and paused.

"Yes, and we've taken care of that."

Ryan cleared his throat. "No, not entirely, I'm afraid. Mr. Lawson did complain to the school, and although some actions were taken, the harassment has continued and gotten worse. She is unable to sleep, her grades are falling, and she feels she cannot learn in this environment," Ryan said.

"She's where? She should be on a plane back to Medford," Frank said.

"She is with her father." Ryan paused. "Apparently, while in California she told her father of the continuing harassment, and he felt it was not in her best interest to return to the school," Ryan said, and he paused to allow the information to sink in. "He further feels that it is best if he keeps her until the custody hearing."

"Well, isn't that convenient? He's just writing his own rules, is he?" Mr. Nordland said. "How long's that going to be?"

"I don't know. He wants to assure you that he is not trying to keep her from you. He understands that you and your wife are important in her life, and while he doesn't want to impede that, he simply did not find it conscionable to send her back to the school." Technically this all had to go before a judge, and Ryan was fast at work to make that happen, but for now he wanted to buy time.

Mr. Nordland said, "I know there was a problem and that the principal handled it. The troublemaker has been suspended. You know, if Brady'd talked to me first this would have been settled long ago. I had to learn about it from the school last time, and now I have to learn it from you this time. We raised this girl. It's frustrating to have such a complete breakdown of our family. I think the problem is him—Richard, I mean," Frank said.

"It's good that your granddaughter has someone in whom she can confide. Harassment and bullying are destructive to a child's self-esteem and can have disastrous consequences. She's already made one suicide attempt. Richard's instincts are good in protecting from another one." Ryan had more to say but didn't. *If Brady's grades were falling and she wasn't sleeping well, why didn't you notice it?*

"Mr. Stephens, you don't understand," Mr. Nordland said, his voice rising. "Richard is stirring up trouble. If he hadn't gotten the harebrained idea of coming into her life and wrecking everything, this wouldn't be happening to her. It's not her fault he's a homosexual. So now he wants to keep her until the hearing? That gives him the upper hand; it seems to me that she's already moved in with him. What about falling behind in school? Is that in her best interests? Is she just going to sit around and watch TV for two weeks? How come you're not calling my lawyer?"

"I have left a voicemail for your lawyer detailing what I've told you. I wanted to save you an unnecessary trip to the airport," Ryan said.

"Thank you for your concern. There are other planes, Mr. Stephens, and she's going to be on one of them eventually," Frank said.

"We're filing a complaint against the school for not acting fast enough to protect Brady. We didn't think this could wait for the courts to take action. It is not in her best interests to remain in the school where she is being ostracized and systematically harassed. She'll be out until it is resolved satisfactorily. I'm sure that you can understand, Mr. Nordland. You mentioned your concern that she might fall behind in class; her father is going to enroll her in their local school, so she won't be idle, Mr. Nordland. You don't need to worry about that," Ryan said.

"They're actually enrolling her in school there?" Mr. Nordland asked.

"Yes, sir, they didn't want her to fall behind any more than you did," Ryan said.

"I'm calling my lawyer," Mr. Nordland said.

* * *

Frank dipped the receiver to the cradle for a count of exactly three and then punched in Evan Cory's number.

"They're violating a court order," Mr. Cory assured him on the phone. "It is clear that they are unreasonably denying contact between you and your granddaughter and that she will suffer from the loss of contact with you and Kathleen. The problem is the school, not you. Is there a school other than Valley Christian in which you can enroll Brady? Just a neighborhood school will do. She's no more bonded with a school in California than she will be with a school in Oregon. That is, if there really is a problem. I wonder if this isn't just something conjured up by Dad as a way to hang onto her. What evidence did they have that this harassment was real?"

"They're going to fax you a whole list of things that happened to her and how they complained," Mr. Nordland said. "According to the lawyer, it's already being sent. He said it was lengthy and specific."

"While she won't be back tomorrow, she will be back soon. Let me know when you have chosen a school for her. The sooner the better on that," Mr. Cory said.

"What's happening, Frank? I've been waiting for you in the car so we can pick up Brady."

He sighed heavily. "Well, Brady's not coming home tonight."

"But what about school tomorrow?" Kathleen asked. "She worries so about not having her homework done."

"I know. I guess that doesn't matter anymore," Frank said.

"But how can they do this? We have custody of her," Kathleen asked.

"It seems some of the kids are teasing her again," Frank said.

"Seems like they're overreacting to me. Kids tease and get over it."

"Yeah, that's what I thought," Frank said, sitting down at the kitchen table, "but now teasing isn't teasing anymore. It's harassment, *systematic* harassment, and it is illegal. Kids can't tease each other anymore or they get evacuated to some godforsaken state like California."

Kathleen leaned toward Frank across the table and said, "I don't understand this. We were a fine family before. Brady had friends, and good grades. She was happy. He came into her life and now she's lonely and getting bad grades." She paused. "It seems to me that the source of the problem is the father."

Frank nodded. "She'd be better off without him. And that's exactly what we need to say if we can get anybody to listen."

LIMIT SETTING

They had shopped for new Ticonderoga pencils and Five Star binder paper and a backpack that Richard said had been hand-woven by Tibetan monks. She had practiced the five-block walk to Pacific School with Richard and then Michael and was more than ready to go alone. She'd been so excited last night that it had taken forever to fall asleep. When she finally did drift off, she realized it had been a long time since she had felt homesick at bedtime. She was home.

* * *

The next day, she peered into her classroom through the small square glass pane at the top of the door. Even with the lights still off, she could see pictures of the students on the "All About Me" bulletin board. The students were darker than her classmates in Oregon. One boy had his hair drawn up in a covered bun on the top of his head. She felt a tingle of excitement about making new friends who were different from the ones back home. A hand touched her sleeve, and Brady turned to see the girl from the beach.

"Fiona!" Brady said.

Fiona smiled, and Brady noticed she had chipped a tooth but her hair was carefully braided. She seemed so happy to see Brady that it made Brady squirm with pleasure.

"Hi, Brady. Are you in Mrs. Patterson's class too?"

"Yeah." Brady smiled.

"Sit by me?" Fiona said as the teacher unlocked the door and everyone crowded in. Brady followed her to the first row.

* * *

Life gradually settled into a bumpy routine of lunch making, homework completion, and getting to school on time. The hearing had been rescheduled twice, and Brady had been with Richard and Michael for over a month. Michael, for fear of being noncompliant, had made it his mission to see that Brady stay in contact with her grandparents. He did notice less chatter from Brady during the calls and that she talked about them less. This seemed like it should be good but still felt sad.

Today was Saturday, and although it was early in the morning. The late-May air was giving way to summer as it warmed the bedroom where Michael and Richard slept. Michael realized Richard had completely encircled him with his arms around his torso and his cheek resting contentedly against Michael's head. Although this was sweet, it was also hot, and Michael pushed Richard off of his body gently. Richard appeared, even in sleep, to be smiling. Michael eased toward him and brushed his lips softly over his partner's neck and cheek, relishing his scent. He reached down and ran his hand from Richard's knee up his thigh to his bare stomach, coming to rest at his waist. Michael nuzzled his mouth into Richard's neck and inhaled deeply. He was considering how to proceed when the door burst open.

Michael leapt to his feet, grabbing a shirt from the chair and throwing it on. "What do you need, Brady?" He hoped his erection wasn't as visible as he was imagining it to be.

"I'm hungry."

"If you'd eaten dinner, you wouldn't be."

Brady shook her father's shoulder. "Daddy, I'm hungry, and Michael won't let me eat."

Richard squinted up at the two of them. Each petitioned him to his and her side with glaring eyes.

"I ate at mealtime, and I'm still hungry." Brady met Michael's eyes defiantly.

Richard rolled his legs out of bed and grabbed her around the waist, playfully lifting her up and tossing her onto the bed. She laughed, clearly delighted.

He began to tickle her slightly exposed tummy, causing her to pull her legs up and twist contentedly in his grasp. "No, you cannot be hungry," he stated, affecting an Austrian accent. "Vee vill not allow it!" He flipped her over on her stomach, buried his lips in the small of her back, and blew out, creating loud, resonating sounds, like an uncontrolled fart.

Michael grimaced at both the offensive sound and the intimacy of having Brady in their bed. Brady cackled loudly, legs pulled to chest, eyes squeezed shut. Michael felt invisible.

"Do it again!" she squealed, and Richard happily complied. It was cute the first week or so, but as he realized this was becoming a morning ritual, it felt invasive. He walked quietly into the bathroom and firmly clicked the door shut behind him.

"Go down and eat some fruit," Michael heard Richard say.

"As if that's gonna happen," Michael muttered under his breath. Then he distinctly heard Richard say, "Or a couple of bowls of cereal." Michael heard Brady galloping down the stairs, banging her hand against the wall with each step.

"That's exactly why she doesn't eat at mealtime," Michael said to Richard through the bathroom door. "Don't eat anything. I'll make breakfast very soon," he shouted to Brady.

Michael opened the bathroom door.

"I think we need to engage in a little limit setting."

"What we have here is a failure to communicate," Richard said in his imitation of the warden from *Cool Hand Luke*. The impression seemed to amuse Richard because he smiled and looked up at Michael. His smile vanished. "What kind of limit setting?" he asked.

Michael reviewed a multitude of infractions.

Richard sat up and placed both feet firmly on the floor, as if bracing.

Michael sat down on the bed next to Richard, who rubbed his hands together and then secured them between his knees.

"Well, first of all, I think it's reasonable to ask Brady to knock on our bedroom door, don't you?" Michael said.

"Yes. It might also be reasonable for us to lock our door. I mean, if we're thinking about having sex with her across the hall. Right?" Richard asked, tilting his head in a mincing manner that irritated Michael.

"She really needs to eat at mealtimes, and she needs to eat healthy food. She should at least *try* new foods before she rejects them so rudely."

"Okay, we'll work together on that," Richard said, but Michael noticed that he seemed unsure, and it aggravated him.

Michael sighed heavily as he considered his next comment. "She should never be in our bed, never. It makes me feel, I don't know, squeamish, uncomfortable."

Richard looked at Michael quizzically. "It's not like she's sleeping with us. We were playing, wrestling, tickling. Those are fun things, acts of affection. I loved wrestling with my father and brothers. Is that what you're talking about?" Richard asked.

"Yeah, it is, and it's every morning now. Maybe I never wrestled with my father, but it looks bad to me. That and whatever you did with your mouth on her back—what was that?" Michael asked.

"Slobber-dobbers? Phoofing? I don't know what they're called. I just remember that it was funny. What's wrong with that? She loves it. Couldn't you hear her laughing? It's affection, cuddling, and snuggling. I guess we're making up for lost time, both of us." Richard shrugged.

Michael felt self-conscious. Was he overreacting and being too rigid? "Maybe I'm jealous?" he asked.

"You want me to push up your shirt and make farting noises on your back?" Richard covered his mouth to stifle a laugh.

Michael stood up and returned to the bathroom, saying, "I don't know what I want. I just feel a little left out, I guess. I liked it the way that it was. I mean I want her here, but I miss us. We used to read in the evenings and have people over and go out to clubs. Now I have to read with my fingers in my ears to hear myself over your reading to her. By the way, she is reading what you are reading. I can see her eyes move in synchronicity with yours. It's eerie to watch. Why are you reading to a child who does nothing but read?" Michael asked, arms across his chest and eyes averted.

"I read to her because it is fun and soothing," Richard said. "She sits in my lap and is relaxed. I can feel it. She isn't always. A lot of times she is anxious. It feels good to have something that helps. It may seem over-the-top, but when we read I feel like all the bad stuff, shame, and guilt are erased. I'm sorry it bothers you, and we can go to another room, but I'm not going to stop." Richard paused and looked directly at Michael. "It's unfair of you to ask. It feels selfish—maybe a little *childish*?" Richard's voice was rising and he glared at Michael.

"Is everything okay?" Brady asked.

Both men turned to see her standing just inside the room with her hand on the doorknob. Her eyes were wide.

Michael thrust himself off of the bed and stormed back to the bathroom. "No, everything is definitely not okay," he said, and he shut the door behind him.

"This won't work," Richard said to the closed door. "We need to talk." He turned to Brady. "Please go back to your room. Everything will be okay. Michael and I just need to talk."

Richard closed the door behind her and walked to the bathroom. Tapping lightly, he said softly, "Please talk to me."

Michael opened the door, brushed past Richard, and dropped into an armchair in the corner of the room. He folded his arms across his chest.

Richard picked up a pad of paper from the bedside table and a pencil and wrote down the complaints that Michael had mentioned. "We can change these things," he said.

Michael looked unconvinced. "I'm not happy. Are you?"

Richard shrugged. "There are bound to be adjustments that have to be made. We're not used to having a child in the house."

"It's weird, but lately I feel that she is working to drive a wedge between us," Michael said. "She doesn't always appear to want this to work."

Richard motioned with his hand for Michael to lower his voice. Michael snapped his head away from Richard in frustration and crossed his legs.

"Do you want this to work?" Richard said.

A long silence followed. "Yes," Michael finally said, but he didn't look at Richard.

"With Brady, I mean," Richard tentatively pursued.

"Yes," said Michael. "And no."

Richard sighed and sat down on the bed. "What's that mean?"

"Right now, she's here, we've gotten that far, and after that, frankly, nothing is working. Richard. It isn't," Michael said.

"Some things are working for me," Richard said. "I feel like I'm finally doing what I should have done when she was first born. The guilt was keeping me from ever moving forward."

"Oh, that's great to hear. So the last three years of us were just you going through the motions, but now that she's here, it's all just sheer bliss for you?"

"God, not this again," Richard said.

"Yes, this again. It has never been resolved. You've used me so you could bring her home and raise her. You don't care about me," Michael said, staring evenly at Richard.

"Stop. You know that's not true. I love you," Richard said.

"I don't know anymore. I used to think that you did. But lately I've seen you do things that separate us. I've seen you joining ranks with her and making fun of the food and the rules that I want observed. Sorry if that doesn't feel like love. What I do know is that I'm not happy. I'm often, very often, angry, and I dread dinner, which I used to look forward to. Dinner used to be a time to enjoy each other and the food. Our haven from the world. Now it's all centered on her. And worse, you and I are picking away at one another. You think I'm being inflexible," Michael said, and Richard looked up and nodded. Michael continued, "But you need to grow up and be an adult, actually parent."

"I parent every day," Richard said.

"Give me one instance in which you stood up to her and made her do what she should do."

Richard shrugged. "I make her brush her teeth. She hates that."

"Impressive." Michael snorted, adding, "What about what just happened last Sunday at that Hyatt? She just got up from a huge meal in which she ate no fruits or vegetables, which didn't appear to be a problem for you, and I've quit saying anything because it humiliates me to be disregarded. I watched, Richard, did you?"

"Yes, I watched." Richard shrugged. "She ate muffins and desserts. It's a one-time event."

"No, we're eating there or some place like it every Sunday, and every time she does the same thing. I can't stand to watch it. At breakfast she eats an entire plate of sausage and bacon followed by muffins. And you never say anything. Of course her body burns it up in a couple of hours, and not to worry, she gets up and pounds down more sugar-covered cereals. Who cares? Apparently not you."

Despite the fact that both men were now standing toe to toe, their voices were rising with each syllable. Richard pointed his finger at Michael's chest to punctuate his speech. "Is it the food that she eats or the fact that you don't get to control every bite she chooses and swallows? That's why I've chosen the buffets. It sidesteps the control issue. She goes to the table and gets what she wants, and we get to have a meal free of confrontation for once in our lives. You complained about how everything is centered on her. Well, that's because you want her to eat what you eat, and she doesn't like it. No kid would. And at first I thought, 'Oh he loves her and wants to see that she eats right.' Then it evolved into, 'Just eat what I give you and shut up.'"

"I have never said, 'shut up.'" Even though it was hot, Michael began shutting the windows to keep the neighbors from hearing.

"But that's the message," Richard said.

"You're so preoccupied with pleasing her," Michael said, "I

really think if I weren't here, you'd break out a box of Twinkies and eat them with her for dinner." He paced between the bed and the bathroom. "You're having this extended slumber party with her, and I'm waiting to actually see you be the adult in the room."

"Is parenting only about control in your mind?" Richard asked. "Is it ever about affection and relationships? You know, she's a good kid. She has straight As at school. No one has to get after her about homework. Doesn't that earn her some liberty in the food department?"

Now that the windows were closed, Michael could feel perspiration beading on his upper lip. "No, food is different from homework. It makes her grow and stay healthy. It shouldn't be negotiable."

"We're not getting anywhere," Richard finally admitted. "I'm not willing to parent the way you want."

"That's not what I'm asking for. You're right, we are not getting anywhere." Michael started back into the bathroom and shut the door again.

This time Richard didn't knock on the door. Very swiftly he pulled on running clothes and sprinted down the stairs and out of the door.

* * *

Brady closed her book as soon as she heard her father run down the stairs and out of the door, slamming it behind him. She hadn't been reading anyway. She waited as long as she could stand, listening for sounds from across the hall. She'd heard parts of the fight when they yelled. She had heard her name. What was going to happen to her? She stepped quietly into the hall. The door to her fathers' bedroom was standing open, and no one was in the room. She walked downstairs and across the living room to where she could see Michael cooking in the kitchen. He moved more quickly than usual, putting down pans on the stove so that they banged as they hit the surfaces. She turned to go back upstairs.

"Now is the time for breakfast. What would you like, Brady?"

Her breath caught. How had he known she was there?

"Are you talking to me?"

He turned to look at her sharply. "Is your name Brady? Do you see anyone else in the room?"

She drew closer to the kitchen. Michael was scrambling eggs and didn't appear to be adding any bumpy vegetables. Her stomach growled.

"You really are hungry." He didn't look up from the eggs.

Brady nodded.

"This is the right time for it and it's ready, so you're in luck." He brought plates to the table and poured glasses of orange juice.

Brady looked at her dad's unset place. "Where's Dad?"

"He went running."

"Why didn't he eat breakfast?"

"He wasn't hungry," Michael said, staring at her.

"He never runs on an empty stomach. It makes him throw up."

"He was upset, okay? He and I had a disagreement, which I'm sure you heard, and running calms him down."

Without looking at him, she asked, "What was the fight about?"

"You, mostly. And life in general." Michael paused. "Does that bother you at all?"

"What did I do?" Brady asked, trying to hear over the crunch of toast. Butter coated her lips, and she licked it off.

Michael looked away. "Oh, any number of things: eating the wrong things and at the wrong times; walking into our room without knocking; leaving clothes, books, and dirty dishes out."

Brady, hungry and uncomfortable, snapped at the food on her fork. She sensed Michael's disapproval as he stared at her and then away.

He made no attempt to eat and didn't even look at his plate.

Her discomfort grew into anger, causing her to tear at the toast with her front teeth.

"It's not just that . . . it's . . ." Michael paused, smoothing his hands over his face. He pushed his glasses up and rubbed his eyes. "Sometimes I feel that you do things deliberately to provoke me. Do you know what I mean by that?"

"On purpose, to make you mad," she said through a mouthful of toast. She knew he was right but stuck her raised chin out anyway and met his eyes.

"Do you think that you do that?" Michael asked.

Brady shrugged. She knew this irritated him, but she thought she'd cry if she spoke.

He slid back in his chair. "We're not doing well here. I'm not enjoying my life right now. I feel like you want me to go away. Is that true?"

Another shrug was all Brady could muster.

Michael pushed her hair out of her eyes. He pulled away from her and got Kleenex from the counter and held it out to her.

Taking the Kleenex, Brady asked, "Do you want me to move back with my grandparents?"

"No. I do want us to get along. Do you hate me?" he asked.

She gave a big shake of her hair and pushed out, "No."

"What is it that you do want, Brady?" Michael asked, handing her several more Kleenexes.

"I don't know," Brady said.

"Why do you think that you do things on purpose to annoy me?" Michael asked.

"I . . . hate . . . the way you talk to Dad," Brady said, raising her head.

"What do you mean?" Michael asked. His face reddened. He opened his mouth and then shut it.

Brady could tell she'd made him mad. She stopped herself from smiling.

"How do I talk to him?" Michael asked. He pushed against the table like he was going to stand up but then didn't.

Brady leaned toward him. "You tell him what to eat and what to wear, and you tell him he's ashamed of being gay." Brady watched Michael's face. "I hear everything, you know." She pointed upstairs toward her bedroom door.

"It's true," Michael said. "These last few evenings we have had some disagreements about those things." Michael's brow furrowed. "But we used to be happy."

They looked away from each other.

"You did it," Brady said in a burst. "You made him gay. He couldn't have always been gay because I'm here, right? You can't deny that. I am here." Brady pounded her fists on her chest. "He was married to my mom, and they had me. You made him gay." She pointed into Michael's face, watching him pull his head in as though she'd slapped him. She lowered her finger but not her eyes.

"I did not *make* your father gay." Michael's voice was steely cold. "Your father was born gay, and he married your mother because she was already pregnant. He hoped he would appear straight and fool everyone around him. But he couldn't. He was miserable. Do you know that he nearly drank himself to death trying to live that lie? His love for me made his life worth living, even during the worst days of his recovery. You know how I know that?" Michael looked at Brady, who shook her head. "He told me. And let me offer you one more reality check: I own everything you see." Michael fanned his arms out and looked around the room. "The house is mine. I pay for the food, your clothes, your bedding, all of it."

"But Dad picked out the stuff in my room, and he has credit cards that he pays for things with," Brady said, her chin jutted forward.

"Yes, and at the end of the month, I pay the bill for those credit cards. I'm happy to do it. I wanted him to be happy. I wanted you to be comfortable here. I wanted a family, and believe it or not, I wanted to be your father," Michael said. Looking away from her, he crossed his arms over his chest. "You wanted a father. I wanted us all to be happy together." Michael's hands lay open on the table.

Brady watched a muscle in his cheek twitch.

"We aren't," she said.

Richard burst through the front door gasping for breath and asked, "How's it going?"

Brady and Michael stared at him.

Finally Michael spoke. "I haven't been happy recently. I don't think this is working for us."

"What are you saying?" Richard gasped.

"I need space, time alone; I need to think," Michael said. "I need for you—both—to go somewhere else and let me figure out what I can handle."

"But we live here," Brady said, and she stood up.

Richard circled the table and put a hand on her shoulder. "Just like that, you expect me—us—to move out? What happened here?" he said, looking from Brady to Michael.

"Are you happy, Richard?" Michael asked, pinning his eyes on Richard's.

"I'm okay." Richard shrugged and looked at the floor. He jerked his head back up and looked at Michael. "It's been rocky, but we can solve this. We've gotten through things before, Michael, we have."

Michael shook his head as he said, "I don't know. This seems too much. What I know for sure is that I need time alone now."

Richard stepped back and rested on the back of the couch. Brady stared down at her hands and listened to her father exhale. She glanced up at him willing him to fight back, fight for her. Say something. Instead, she saw him draw a deep breath, and shoot a glance at Michael who stared straight ahead. Her stomach clenched with anxiety. *Had she caused this? They'd been so happy.*

"How much time?" Richard asked. "An hour? Two? A night, a week, more? Should I find another apartment? What are we talking about?"

Brady turned and looked over her shoulder at her father, who held his hands out as he spoke.

"I don't know, Richard. I can't think. At least a night. I'll call when I'm ready," Michael said.

"Where?" Richard asked. "Hotel rooms are expensive."

"Call Tom and Vince. God knows they have room to spare," Michael said.

Richard grimaced.

"And what about court?" Brady asked.

Michael looked at Richard and shook his head. "I don't know anymore."

Richard straightened his glasses. "Well, I'm going ahead with the custody effort," he said, starting toward the stairs. "And I will call Tom. I am that desperate."

"Should I pack?" Brady asked from behind him on the stairs.

"Yes," Richard said, nodding his head.

Brady stood in her room and looked around. Michael's "I own everything" speech played through her mind. Were any of the clothes hers? She looked at the bedding, matching towels, and bathrobe. Finally she packed all of the clothes, thinking, *What is Michael going to do with a bunch of dresses, anyway?*

* * *

Richard saw Brady struggling with her suitcase down the red brick steps and lurched forward to unburden her.

"Where are we going?" she asked, releasing the suitcase with obvious relief and heading toward Michael's Acura.

Without a word, Richard circled around her and walked to his bright yellow 1986 Vega. He couldn't remember the last time he'd driven it. Praying that it would run, he brushed dirt and leaves from the windshield. Finally he climbed inside and used the wipers to finish the job.

"Dad, where are we going?" Brady asked again.

Richard ran his hand over his face. "Tom and Vince's. You don't know them. They have a huge house and a dog. You'll like it."

Brady peered unsmiling through the pine needles and dead leaves. "Don't you have to get a divorce and counseling or something?"

"We were never married," Richard said.

"Aren't we ever coming back?"

"I don't know."

"Don't you feel sad?"

"Yes."

"I like my room," Brady said.

"We'll handle it," Richard said.

"What does that mean?"

"Oh, Brady, you'll be okay. Okay?" Richard said, his eyes pleading for her to be quiet. He ground the transmission into reverse.

Brady closed her eyes. "I like my room," she repeated.

EXILE

Richard peered through the grimy bug-smeared windshield of his Vega as he joined the endless line of cars speeding nowhere. Whatever the destination, Richard was racing to get in line.

"Shit! Goddamnit! That was where we were supposed to get off." Richard tried to force his way into the lane, but it was too late. The driver of the car he was trying to crowd in front of laid on his horn and made an obscene gesture. "Oh, right back at you, asshole!" Richard gave him the finger, too.

"Dad!" Brady said.

"Sorry," Richard said, blushing and raking his jaws against one another. "Just get over it. Now, how do we get back on the freeway?"

"Why did you get off if you wanted to keep going?" Brady asked.

"I got off so that I could turn around and go back to where I should have gotten off in the first place," Richard said through clenched teeth. He fought the impulse to tell Brady to be quiet.

"Are we lost?" Brady asked.

"No, we are not lost. I just need to find the freeway," Richard answered.

"It's up there." Brady pointed to the overpass above their heads.

"No kidding, let's just take flight and airlift ourselves, shall we?" *Why don't you be quiet?* he thought, but his tone seemed to have silenced her.

He negotiated the unfamiliar streets with difficulty, noting the idle people on the sidewalk and the proliferation of gang graffiti. Richard observed a particularly intimidating group of large men staring through the windshield at him. He glanced at Brady, but she was staring through the dirty glass at dilapidated buildings with boarded-up windows. People were already settling their bedding in the doorways to sleep. Some were just sitting on the sidewalk with all of their belongings next to them in shopping carts. Brady's jaw appeared to loosen as she watched.

Richard wasn't shocked. He remembered it; only this time he was facing homelessness with a child. He thought grimly of all the logistics he was now going to have to master. How was he going to get her to school? How would he pay for gas? How long would Tom and Vince allow them to stay? How long could he stand them? Most importantly, how long was Michael going to keep them exiled—or was it really over between them? He squeezed the steering wheel to suppress his panic. He fairly sang when he saw the freeway on-ramp and steered erratically into a left-turn lane to make a U-turn and get away from this seedy encampment.

"Dad, watch out!" Brady said, and she ducked her head reflexively.

Richard swerved out of the path of a glistening Black SUV. "I thought the light was green." He stared at the light in his review mirror. They could hear the driver honking all the way down the block. Richard shrugged defensively but didn't apologize. He sped up on the freeway, anxious to put the scene behind him.

"This looks familiar," he stated as he read the freeway signs. "I don't want to miss it again. There it is." The freeway was wide and fast moving. The desolation was quickly replaced by rolling hills with ranch-style homes that seemed to grow larger as they progressed. Richard breathed deeply for the first time this morning as they pulled off of the freeway and into Tom and Vince's neighborhood, Palos Verdes Estates.

Both Tom and Vince were in the front yard with the pug as Richard and Brady pulled in front of the imposing estate.

"Even the dog looks worried," Richard said.

Brady giggled behind her hand.

Tom cradled Pugsly in his arms and approached the car with the care one might give a trauma patient. Tilting his head to one side, he asked, "How *are* we?"

In contrast with the tension of the morning, the image was so comical to Richard that he burst into uncontrolled laughter, which even he could sense was very close to crying.

UNLIKELY ALLIES

⸺

"Welcome to our home." Tom spread his arms out and bowed slightly from the waist, allowing the two travelers to admire the manicured lawns punctuated by flowering birds of paradise. Brady and Richard followed their two hosts through the imposing hand-carved double doors and entered the reception area of the house.

"Wow, this is a huge room." Brady craned her neck to take in the exposed beams of the cathedral ceilings that rose two stories above their heads. She looked from side to side at the mahogany shelves that lined the walls with leather-bound books. The plush antique Persian rugs in their various shades of red adorned the highly polished hardwood floors under the heavy brocade couches that reminded her of pictures of rooms in castles in France that she had seen in Social Studies. The room was dotted by small mahogany tables with carved legs that sloped gracefully to the floor and appeared to end with metal dog's feet. They looked creepy to Brady, and raising her eyebrows, she looked at Richard, who shrugged.

"Don't you like them?" Tom asked, frowning. "We just love the way they look, like they could dance if the moment called for it. They are over three hundred years old and date back to the time of Louis the Fifteenth," he said and then muttered to himself, "You can't find that kind of detail work anymore. The labor would cost too much. There is so much you can do with pressed labor." He patted one of the tables and, glancing up as an afterthought, smiled at Brady. *Why does he seem proud of his little tables? Weird.* Brady forced herself to smile back.

Skirting the table, she walked to the stained glass window of gold, blue, deep green, and red that ran from ceiling to floor. The sun was flowing through the window, sending flecks of color twinkling around the room. She traced the metal in which the dazzling glass was inlaid. The pieces of glass, smooth and warm, soothed her fingertip.

"Everyone loves our stained glass," Tom said. "We had it commissioned by an artist in Beverly Hills."

"The glass was flown in from Italy," Vince said from her right.

Brady nodded. "It's warm, and the colors look like crayons."

"That is exactly our intent," Tom said, punctuating his speech with his hands. "It's dazzling when it catches the sun and warms the whole room even in winter. A very nice touch, I think, visually and tactilely, yes?"

Brady didn't understand all of his words but nodded anyway.

"Wait until you see your room. I think you will be very happy with it for whatever length of time you're in it," Tom said, motioning for her to follow as he turned and rushed down the hall with Pugsly neatly tucked under his arm like a football.

Brady followed. How long would they be here?

They waked down seemingly endless hallways, their steps muffled by plush rugs. At one juncture in the hall, Brady was startled by a suit of armor standing at attention.

"Is this real?"

"Oh, don't touch it!" Vince pulled her hand away from it. His palm was as soft and smooth as a baby's.

She looked over her shoulder at Richard, who seemed not

to have noticed. She wrapped her arms around her chest and held onto her elbows as they kept walking. She'd caused enough trouble already.

"Sorry," Vince said, "it's as old as the tables, and it falls apart easily."

From farther up the hall, Tom's voice beckoned. "We put you across the hall from one another. This is your room, Richard, and this, Little Miss, is your room." He flourished his hand through the doorway of the room, and Brady turned the corner and beheld what appeared to be a lot of oversized caterpillars in a bedroom. Looking more closely, she realized they were all just a huge amount of very large, very pink ruffles. There were ruffles on the edges of curtains, every pillow, and every comforter and sheet; even the bedside table was topped with a cloth that swept the floor with three layers of ruffles. The bed was covered by small pink ruffled cushions. A canopy topped the bed, and its drapes were trimmed with ruffles. The walls were painted a harsh Barbie pink.

Tom, who had stepped just inside of the room, seemed to be holding his breath and watching her.

Brady's scalp itched, and she didn't know what to say. "It's perfect!" she said, watching his face.

Tom smiled and tilted his head back. "We knew you'd love it. Any girl would." He bent down and put Pugsly on the floor. He took a step forward.

She'd been thinking there was something wrong with the dog's legs, so she was relieved that he could actually walk. After that one step, however, it sat down, looked up at Tom, and whined. So he *could* walk—he just didn't want to.

Hoisting the dog to his shoulder, Tom said, "You are the room's first guest. We wanted to have at least one accommodation in which a woman could be comfortable. I'm glad you like it." He looked around the room nodding at his handiwork.

"You," Vince pointed a finger into Richard's chest and said in mock deep voice, "are in the hunting room."

"Hunting room?" Brady repeated, wondering if it would be decorated with deer heads. She heard Richard exhale as he walked

behind her into the room across the hall. It turned out to be decorated with ducks on forest green walls with dark brown wainscot-
ing. It smelled woodsy, and when Brady asked why, Tom pointed
to a dark brown clay pot filled with cedar potpourri on a plain
wooden table near the door. The bed was king-sized with cannon-
ball posts of polished cherry and was covered by a thick comforter
festooned with flying ducks.

"You'll probably have to repress the desire to grab a gun and
shoot yourself a bear or a moose, but you should sleep nicely,"
Vince said, raising his eyebrows and staring at Richard. Brady left
the room and began unpacking books in her room.

* * *

Vince, noticing that Brady had left the room, smoothed the bed
affectionately and winked at Richard, conspiratorially. "It worked
for us," he said. When Richard looked confused, Tom chimed in,
lightly patting his partner on the back. "This is where we consum-
mated our relationship."

"Thanks for sharing," Richard said, wrinkling his nose and
clearing his throat.

"Your bathroom is adjoining," Vince said, pushing the bathroom door open. "All of the rooms have their own bathrooms."

Tom and Vince were famous for huge parties with extrava-
gant food and exotic entertainment. They had a constant stream
of guests, and Richard wondered if he was going to have to make
conversation with strangers. "Are there other guests, right now?"
he asked.

"No," Tom answered. "We didn't think you'd be up for it." He
gestured in the direction of Brady, who was in her room pulling
books out of her backpack.

Vince inclined his head toward Richard and said kindly, "You
can stay as long as you like, really. Do you want to talk or anything,
or do you just want space?"

"Space is good right now," Richard said, nodding. "I'll talk
later," he assured them. "Right now I'm exhausted. I think I'll just

read. Maybe go for a walk with Brady later." Richard ended with an uplift tone as though trying to convince himself that he would do these things.

Vince nodded.

"Thank you, really, for everything," Richard said as he gestured in a circular motion.

"We're happy to do it, and tomorrow we can have a nice dinner together. Food and time are always the best healers," Tom said.

The words were simple but so soothing that tears welled in Richard's eyes. He coughed and said, "Well, good night." And with that, he shut the door and realized he had no book. He walked along reusing the titles and finally selected a Shakespeare anthology. His favorite was *King Lear.*He had his own Cordelia and he was upsetting nature by fighting to have her in his life. Was he sabotaging himself? Michael had been the reason to stay sober and now he was without him. The reality of his situation overwhelmed him. Richard never did go for a walk with Brady. He didn't even check on her. He read until his chin hit his chest and then turned out the light, and fell asleep on top of the bed, outside of the covers.

Richard awoke shivering and disoriented. Sitting up, he felt the cold night air pressing his face. He pictured his own bed, where he could snuggle up against Michael, and felt despair tighten his throat. He looked down at the flying ducks and wished he had not been told this was the birthplace of Tom and Vince as he knew them. A wave of jealousy disguised as anger coursed through him, and he asked himself, what right did they have to be so damned content with each other? He and Michael were so good together. Was it a mistake to have involved Brady? Or were they doomed from the start?

He sighed heavily, and it sounded like the groan of an old man. He shivered but felt too tired to close the window. He was weary of the struggle required by being alive and sober. It occurred to him that Tom and Vince would have booze. Liquor flowed at their many parties, and they drank daily, so it would be like a grocery item to them. He could picture a perfectly legitimate cabinet where gin, vodka, and whiskey were stored for the innocent drink now and then.

He tried to remember where the alcohol had been stored. There must be something in that vast kitchen. He envisioned himself going down the hall and going into the kitchen, but from there he wouldn't know where to go. People followed patterns though. His parents always stored the liquor in a cabinet over the refrigerator.

He swung his legs over the side of the bed, noting that his feet hit the floor like weights. His heart accelerated, his hands were clammy, and he struggled to swallow. He had lost Michael already. If anyone had an excuse to drink, Richard certainly did. It satisfied him to know that he could blame his relapse on Michael. Richard wanted to get over the indecision so that he could just drink and be numb. He lurched toward the door on stiff legs and opened it. Everyone expected him to drink. He might as well just get it over with. That would sure show Michael.

Richard stared down the dark hall and listened to the night. At first there was nothing, not even the movement of air, and he took a step into the hall. But gradually he became aware of Brady snoring. He stepped back as though he had been pushed. If he drank, he would lose Brady. He would have provided her with just one more bitter disappointment and proven his father-in-law right. He would certainly lose Michael and then himself. An unwanted slide show of his past began in his mind: aching bones from sleeping on the ground under freeway overpasses; the stench of piss; being hungry, confused, and ashamed. He remembered waking up with his mouth dry and his head throbbing. Even in his most deluded moments he had known he was poisoning his heart, kidneys, liver, and brain.

Richard backed into the room and against the bed. Maybe he and Michael would never get back together, but if he didn't drink, he would have Brady to raise, and he would live. If he could just make it through this dark night.

He closed the window against the cold. The room was lit by the full moon. He stood at the window despite the cold and spoke into the void. "Please, God, just help me get through to morning. Shit, just help get me through the next minute."

DISHEVELED AND DISTRESSED

␣␣␣␣␣␣␣

It was Friday, day seven of the exile of Richard and Brady, and the weather during the day was unseasonably hot for May. During this short period, the two had had to contend with many obstacles. The distance from Palos Verdes to Manhattan Beach was not long, but it collided with many commutes, so Brady had been late to school every day since they moved. Tom and Vince talked to Pugsly in falsetto voices, which got on Brady's nerves, but she had begun to like Pugsly. Originally she found his phlegmatic breathing gross, but she decided it was kind of cute.

What still hadn't settled was her dad, and Brady was frightened at how he appeared to unravel a little bit more every day. His moments of being distracted broadened and were no longer isolated to when he was writing. He appeared to stop writing altogether, only serving time in front of his laptop and staring into space. Brady could hear her father muttering at night and sometimes crying.

Richard, who hadn't been a brilliant conversationalist, was now distant in any conversation, and this added loneliness to

Brady's fears. Being new at school, uncertain of Tom and Vince, and increasingly estranged from her father, Brady had no-one to talk to. She would watch Richard from the side as they drove to school and hear him mutter phrases that didn't fit in the conversation. Brady pretended not to notice and tried to engage him, talking about what he was writing or what she was doing in class, but it never lasted more than two sentences. Increasingly, his eyes grew red, his hair became disheveled, and his clothing was a weird mix of whatever he had slept in or found on the floor.

Tom and Vince noticed as well and treated it as a joke at first. What weird outfit was he going to come out in this time? Over time, they stopped kidding him, however, and began exchanging worried glances.

Brady continued her life in the way children do in crisis; she limited herself to her homework, reading, and Pugsly. Pugsly became her best friend, always looking like he was worried about her. Pugsly was actually waiting for Brady's next gesture, preferably accompanied by treats. She often took him for walks, which Tom and Vince were happy to allow, and in return for that, Pugsly began to follow her from room to room like she was a rock star. His company helped Brady get her homework done on the pool deck, since Brady found the "Barbie" room too distracting. If the dog could have talked, he might have recommended that she talk to a teacher, a counselor, someone who could help.

Friday was a particularly sucky day in which she found she was not ready for school because she had done all of the wrong math homework and forgotten her lunch. At lunch, Brady stood on the edge of a four square game, wishing the noon aid would notice that she wanted to play and that the girls were leaving her out, but the woman looked the other way. Ordinarily, her new best friend, Fiona, would have given her food from her own lunch, but Fiona was absent. So Brady went through the day hungry and lonely.

* * *

It was at the end of this day that Richard's car broke down on the way to pick Brady up after school. After guiding the powerless Vega to the side of the freeway, Richard reached for his cell phone to call Brady's school only to find that his phone was dead. He even tried starting it in an infantile desire to resuscitate it. The screen remained black and lifeless. Now what? Bone-penetrating fatigue that came from self-condemnation invaded his thinking. Why didn't he have a real job so he could afford a reliable car? Bottom line, what was he going to do to get Brady picked up on time?

He forced himself to regroup and attend to the problem of getting the car fixed. Way down the freeway, he saw the yellow call box. It was a little after two and already the traffic was picking up for rush hour. He dreaded walking down the freeway alongside hundreds of huge vehicles driven by hungry, tired, and frustrated commuters. But that was exactly what he had to do if he was ever going to get off this godforsaken freeway and to his daughter.

He began to walk. As the cars rushed by, the vacuum created by their momentum threatened to suck him into traffic, so he held the rail to steady his body. He was almost to the phone when a police car whooshed in front of him. He should have felt relieved, but instead his anxiety peaked. The memory of his last interaction with a cop was unforgettably bad. Richard eased between the police car and the rail to talk through the window.

"Car trouble?" the officer asked from inside his car.

No, just out for a stroll on the freeway during commute hours in the ninety-degree heat, Richard thought but said instead, "Yes, that's my car back there. I'm not sure what went wrong." His car looked like a yellow speck a million miles away.

"I can get a tow truck for you. Are you a member of an emergency roadside service provider?" the officer asked.

"No," Richard answered.

The officer frowned as though this were a particularly egregious oversight on Richard's part.

"Okay, I'll call it to the first truck who can respond." The officer looked critically at Richard's unkempt, dirty hair and mismatched clothes and asked, "You're going to be able to pay for this, right?"

Richard nodded yes.

The officer called for the truck.

Richard held out his cell phone and said, "My phone is out of juice, just when I need it the most, naturally. Is there some way you can get word to my daughter that I'm going to be late? She's at school."

The officer did as he requested and reported that the woman in the office said she would get word to Brady. She said she could see her sitting on the curb out front. Richard felt anxiety growing in the pit of his stomach. He knew he should call Michael and ask him to pick her up, but they had agreed that Michael would call when he was ready, and since he hadn't, he must not have been. Should he call Tom and Vince? He had already imposed on them too much. So in the end, he walked back to his car to wait for the tow truck.

The tow truck arrived with radio blasting, and the over-caffeinated driver leapt out and handed him a clipboard with the charge of $250 already totaled.

"What is this? You don't even know where you're taking me," Richard sputtered.

The driver smiled, exposing nicotine-stained teeth, and replied, "That's what the law says I can legally charge, no more, no less. You don't like it? Call for another truck." He followed this with a laugh that was hard to distinguish from a cough.

Richard thought about Brady waiting at school, sent the driver a look of irritation, and signed the form.

"I need a credit card and a driver's license," the driver said.

Richard pulled out his wallet and handed him both, secretly wishing the man a swift but painful death.

"Thanks, man. I'll be right back!" the driver said, climbing back into the truck.

Michael could have cancelled Richard's credit cards, and he could be stuck here with no way to pay the highway robber.

The rotund but diminutive driver bounced back gleefully to him and proffered the clipboard for a second signature. Richard scratched his name so deeply into the form that it tore, and he shoved the clipboard back at the loathsome man. He wondered if he threw the clipboard into the traffic, would it dampen the driver's joy? Or would he follow it to his death, as a dog might do for a bone?

"Climb aboard, man." The driver appeared to see Richard as his new best friend, which was understandable because he had just made him $250 richer. Richard opened the truck door, hoisted himself into the passenger seat, and slammed the door shut. The driver whistled as he pulled into traffic.

"Do you have a mechanic you want me to take you to?" the driver asked while easing into traffic. Richard looked over his shoulder at his car dangling precariously in its harness and wondered if chains and belts ever broke, sending crippled cars into the windshields of innocent drivers.

"Hey, man, did you hear me?" The driver nudged Richard in the shoulder with his beefy hand. Richard, who hated being touched by strangers, recoiled from the man's dirty fist and forced his mind into the conversation.

"I'm sorry, I didn't hear you." Richard wasn't sorry. He had heard him. He just didn't want to be in a conversation with this grinning gargoyle.

"Where do you want it taken?" The man jabbed a thorny thumbnail at the beleaguered Vega wobbling behind them.

"To a mechanic who can fix it," Richard said.

"I know a guy who can do just that. He's a good mechanic and won't charge too much. Some of these guys can really ream you, you know?"

Kind of like you? Richard thought, but he said, "I need to get on the road to pick up my daughter. Will you be able to get me to Manhattan Beach?"

The driver squinted one eye as though thinking hard before he said, "No, sir, that would present a problem, I'm afraid. See, that is not what I do. I pick up the cars and get them to mechanics. From there, people get their own transport. I am a tow truck driver, not a taxi driver. Know what I mean?" He smiled at Richard, then changed tack. "Of course, if you were to pay me, the way you will have to pay a taxi driver, I could drive you to—where was it again?"

"Manhattan Beach," Richard said. The driver was pretending not to know where Richard was going to impress upon Richard what a huge favor he was asking. Huge favors deserve huge rewards. They had merged onto Highway 10, and even with Richard's unpredictable sense of direction, he could tell they were headed away from where he wanted to go and at a great speed.

"Where are we going?" Richard asked, looking at the signs around him. The signs had that odd effect of being familiar since they could be found on every intersection in the west coast but also being slightly disorienting because they were not his neighborhood signs. At one time there might have been a memorable hamburger joint or coffee shop, but now there was only one long march of Starbucks, McDonalds, and Noah's Bagels.

"This, sir, is beautiful downtown Lawndale." He drew out the two syllables of the town's name in a mocking manner. "Home of motels, hotels, mediocre restaurants, and not much else, except, of course, my friend Dale, the mechanic extraordinaire. He is the doctor of distributors, ambassador to alternators, and a friend to all fan belts. There are none better than my friend Dale."

With the last two syllables, he pulled into a garage, and Richard squinted at the blue-and-white sign circling above their heads. It read, "Dale the Mechanic."

Dale, Richard presumed, ambled toward them, extending his hand for Richard to shake. Richard forced himself not to pull back as he touched calluses and bumps left by years of doing battle with corroded bolts and screws.

"Car trouble?" Dale nodded at Richard, who thought, *Do people come to this mechanic with anything other than car trouble?*

"How soon can this be fixed?" Richard was still clinging to the hope that this could all be fixed without him calling for help from anyone.

"Well, let's take a look-see. It's bound to be the alternator, based on what you have described," Dale said as he bent into the greasy engine. "And if it is, you may be in luck because I have an alternator—not new, mind you, but good, sturdy, and working. Used is good in your case. You don't want to pay for new in a car this old."

Richard nodded, and the work began. Despite frequent reassurances that "We are moving as fast as we can," it was now almost three thirty and the car was nowhere near repaired. Richard knew that Brady had been on the curb for an hour, and there was no way of knowing how much longer it was going to be.

MIND MATTERS

Brady, hungry and furious with her father, slumped on the curb in front of her school. She looked up as a group of kids walked by laughing and watched them climb into a gold-lettered Lexus minivan that had been there when Brady walked up. This never happened with her grandparents. She ducked her head and covered her ears until she sensed movement behind her. Looking up, Brady recognized Jamie, her research partner for the state of New Hampshire. "Bye," she started to say to but Jamie's eyes slid past hers. Brady lowered her head to her knees and wrapped her arms around her legs.

"Excuse me, dear," someone touched her arm.

"Yes," she squinted up to see Mrs. Bretzin standing over her.

"Your dad just called. His car broke down, and he's going to be late, His phone was out of power or he would have called you. the woman said, pushing her long red hair out of her face where it had been blown by the wind.

"Wouldn't have mattered. I left my phone at home this morning." Brady said and then asked, "How late?" How much later than usual?

"He said he'd be here as soon as he could. I'm sure it won't be long." She shrugged, adding, "You're welcome to come in and wait in the office, if you'd like." Her expression was way less welcoming than her words.

"No, I'm good here. I'm sure he'll be here soon." Brady forced a smile, and Mrs. Bretzin spun her double-tied Nikes around and marched back to the office.

Brady watched as trash swirled in the wind. A Taco Bell wrapper blew across the parking lot and against her chest. She wrinkled her nose and picked it off, letting it fly a few feet in the air. The wind stung her eyes, making them water. Although it had been hot during the day, as the sun set, the air became cold. She crossed her arms over her chest and turned away.

She moved to a bench that was blocked from the wind by the custodian's car. She heard footsteps and watched Mrs. Bretzen leaving. Brady stood and raised her hand, about to call out that she was still here and needed a phone, but then she stopped herself. She didn't want to tell the woman her father still hadn't shown up. Staring at the taillights of the large silent hybrid as it vanished, she slumped back down on the bench.

And then she smiled. "I am outta here," she said out loud, heaving her backpack on and beginning the familiar walk to Michael's house.

When she reached the last hill that led to the house, she began to run. Hot despite the cold wind, she gasped for breath as she topped the steps and punched the doorbell. No answer. "Oh, come on," she groaned, and rang it again. Still no answer.

She plunked down on the porch bench, backpack still on and taking up most of the seat. Her shoulders caved, and her hands lay like dead fish in her lap. She stamped her feet and ground her teeth. She caught sight of the sun setting just as a timer turned on the porch light. She eased her backpack off and took out the book *Divergent*. She'd been reading it with Dad since she'd gotten it from the library.

She was immediately sucked into the book and loved the feeling of escaping. She leaned forward in the dim light to concentrate.

Her eyes blurred as time past and her head dipped until she gave up and settled in the corner of bench with her backpack as a pillow.

"Brady, what are you doing here, sweetie? Is Richard here?"

She jerked to consciousness and stared at Michael as if he were from outer space. She rubbed her eyes as they and her mind awakened.

"Sorry," he said, touching her shoulder.

Brady blinked hard and forced herself to speak. "His car broke down, and I got tired of waiting," she said.

Brady lowered her head but lifted her eyes to Michael's.

He smiled and unlocked the door. "I'm glad you came. Come on in. Are you hungry?"

"Starving." She followed him through the door. "I didn't have lunch."

She knew there was nothing that bugged Michael more than not eating. Richard had explained that for Michael, food *is* love. Michael stared at her, and she knew he was wondering how Richard could have let this happen. She was sorry she had said it but not entirely.

He furrowed his brow as he asked, "Why not?"

Brady raised her shoulders in a shrug but remembered that this gesture irritated him, so she froze her shoulders in place. She lowered them slowly. "Just forgot," she said.

"Well, come on in and let's eat. I'm not sure what I have, but I know I'll find something."

Brady climbed onto the creaky wicker stool at the breakfast bar, smiling as she watched Michael study the fridge contents. A tickle of warmth eased her tummy. He was going to take care of her. She swung her dangling feet back and forth before resting them on the wrought iron base of the stool.

Michael was well into slicing cheddar cheese and buttering bread and then crisping them in the skillet. He added sliced Ambrosia apples and slid the meal toward her on a large blue ceramic plate.

She ate with enthusiasm and could tell it pleased him. He didn't have the kind of milk that she liked, so she drank apple juice, even better.

"I have those chocolate cookies you like," Michael said.

Brady could taste the cookies without having seen them and looked toward the pantry.

Michael brought the cookie jar to the table and put it in front of her.

"Wow, there are a lot in here," she said. Standing up on the bar of the stool, she lowered her face to the jar and took a deep sniff. The chocolate smell was so strong, she could taste it. She took out the two she knew she was allowed.

"You kept baking them even though I wasn't here?" she said, taking a bite and staring at the mound of cookies through the Lucite walls of the jar.

Michael blushed and shifted in his seat. "I never knew when you were going to come home." He cleared his throat and stared at his salad.

Michael's baking cookies for her even though she wasn't there seemed sad. She swallowed hard. He wanted them back. Maybe he wanted her back.

"Dad was waiting for you to call."

Michael sighed. "Yeah, I was working on it. So, how are things with Tom and Vince?"

She stared at the jar again and then at him.

"Go ahead," Michael said, and he pushed the open container closer. "They'll go bad."

"Tom and Vince are—" she paused slightly and chose something safe to say—"okay."

"And how is the dog?"

"Pugsly is great. He's cute once you get past the weird noises." She imitated Pugsly by breathing through her nose and mouth simultaneously, causing a long Darth Vader–like hiss.

Michael laughed, which made her laugh.

As he laughed, he seemed kinder.

"Are there, like, different levels of gayness? Tom and Vince are . . . extremely gay," she asked, studying Michael's face for disapproval. "But you and Dad—people would hardly know you are gay."

Michael said, "Well, no."

"You don't talk or walk like Tom," Brady said, staring, shoulders hunched.

"Fair enough. But that isn't what you asked," Michael said. "Do straight boys or girls take lessons in how to walk like straight boy and girls?"

Brady took a fifth cookie and shook her head.

"Neither do gay boys and girls. They walk and talk the way they feel is natural, and it has nothing to do with how gay they are," Michael said. "If the world were reversed and everyone was gay, would you want to have to learn to walk differently than you do by nature?"

Brady shook her head again, this time vigorously.

"Well, neither do Tom and Vince or any other gay men. Some gay men are naturally effeminate; some aren't. Tom and Vince like who they are and celebrate it without apology. They like all that . . ." Michael paused and seemed to be searching for the right word.

"Faggy stuff?" She sat back in her chair and covered her mouth, sending cookie crumbs flying.

"Yeah, faggy stuff." Michael nodded. "Because that's what they are—faggots, if you like, or gay men, or queers, or whatever. They want to be proud of who they are. By being openly gay, they are stopping anyone from making it bad. Does that make sense?"

"Yeah," she said, reaching for another cookie "Sometimes Tom and Vince are more girlie than any girl I know. It's like their idea of what a girl is like is all . . . models or something. You should see the room they have me in. It looks like Barbie exploded in it. How could they think that's what any girl would want?" Brady paused, drew a breath, and blurted out, "They drink, you know, alcohol, every night. Oh, Dad doesn't drink, but he wants to, I can tell. He stares at their glasses and at the bottle. Tom even offered him some once."

Michael hit the counter and rolled his eyes. "Tom!"

"Dad won't drink because I'm watching, and he won't do it in front of me. But it's still scary. He looks bad. He misses you. He doesn't say it, but I know it. He cries at night." She stopped talking and held her fingers over her mouth.

"Does your dad know you're here?" Michael asked.

"No, the office was closed when I decided to come here, so I couldn't call him."

Michael picked up his cell phone and speed-dialed Richard. He sighed in frustration when it went to voice mail immediately. "Call me. I've got your daughter," he said in a menacing voice as though asking for ransom. He smiled at Brady. "She's safe and sound and eating her body weight in cookies."

Brady laughed and picked up a seventh cookie. Michael smiled.

"I wish he would call. We could go pick him up," Michael said, and as if on cue, the phone rang.

HAIR SHIRT TIME

"Brady is here. She's fine. We've had dinner," Michael said into the phone.

Brady pulled out her math book, held it up, and mouthed *homework* to him.

"We are now going to do homework—on a Friday?" Michael looked like he couldn't believe it.

Brady whispered, "It'll make him feel better."

"Impressive," Michael said, but his tone was flat.

Brady stared at Michael as he listened and tried to figure out what her father was saying.

"Right, don't do her math for her," Michael said, raising his eyebrows and staring at her.

Brady rolled her eyes.

"When are you going to be home?" Michael continued. "Do you need me to come and get you?"

Brady nodded eagerly. She needed her father home—with Michael.

"It's okay, really. She was asleep on the porch bench when I came home. It's been good, I think," Michael said, lowering his voice, turning away from her.

Brady was feeling very full, so she busied herself with replacing the lid on the cookies and returning them to the shelf.

"Would you like to ask her yourself?" Michael handed the phone to Brady.

Brady took it while looking at the math book. "Hi, Daddy."

"Are you okay?" Richard asked. "I'm really sorry."

"I'm okay, Dad," Brady said, drawing out the "kay" in exasperation. She'd been left at school and now she was comforting him. It's not like it was not going to happen again. "Really, I'm fine, Dad."

"They're done. Gotta go. I'll be there as soon as possible," Richard said.

"Bye," Brady said, and she hung up the phone.

Michael turned and rubbed his hands together. "So, what do we get to do for math?"

Brady sighed. "It shouldn't be too bad. I did a lot of it already. That's the good thing about Dad being late—I get most of my work done at school. I just have this stuff left, which I don't get." She tapped her finger on a section entitled "Mixed Fractions."

Michael turned the book toward him and read the directions. "Maybe my MBA will get me through fifth-grade math. He squinted and leaned closer to the book. "What a complicated approach. You don't need to do all that. Just do this." He pulled out his financial calculator.

"We can't use calculators," Brady said, sitting back in her chair.

"Why not?" He pulled his calculator to his chest as if to protect it.

"Mrs. Patterson says we need to know how things work, and unless we can show our work, she can't tell what we understand."

"How about if you show your work on one problem, which will show that you understand the process, and then just do the rest on the calculator?" Michael said.

"Nope, we have to show it all." Brady frowned.

"Nobody does this kind of work without a calculator in real life. There's too much of a risk of making a mistake and it takes too long. Not to mention that it's unbelievably tedious!"

"You want to write Mrs. Patterson a note saying her homework is too hard?" she asked, smiling as she pushed a piece of binder paper toward him.

Brady couldn't believe her good luck. This would be a get-out-of-math-homework-for-life card.

Michael shook his head. "How many problems do you have to do?"

"All of these." She ran her finger across the page and turned it. "And these. I already did these. Do you want to check them?"

"Can I use a calculator for that?" Michael asked.

"Yes." She pushed the book and her paper to him.

Taking a deep breath, he began.

"Your dad is able to help with this?" He peered at her over his glasses.

Without looking up, Brady shook her hand slightly. "Mostly he just checks my work with the calculator like you're doing, and then he goes running." She laughed. "There's something about my math homework that really makes him need to go running. Hmm?" She puzzled with mock concentration.

Michael laughed with her, a deep, happy laugh. She stared at his open smile and the creases at his eyes and felt the opposite of lonely—whatever that was. Like she really truly belonged and fit in here.

She was aware only of the ticking of the clock as she mastered one math problem after another. She loved the satisfaction she felt when Michael checked her work and declared it correct. "Bam! Done." She announced.

He checked it and offered her a celebratory high five.

"Looks good." He glanced at the clock and his face changed. He looked worried. *Where was Dad?*

Brady sighed. She wanted a reward for having done her math homework on a Friday. "And now we read!" She hoisted *Divergent* out of her backpack.

Michael's face looked blank.

But she was so excited about sharing the book with him that she overlooked his reaction. *Divergent* was way above her grade level and had complicated ideas. She could read it, but reading it with Dad had made it much easier. Now she could be the expert and explain the book to Michael.

Michael settled on the couch.

Brady scrambled up to him, holding the big book in front her, and then plunked herself in his lap. She nestled deeper.

"Where is your dad?" Michael asked.

Brady was leafing through the book, finding where she left off before she fell asleep. "I don't know."

"Brady, I think you need to take a shower first."

"Oh? Do I smell bad? The kids say I smell bad." She kept her eyes on the open pages of the book. She just thought the kids were being mean. She didn't want to know that they were right.

"In America, people are preoccupied with cleanliness, which I suspect is due to the fact that we were settled by Puritans. Most Americans shower daily, which is probably a waste of water—but nonetheless, most Americans do."

She turned her face to look up at him and bumped his chin. "What?" she asked, brow furrowed, lips pursed.

Michael pushed her off his lap and away from him a good foot. "You need to take a shower," Michael said.

"But do I smell bad?" Brady asked, pulling a strand of hair to her nose. She raised her eyebrows and looked at Michael, who stared back at her with large, unfocused eyes. She could tell he didn't want to have this conversation either.

"You smell like you need a shower," he said very carefully.

Brady felt as if he had slapped her face. It was true. The kids were right. She could feel her face get hot. How could she have let this happen? She lowered her head and wanted to crawl out of the room. Would she ever be able to look at Michael again?

And then he asked, "Didn't you take a shower at Tom and Vince's last night or this morning?"

It had been way longer than that. "I can't figure the showers out. They have this one weird handle with no hot or cold markings, and I've tried to get the water to run but I can't. And now the kids say I stink!"

"Why didn't you ask your dad?"

Brady forgot herself and shrugged.

"I'm sorry. I don't speak *shrug*."

She took a deep breath. "I just didn't."

"Why don't you go upstairs and take a shower? I'm sure it will feel really good by now."

She nodded her head enthusiastically, causing her matted hair to flap back and forth.

Michael guided Brady by the elbow up the stairs, where he turned on the water for her even though she already knew how.

Did she imagine that he groaned in disgust as he walked away?

A half hour later, Brady emerged from the steamy bathroom to find that Michael had laid out her nightgown and slippers, which she had left behind. Red faced and fragrant, she struggled to pull a brush through her wet hair. She wasn't able to get the brush out. She groaned.

She stood on the landing looking down at Michael, who was settled on the couch with *The New York Times*. She didn't want to bother him. She sighed very deeply.

He looked up and smiled.

"I can't get it out," she said, turning her head so he could see the brush so stuck in her hair that she didn't have to hold onto it.

"I can, come on down," he said. He worked the brush free and had her sit on the footstool while he slowly edged the brush through the wet strands. His hands were gentle but strong, and she could feel the knots easing into strands. Finally, every last strand of her hair lay subdued in perfectly straight, sopping strands on her shoulders. She felt the tickle of comfort that comes from knowing someone loves you enough to take care of you.

"Where's Dad?" she asked.

"I don't know, and since his phone is out of power, I can't call him," he said. "He may still be waiting for the repair, or he may have gotten lost. He'll get here eventually." He squeezed her shoulders and then asked, "Would you like to read?"

She nodded and handed him the book. Something had changed. She felt awkward with him. She pushed back into the couch where she sat.

He eased deeper into the cushions and made a tiny gesture with his hand.

She took this as an invitation to move closer, and although she wasn't sure she still wanted to, she snuggled in and then nestled under his arm. She took a very deep and relaxed breath for the first time that day.

* * *

Four hours from when he had called, Richard opened the door and saw Michael and Brady nestled into one another, heads nearly touching. He had forgotten to call before he left, despite having said that he would. He had not thought of getting gas in the car because he was anxious to get home to them. He had started off in the wrong direction and then run out of gas. He had to find his way back to his car because in his panic he had not made a point to remember where it was. When he did find his car, and put the gas into it, he realized he was still lost.

During Richard's second attempt to get home, he noticed a marked change in his own behavior. He realized that there was a difference between *appearing to try* to get home and actually getting there. This time he asked for exact instructions, wrote them down, and read them back for confirmation. He felt that he had broken out of some kind of purgatory of good intentions that never accomplished anything but left him in a perpetual state of apology. No one ever cared that he was sorry. They cared that they were disappointed and inconvenienced. But here in the dark on some huge freeway in Los Angeles, Richard found it vitally important to pay attention so he could navigate home to Michael and Brady in his repaired Vega.

And now he stood listening to Michael read out loud to Brady. The scene was so serene that he didn't want to interrupt.

"Daddy, where were you?" Brady said, climbing over the couch and leaping onto him in a full-body hug. Brady's hair smelled of Michael's shampoo.

"What took you so long?" Brady demanded. "It would be

nice if you charged your phone so you could use it at times like this! Where were you?"

"It's complicated. I'm sorry I was late," he said, and then he paused. "I am very glad to be home and with you." Richard directed his words at Michael.

Sensing that they needed to talk without her, Brady took the book and, running upstairs, yelled good night over her shoulder.

APOLOGIES

M ichael looked Richard over. Had he too had trouble making Tom and Vince's shower work? Richard's pants, usually taken to the dry cleaner by Michael, were wrinkled from being stored in a pile on the floor. He had lost weight and was compensating by tightening his belt, but since his jeans were too big, they bunched around his waist and hung formlessly to his shoes. The flannel shirt that he wore to keep warm when he wrote appeared to have been buttoned by a blind man.

Richard shifted his weight and attempted to tuck in his shirttail but gave up halfway around his front. He dragged his hand through his dirty, overgrown hair and peered over his glasses at Michael, offering fleeting eye contact. But then he stared off to the side at nothing, making him look penitent.

"Have you been drinking?" Michael asked, eyes narrowing.

"What?" Richard seemed stung by the accusation. Michael motioned for Richard to follow him into the den. Shutting the door, Michael whispered, "Brady told me she hears everything we say. Have you been drinking?"

"No, I wanted to, but I didn't. I had to walk by a bar tonight twice, once to get gas and once to bring it back. But I did not go in. I did not drink alcohol. The only thing that kept me from going in was getting back to you and Brady, and I knew . . . I knew that if I took a drink it would all be over. I know I'm late, that I should have called, and I should have gotten gas before I took off. I know all of it. But I did get here, and I did not drink. I put some whopping repair bills on the card, but I have some money and I'll pay you back. I will, I swear, I will."

Michael held his hands up to stop the barrage of apologies. "It's okay, Richard. Really, I don't care about the money. But I swear to God, if you'd come in with even a hint of alcohol on your breath, I'd throw you right out. That, I can not afford."

"I didn't drink. You have to believe me. It doesn't mean anything if you don't believe me."

"I do believe you." Michael hugged Richard as though he were going to consume him.

Michael continued, "I heard Tom offered you a drink. Some friend." Michael shook his head in disbelief.

But Richard said, "I don't know, but it's sort of a badge of courage. I mean, I lived in a house with all kinds of booze, and I didn't drink. I've even come to like them. They're loyal to each other and were very kind to Brady and me. They cared about us, and I came to care about them. I should call them. They'll be wondering where we are by now. See, I'm being responsible. This is me being responsible." Richard brandished the phone and left a voice mail.

Michael made a second dinner for the night, and no one said a critical word to Brady when she crept down the stairs to join them for her additional dessert that evening.

In the middle of all of this happy sentiment, Brady, with her mouth full of cookies, said, "I want to get a dog."

Richard sat back from the table, bracing for Michael's veto and the emotional fallout that would follow.

Michael leaned back in his stool, stroked his chin, and said, "I like dachshunds."

ANTICIPATION

⁂

In the week since she and Dad had been back, rules had been clearly set: If you take something out, put it back when finished. Eat when and what you are served at mealtimes. Snacks must be healthy. Teeth must be brushed and flossed twice a day, and hands must be washed before meals. She needed to shower and wash her hair daily. Screechy cartoons were never ever to be heard by Michael. And she was expected to knock before opening any closed door—and never before nine o'clock on a Saturday morning, like today.

What they didn't know were the unspoken rules she had figured out, like: When everyone was in a good mood, a lot of the rules about food stopped. She could fake brushing her teeth by putting a little bit of toothpaste in her mouth, and this was important on school days because it was faster. The door-knocking also applied to coming downstairs, which she learned to do by making noises like coughing, stomping her feet, or talking before leaving her room. These noises sent the two men shooting away from each other—even if they were only reading the paper. The precautions

seemed to make everybody feel safer, especially her. She sometimes wondered if kids of straight parents had to go through this.

Also, if she really wanted an answer to a question, she should
never ask when both Dad and Michael were in the same room.
She found that if she did, they would start arguing with each other
using words she couldn't understand.

One school night Brady was finishing up math homework at
the kitchen counter while Dad and Michael cleaned up after dinner.
They had *NewsHour* on, which had two men debating about a trade
agreement between America and Asia.

"So a trade agreement with no workers' rights and no pro-
tection for the environment? What kind of an agreement is that?"
Dad snorted.

"Richard." Michael sounded like Brady's teacher when she
was explaining a math problem for the third time. "You have to
understand how large a market Asia represents."

Dad interrupted. "It's not Asia. It's China they're talking about—
the ones who rolled over their own people in Tiananmen Square."

"Okay, yes, and this is a chance for the United States to write an
agreement that isn't written by China and represents our core values."

"What core values allow people to live in a place where the air
can't be breathed because it's so polluted? Our core values seem to
be sold to the highest bidder. Let me think, who does that?" Richard tipped his head back and stroked his chin. "Oh yeah, whores!"
he snapped the dish towel at Michael's butt.

Brady stood up on the iron bars of her stool to watch.

"That's us, Beijing's *hoes*." Dad cornered Michael and pressed
him against the counter, bending him back, his face nearly touching Michael's.

"Richard." Michael said, directing his eyes over Richard's
shoulder.

Brady almost got whiplash from lowering her head and body
so fast.

Dad looked toward but not at her. "Right," he raised his
hands and nodded. "Right." He turned back to the counter and
dried dishes as though trying to get a genie to emerge from them.

Brady pretended to do her math, but she was too excited by what she had seen and very sorry she had wrecked it.

So now at eight thirty on a Saturday, she had to wait for them to get up so she could get a dog. Brady twitched with excitement at the breakfast table, forcing cereal down her throat even though she wasn't hungry. Michael had promised they'd go see the dachshund breeder today, and she wanted to be able to say she had eaten.

She stared at the silent television. She took her cereal spoon and allowed a drop of milk to slide down the wall of her now-empty orange juice glass and counted the seconds it took to reach the bottom. She was on the third drop when she heard Richard on the stairs. She stood up. "I've eaten. And I have the directions to the breeder." She held up the paper she had printed out last night. "Where's Michael?"

Dad walked past her without pausing and headed for the coffee pot. "He's coming. Nothing happens without coffee," he said over his shoulder.

"I know. I already pushed the button to make the coffee," Brady said.

Dad's eyebrows rushed together, but after he took a sip, he said, "Don't tell Michael you started it so early. He'll say it's too cold."

Brady slumped in her chair, arms hugging her body, and kicked the table leg. "I hate the smell of coffee."

Dad stared at her before leaning forward to kiss her forehead.

His face was rough. He still needed to shave.

She looked up to see Michael coming down the stairs still in pajamas. She groaned silently through clenched teeth as she watched her father walk to the front door to get the paper. Was he really going to read the paper? She knew better than to say anything more, or the whole morning would unravel. Michael sat down across from her, took a long drink of coffee, and stared at her.

"How are you going to tear your dad away from the paper? It's what he lives for," Michael asked.

Michael seemed energized by the coffee. "I will dress, but don't put milk on my oatmeal. It makes it soggy." He grimaced.

Brady, happy to have something to do, poured two bowls of oatmeal and placed glasses of soy milk and orange juice on the sides.

Richard lowered the paper, moved his glasses from his head to his eyes, and stared down at one of the cereal bowls, which she had placed in front of him. He started to reopen the paper.

"Eat, Dad," Brady growled, giving the table a big jarring kick that caused the glasses to jump.

"I just have to finish this story. They buried the second half somewhere—oh, here it is."

Michael returned and began eating with a purpose. As he scraped the last bite from the bowl, Brady grabbed it and took the spoon from his hand, heading to the sink.

"You are torturing your daughter, you know?" Michael said to the newspaper barricade. "Think you could pick up the pace a tad?"

"The woman told me she had several litters. So it's not like they're going to sell out by nine," Dad said to Brady, who fixed him with an angry squint.

Dad put down the paper and sprinted toward the stairs. "I bet I can do this in nine minutes and thirty-seven seconds. Time me!"

Brady fixed her eyes on the clock and began counting down the minutes. As Brady counted the final seconds, Dad took the stairs two at a time. In desperation, he catapulted himself over the banister, landing in a heap in the living room.

Dad pulled himself to his feet and sprinted for the door, announcing gleefully, "Beat you to the car!"

Brady cheered and followed him.

* * *

They pulled up in front of a ranch-style house and were welcomed inside by a very large and rotund blonde woman with scarlet lipstick. Her tent-like dress matched the color of her hair. She spoke with a southern accent.

"I noticed that your family name is Getty. Any relation to the famous Getty family?" Michael asked.

"If I were, would I be picking up dog poop all day?" she answered in a practiced manner.

"Where are the dogs?" Brady asked.

"You wanna see dawgs?" the woman bellowed.

"Yes, ma'am, very much," Brady said, rocking forward on the balls of her feet as though ready to jump in place.

"What kind of dawgs?"

"Dachshunds, please."

"Red, black-and-tan, long, short, or wire haired?" the woman asked.

"They come in all those ways?" Brady asked.

"They do, and we got 'em all," Mrs. Getty answered.

"Can I see all of them?" Brady asked, wide-eyed.

Mrs. Getty nodded. "Hal, bring 'em all out."

A red-faced man in cowboy boots with a Band-Aid over the bridge of his nose came in carrying a laundry basket filled with black-and-tan puppies. Soon the room was full of the movement and sound of barking puppies.

Brady thought this had to be as good as it could get. The puppies were all over her with their floppy ears and wobbly legs. Hal returned with another basket, and these were red puppies. The puppies knocked over the basket and tumbled out. Their heads were big and threatened to make them pitch forward. But their stomachs were even bigger and swung from side to side as they wobbled on their tiny paws. Hal entered with a third basket, and Brady let out a delighted gasp. She laughed out loud at Dad and Michael, seated on the floor, greeting each wiggly puppy with falsetto voices just like Tom and Vince.

Brady noticed one little red dog that was obviously bigger and older than the others. It had a weird nose that bent slightly but visibly to the side. It made him look like an old man.

"What happened to that one?" Brady asked Mrs. Gettty.

"Oh, that ol' dawg." The large woman scooped up the puppy with such speed that it sat down in her hand. She brought it close to her face and spoke directly into its eyes. "You an ugly ol' dawg, aren't you? No one's gonna want you, are they? Now, what am I going to with an ugly ol' dawg like you?" The puppy stared into the big woman's face and wagged his tail. Brady pursed her lips as she watched the breeder bully the pup. She looked at Dad and then

Michael, who were also staring. Brady shot forward and took the puppy from the breeder.

"I don't think he looks so bad." Brady smiled at the scruffy pup, and he looked up at her with large brown eyes that made her feel soft inside.

She realized that Dad was beside her when he spoke. "There's something very appealing about him. Come look, Michael."

Michael hesitated, which worried Brady.

"He's come from a long line of champs, of course." Mrs. Getty squinted at a paper before grabbing glasses. "Despite his unique face, he has a grand pedigree. Sired by Mardex Centurion, and his dam was a dappled bitch named Demeter's Persephone. They don't come any better." Mrs. Getty finished with a wave of her hand and grinned widely at them.

"How much for one of those?" Michael asked, pointing to the perfect puppies, wobbling and climbing all over one another as though they were still the main event.

"Well, they don't have his lineage, you know," the breeder began to backpedal.

"How much?" Michael repeated, standing up.

Mrs. Getty squinted at Michael and tilted her head. "$250, but as I say, they don't have his lineage."

Michael took one step closer, leaned toward the woman, and lowered his voice. "No, and they don't have his nose either. You and I both know that dog didn't sell because he looks bad and can't be shown. I don't care who his parents are; you're never going to get $250 for him. Besides, he may require medical treatment for breathing problems. We'll give him a good home and take him off your hands, but . . ." he leaned closer to the woman and said something Brady couldn't hear.

Mrs. Getty drew back, snapping her mouth shut as though slapped. "I can raise him myself, breed him, and make more money than that."

Oh no, we're not going to get him, and he'll be alone with that mean lady, Brady thought, leaning over the dog as if to protect him.

Michael sounded angry. "You won't, because it wouldn't be

worth the risk. You wouldn't breed him because he's defective. You'll be lucky to get $100 for him. See that little girl over there? She'll make him feel like a champ."

Brady couldn't believe Michael was saying all this about her. She straightened her shoulders.

"For you to keep him would just be pigheaded," Brady heard him say, and she pulled the dog closer.

"$150," Mrs. Getty said.

Michael narrowed his eyes and said, "$125." He started to say, "That's my final offer," when she interrupted.

"Deal," she said, and without smiling, she extended her hand, which he shook.

"And now our family is four," Brady said, smiling, as she carried her puppy to the car.

* * *

On the way home they tried out different names for the dog. Brady rejected any food names, such as Wiener or Hot Dog.

Michael suggested Quasimodo, but Brady had seen the Disney version and said they were making fun of him, which was just as cruel only for different reasons.

Dad came alive with the idea of Cyrano de Bergerac. He said that Cyrano was a great soldier for the French, an inspiring poet, a true friend, and a devoted lover of Roxanne, a woman half his age. He also had a very long nose that he allowed no one to ridicule. With the puppy on her lap, Brady went off to sleep, saying, "Cyrano is the perfect name."

CONTRETEMPS

"Brady, that dog made a mess in the kitchen again. It must be cleaned up before you go to school," Michael said as he stepped past her on his way up the stairs to get ready for work.

Brady sighed and glanced nervously at the clock. She already had her backpack on and her lunch in her hand. Michael hated messes, and Cyrano made a lot of messes. She remembered how easily she and Richard had been ordered out of the house before. It would be even easier to get rid of a dog.

She needed to clean up the smelly mess in less than two minutes in order for her to meet Fiona on the way to school. If Cyrano was to stay with them, he was going to have to be house-trained. Just not right now.

Brady held her nose, placed a paper towel over the mess, and scooped it into the garbage. She watched as it slid among eggshells and soiled napkins before disappearing underneath a coffee filter, heavy-laden with grounds. Shoot, she was supposed to flush it! It would smell bad in an hour, and she would hear about it.

She glanced at the clock. She could take the garbage out to avoid Michael's anger, but then she'd miss Fiona and have to walk into class alone. She slammed the cupboard shut, hiding the garbage can; washed her hands; and bolted for the door. She'd take out the garbage when she got home.

Running with a backpack full of books was hard and made Brady feel off-balance. It slowed her down. But she wanted to meet Fiona so they could walk in together. She was breathing hard and her heart felt like it was beating in her throat, but she kept going faster. Still, as she rounded the corner, she could see from a block away that Fiona wasn't there.

"An 'us' day," Brady muttered to herself, already feeling lonely. She asked Fiona one time, "You're absent a lot. Are you sick all the time?"

"No." Fiona ducked her head and smiled as she answered, "My mom and I have an agreement. I'm the baby, and I've been going to baseball, soccer, and ballet lessons for both my older brothers and both my older sisters all my life. So now, when I need to, I can stay home and we can have 'Just us time,' now that everybody else can drive themselves."

Brady felt again the stab of jealousy, since she didn't have a mom, and anger because Fiona should know how much Brady needed her.

Brady raced the rest of the way to school because now that she knew she was to enter the classroom alone, she didn't want to make it worse by being late. Brady never quit hoping Fiona would show up and was scanning the playground when the bell rang, and then she raced to be first in line.

It was Wednesday, which meant there would be a spelling test, which she always aced. But what really made Wednesdays important was that school got out an hour earlier, so Brady would go to Fiona's house to do homework and play.

Brady loved the chaos of Fiona's house and sometimes imagined living there. Backpacks were scattered in the living room, and no one complained. Books and papers of all sorts were stacked on every piece of furniture until they fell over. Meals at Fiona's house were like shark feeding frenzies. They served food Michael would never allow—fish sticks and hot dogs, and doughnuts for breakfast. Nobody forced her to eat bumpy fruits and vegetables.

But today Brady was at school alone. The class was fully assembled and looking expectantly at Mrs. Patterson. She smiled and waved them in, ready to start the day. Brady couldn't help staring at Fiona's empty desk.

Brady gathered class work for Fiona from Mrs. Patterson and put it in a folder.

"Fiona is lucky to have such a loyal and responsible friend as you," Mrs. Patterson said to her, patting her shoulders with both hands.

Brady blushed and ducked her head, saying, as she sped out of the door, "I'm lucky to have her too."

She held the file in front of her as if it were a prize as she jogged the way to Fiona's. She ran faster as she got closer to the house and was happy to see the big blue van that Fiona's mother drove parked in the driveway. If her mother was home, Fiona was with her; of that, Brady was sure.

Brady sprinted to the door and knocked and waited impatiently and out of breath. She was just about to give up and leave the file in the mailbox when she heard the door being opened.

Fiona's mom peaked out, blinking in the bright sunlight. "Oh, Brady, Fiona has very bad strep throat, and you shouldn't come in. I'm sorry, sweetie," she said.

"Well, here is her homework, and I can get it for her tomorrow, too, if you want. Will she be back tomorrow?" Brady asked.

"The doctor excused her for three to five days. So she won't be back for a while."

Brady held the file higher for Mrs. Sanchez to see. She needed Mrs. Sanchez to take the file and give it to Fiona.

Mrs. Sanchez opened the screen door and took the file. "Thank you, Brady, I'll give it to her."

"I can help her do the homework." Brady needed to see Fiona.

Mrs. Sanchez closed the screen. "Not today, dear, but she will do it before she comes back. She's very responsible, my Fiona."

"Can I see her?" Brady asked, embarrassed by the pleading in her voice.

"Oh no, dear, she is very sick, and she's sleeping right now.

You don't want to catch it if you can avoid it. You should watch out for it. Really high fever and a terribly sore throat." Mrs. Sanchez was stepping back in order to close the heavy door.

Brady did not want to be alone on that porch. "Well, tell her I hope she feels better soon. I'll be back tomorrow," she said, turning and running from the door as though she wanted to be far away quickly. She still heard the door click shut, and her throat tightened as she ran down the steps. She felt hot tears on her cheeks. What was wrong with her? Her friend was sick but would get better. Why was she so upset?

On the next Wednesday, Zach Webster, who sat behind her, hissed in her ear, "Why are you staring at Fiona's desk?" Brady hadn't realized that she was and felt embarrassed.

"I don't know," Brady said.

"I do," Zach's rasped in her ear. "It's because you're gay! That's why you miss her so much. Because you're in love with her."

Brady's face grew hot as she felt the vibration of his suppressed laughter. She slumped in her seat pretending to concentrate on Mrs. Patterson's math lesson. *Here it is again*, she thought. *Why do bullies exist? Am I going to have to live through it all over again?* The memories of the bullying in Oregon came flooding back. Her vision blurred, and she blinked hard. She did not want to cry.

"She's crying," Jessica Dolman said to Mrs. Patterson.

Mrs. Patterson stopped her math lesson and looked at Brady, and all of the students did the same. Brady clamped her eyes shut.

In case Mrs. Patterson had missed it, other kids joined in: "Brady's crying."

Capping her pen, Mrs. Patterson said to the students, "Let's take a break, shall we?" The class went into recess mode, divvying up jump ropes and balls for four square, and stampeded out of the door. In a split second, Brady was alone with Mrs. Patterson, something she ordinarily enjoyed. Now she just felt embarrassed.

Mrs. Patterson knelt down in front of Brady's desk, gripping the edge, and asked, "What's the matter, Brady?"

Brady struggled out with, "I don't know."

Mrs. Patterson sighed, and Brady could feel her teacher's breath on her face. "Do you miss your friend?"

Brady nodded her head vigorously.

"You know she's just going to be sick for a little while and then she'll get better. Really, it's just going to be a day or two more. Do you understand that?"

Brady nodded.

"So why are you so upset?" Mrs. Patterson glanced at the door. Brady erupted, "Zach says I'm gay because I miss Fiona."

Mrs. Patterson rested back on her heels and looked Brady in the eye. "I am very sorry, and I will talk to him immediately. We consider this bullying, and there are consequences for him. So I need to talk to him, okay? You can come out with me and help me out there. How about that?" Mrs. Patterson smiled at Brady.

Brady looked at Mrs. Patterson apprehensively but followed her onto the playground. As soon as they reached the yard, Mrs. Patterson approached Zach, but Brady hung back, then backed away several feet more. Brady held her breath and watched Zach put his hands in his pockets and lower his head while Mrs. Patterson continued to talk. At the end, they walked to the principal, who was standing by the swings. Brady wished she could believe this would stop Zach.

When she came in the door at the end of the day, the garbage can was placed in the entry with a note on it: "Clean up after your dog." She took the smelly thing out and slipped into her room. She didn't want to talk to anyone.

SICK

When Brady opened her eyes the next morning she knew immediately something was wrong. She felt hot and ached all over, and when she swallowed, it felt as though there was a rock in her throat scraping up and down. She found that she had to prepare herself for the act of swallowing by drawing her neck into her shoulders and bracing herself for pain. The room moved when she sat up, and she struggled to get to the side of the bed. As her feet hit the floor, she felt that she would follow them right over. Pulling herself to a standing position, she became aware of an unrelenting throb in her head. Should she bother to try to dress for school?

Her father pushed her door open, saying, "Oh good, you're awake. I didn't hear you, so I was worried."

Before she could say anything, he left. She wavered on her feet alone in her room. She steadied herself against the bed as she walked to the chair where her clothes were laid out. She tried to pull them on, but the texture of the cloth raked against her skin. When she got to the top of the steps, there seemed to be two sets of stairs, and she felt unsure of which banister to grab. She teetered on her feet and leaned against the wall.

Her father walked up the stairs, carrying a cup coffee. He squinted at her and asked, "Are you okay, Brady?"

"I don't know, I just feel so weird." When she spoke her voice sounded deep and garbled, as though something was in her throat. As the words left her mouth, she started to swallow, but the pain of the effort brought tears to her eyes and caused her to pull her arms into her body in sympathy with her throat.

Richard reached forward to steady her, and his face immediately registered surprise.

"Geez, Braid, you're burning up. You need to go back to bed. I'll call the school and bring you something to drink," he said.

Brady nodded rather than speak, and without changing clothes she staggered back to bed and under the covers. Michael arrived with water and orange juice and a worried look. His hand felt cool and comforting. And at first a cold drink looked appealing, but when she tried to swallow, the pain overwhelmed her and it came spewing back up. Brady fell back against the pillow, and Michael took the wet comforter away.

"You are going to have to drink something. You're burning up with fever, and your body will get dehydrated, okay?" Michael said, touching her face.

Brady struggled to raise her eyelids and nod.

"Okay, sweetie, sleep for now," Michael said, murmuring a sympathetic sound as she had heard him do during sad movies.

It appeared to be the middle of the night because it was very dark, but Brady had lost track of time. She awakened to feel the thermometer in her ear, followed by the beep.

"Oh God!" Michael said. He threw the covers back, and she felt herself being picked up. She also felt weirdly weak and shaky, almost jumpy. She couldn't focus her eyes or control her head. She realized she was being carried into the hall bathroom and that her father was running water, but when she was put into the tub with her pajamas still on, she knew something was really wrong. The cold water soaked into her clothes and hit her skin with such a shock that she gasped for air. Her head, which had been lolling back, snapped forward, and she felt her eyes instantly open, offering her a view of the harsh lighting in the bathroom. She wanted to end this, to tell them to get her out of this, but her tongue seemed swollen and that made it hard to talk. Her teeth were chattering and her body shivered. She tried to put her feet under herself to propel her body out of the cold tub, but nothing seemed to be obeying her commands. Her eyes flashed open again, desperately appealing to them to get her out of the tub. Instead they poured the water over her, even running a wet washcloth over her face. She reached up and grabbed hold of the washcloth.

"That's progress," Michael said.

Finally she spoke: "Get me out."

Her father laid out a large towel and said, "You got it."

Michael, his shirt thoroughly soaked by all the splashing, picked her up and laid her on the towel while her father wrapped it around her. This felt briefly soothing, but as the towel absorbed the water from her pajamas, it became cold again. She began to tremble, and her teeth started to chatter. Her father had left but returned with new pajamas. They slipped her out of the wet and into the dry, toweling her hair in the process. They settled her back in the bed, but just looking at the comforter made her feel hot. Brady pushed it away when Michael tried to put it over her. She shook her head, saying one word: "Hot." She sounded as though she were gargling.

"In a few minutes, you'll be too cold. Here, take this." Michael held out a measuring spoon of liquid Tylenol. Looking at the spoon made her throat hurt. She shook her head more gently this time.

"You have to, or you're going to go through that again." Michael jerked his thumb toward the bathroom. This seemed mean, but his eyes were begging. He pushed the Tylenol to her mouth and, closing her eyes, she opened her lips and braced for the agony that would follow this simple action. She got it down and noted with satisfaction that it stayed down. She smiled at her two fathers, but they only stared back at her. After that she remembered nothing.

* * *

She's swallowed the Tylenol, thought Michael as he as he left her room, leaving her door open so he could hear. Richard stood in the door of their bedroom just feet from him, outlined by the bedroom light, his shoulders caved. Michael held a tray bearing the medicine spoon and Brady's glass and tried to sort out what needed to happen next. They were all exhausted, and tomorrow would be so much better for making decisions, but tomorrow might be too late. They had bought time with the cold bath, but her fever would surge back up. She was already kicking off sheets and blankets.

"We have to go to the hospital," Michael said.

"I've got insurance information from Frank somewhere," Richard said, looking around the empty hall.

"Find it now. We have to get her to the hospital while the Tylenol is doing its job," Michael said, mapping the fastest way to the hospital. He needed his wallet, checkbook, and water and a blanket for Brady. He pushed away from the wall and, throwing a blanket over his shoulder, grabbed his wallet, keys, and checkbook; he scooped Brady's limp body out of the bed and carried her down the steps.

"I could call Frank," Richard said as he followed Michael out of the door. "I mean, if I can't find the insurance card."

"We have to get her there now," Michael groaned. "Find it later." Michael struggled with the front door and Brady at the same time. The door fell shut before he could get through it. "Goddamnit!" Michael said.

"I can help, if you'll just let me." Richard reached for the door handle, but Michael pulled it open.

"I've got it!" Michael said. "Let's just go."

Richard slunk to the passenger side of the car and lowered himself into the backseat so Michael could hand him Brady in his lap.

Michael felt the heat of Brady's fever through the blanket as he handed her to Richard. His heart ticked faster with each second. He started the car and pulled onto the freeway in record time. Even though it was three in the morning there were other cars on the road. "Only in California will you find traffic in the middle of the night," he said, stomping on the accelerator.

"There's the sign for the hospital," Richard said.

"I can see it," Michael said, and he snapped down the turn indicator. They parked in front of the emergency room. Michael pulled open Richard's door, twitching as he watched him gather Brady into his arms and struggle to stand. Michael surged forward to grab Brady from Richard. "I'll get her," he said.

But Richard pulled Brady closer to his chest. "I've got her, Michael. Just stop and let me handle this for once."

Michael snorted and marched to the automatic sliding door to the emergency room. When it did not open as fast as he wanted, he groaned and put his hands on it as though he might force it open.

* * *

Richard struggled out of the car with Brady's flaccid body. The car door fell shut on the blanket, and as he walked, it pulled away, revealing her face. Richard gasped at the sight of her eyes rolling back and her mouth working on nothing while streaks of saliva formed at the corners of her lips. Her body jerked spasmodically.

"God," Richard gasped, and he broke into a run. The door rolled open, allowing Michael and the nurse behind the counter to see him.

The nurse rose and circled the counter, pulling a gurney from the side of the station. "Okay, sir, I'll take it from here. What's been happening with her?"

"She's running a fever and has a sore throat." Richard struggled to reconstruct the events. As they walked, the nurse listened to Brady's heart, and then asked, "How long has she been running a fever? Is she allergic to any medication?"

"Just today and . . ." Richard was winded from running and anxiety, and his voice shook. He had no idea if she was allergic to any medication. What else didn't he know? He struggled to catch his breath.

The nurse looked at him. "Okay, you're in the right place." She glanced at a chair. "Why don't you have a seat, Dad?"

Richard sank onto the chair and sucked air into his lungs.

"Am I right? Are you her father?" the nurse asked, pulling the stethoscope away from her ear.

"Yes, yes, I'm her father," Richard said.

"Have you given her anything for the fever?" the nurse asked.

"Yes, not me, but my partner—Michael?" Richard said, gesturing toward Michael, who came into the room.

"I've been giving Tylenol to her every six hours," Michael said.

"For how long?" the nurse asked.

"Just for today," Michael said.

"Has she seen a doctor?"

"No. I kept thinking the fever would break. Sometimes it appeared to be going down, but then it would surge back up again. It was 106 when we decided to come here." Michael stood with his hands in his pockets and stared at Brady.

"It's still 106," the nurse said, typing on the computer.

Michael looked at her. "Even with the Tylenol?"

The nurse nodded. "Has she been exposed to strep?"

"Yes, her best friend has strep," Richard said.

"We'll do some tests. It's of some concern that we can't wake her up, but she isn't unconscious, just sleepy. It looks different," she said, stroking Brady's cheek.

Brady turned toward the touch, her eyes briefly fluttering open.

"I have a doctor coming, so you can see what she says," the nurse said.

She picked up a clipboard and looked at Richard this time, asking, "Got insurance?"

"I have to call to get the number," Richard mumbled.

The nurse stopped and stared at them.

Richard looked at Michael, who answered, "No, my insurance won't cover her because she is not my dependent yet."

"Credit cards work," the nurse said. "I mean, until you get that number."

Michael handed her his credit card.

As the nurse took the card and walked out, she said over her shoulder, "And you are the biological father with custody of her, right?"

"I am the biological father, yes," Richard said.

She stopped at the door and turned to face him. "With custody?"

Michael answered, "Yes, with temporary legal custody."

She stared at the two men for a long time before saying, "I need ID for both of you. Who does have custody of her, normally?"

"Her grandparents."

"Is there any way I can call them?" she asked.

"Why would you need to? He is the biological father." Michael jerked his thumb in Richard's direction.

"Look, I don't make the rules. I just don't want to be the one who didn't check."

"Check what?" Michael asked, his voice sandpaper rough, lips curling.

"Hospitals are often the first ones to know where a . . . missing kid has turned up."

"She's not missing," Michael said, stepping closer to the nurse. "She's sick and needs medical treatment, and nothing else." He made a slashing movement with his hand as he spoke, which the nurse followed with her eyes.

Richard circled around Michael, speed-dialing Frank Nordland. "Hello, Frank—I have him on the line," he said to the nurse while pointing to his phone. "Sorry to call in the middle of the night. This is Richard."

"What's wrong?" Frank's voice made Richard's heart pick up speed.

"Everything is fine," Richard said.

"Everything can't be fine, or you wouldn't be calling me in the middle of the night. Now what's going on?" Frank growled.

"Brady is running a temperature, and we're here in the hospital and—"

"Hospital? She's lived with us for five years and has never been to the hospital. My God, what happened?"

Richard could hear Kathleen's voice in the background. His face felt hot. He wanted to hand the phone to Michael, who stood poised to take over.

"She's running a fever."

"You took her to the hospital just because she's running a fever?" There was a muddle of voices at the other end.

Richard heard Kathleen ask, "How high?"

"106."

Frank repeated it. Quiet. "How long?"

"I don't know—for the amount of time it took for us to get her here. She's fine now." Actually, she wasn't any better off, but they had gotten her to help, so Richard felt better. "We need your insurance number."

"Kathleen's getting it. Give her lots of fluids. It's easy to dehydrate with a fever that high. I've never heard of anyone having a fever that high. I wish she were here. We'd have taken care of it. She probably got it from someone in school. You have to watch out for these things."

Shit happens, old man. "That's why we're asking for the insurance number, so we can get her treated—quickly? We'd take care of it ourselves, but she's not our dependent."

Frank interrupted with the number, reading each digit loudly and slowly as one might to a child.

Richard sensed movement and looked up. A diminutive, young blonde woman entered the room in a white coat, with a stethoscope slung around her neck. This was the doctor, Richard surmised, and he gave Michael a sidelong look. She looked more like a high school graduate. Richard would have been so much happier with an old graying male doctor, but then that kind of physician didn't work at three in the morning. They had been told by friends in medical school never to get sick at night in June when the freshly graduated were unleashed to treat the public. Now they were doing exactly that.

Richard looked up to see the nurse gesturing to Doctor Kendall and saying, "You need to get authorization from the grandfather."

The doctor forced a smile and approached Richard, extending her hand. "I'm Doctor Kendall." Richard shook her hand and watched her wipe his perspiration off on her white coat. "I'm told you're talking to the grandfather? I do need authorization from him."

Richard wanted to protest, but he didn't want to delay Brady being treated, so he obediently handed the phone to the doctor.

"I want to make sure you are giving your authorization to treat your grand daughter," Doctor Kendall said to into the phone, turning away from Richard.

Richard shoved his hands in his jeans pockets. He couldn't even look at Michael, and Michael was not looking at him.

Listening to the conversation was galling, but Frank made it worse by verifying everything Richard had just told him. Did he think Richard was making up information or that he would lie?

"Good to go." Doctor Kendall handed Richard his phone and gave him a tiny smile but no eye contact.

Finally released, the men surged with questions. Michael nodded at Brady and asked, "How come she hasn't awakened? Is that normal?"

"Seizures are exhausting. They are a complete upheaval of the whole body, and that coupled with fighting infection makes the kid sleepy." She smiled down at Brady, adding, "There's a lot going on in that little body." She stroked Brady's foot through the blanket.

"How long is this going to take?" Richard asked.

"We can get the tests back in an hour or two, and from there we will know what to do next. If it is just strep, we'll give her heavy-duty antibiotics, and if her fever goes down, she'll be able to go home around noon, I'm guessing. You don't have to stay. She's just going to sleep. We'll call you with the diagnosis."

Richard and Michael exchanged glances, but neither moved.

Michael volunteered to stay in the room with Brady. Richard left for the waiting room.

✳ ✳ ✳

And so began the nighttime vigil. Although Michael tried to sleep in his lounge chair, the harsh overhead lighting and beeping of various monitors combined with the tension of the circumstances made it impossible.

Richard was slumped on a couch in the waiting room when Dr. Kendall brushed by him, brandishing a piece of paper.

"She's got strep," she said as she passed through the door to the dark examining room. "We can treat it easily."

DOING PUGSLY

Cyrano the Dachshund was especially pleased to see Brady when she came home from the hospital. Since she was sick and recovering, the dog received something like papal dispensation that allowed him to sleep in Brady's bed. Everyone, including Michael, agreed that the dog had medicinal qualities and that Brady would heal much faster if he were with her. Having the dog happily housed and Brady recovering in her own bed created a psychic salve for their family. Michael cooked as he never had before, learning to combine foods that Brady did like with what he knew to be healthy so she improved in color and energy.

All of this good news called for a celebration. Vince and Tom were eager to have them over, saying that Pugsly missed Brady. Brady, in turn, wanted to let Cyrano have a formal introduction to society. They set a date, Michael made a dish, and they took off for "P.V. Estates" one evening at six.

"It looks better somehow this time," Brady said, looking up at the imposing estate as she climbed out of the car.

Pugsly came catapulting down the brick steps, followed by Tom and Vince. Brady held Cyrano in her arms and crouched to greet Pugsly.

"I really do not see what you like in this dog," Michael whispered in her ear, adding, "he sounds like a death rattle."

"That's mean," Brady said, and they all looked up to greet Tom and Vince.

"There's something wrong with his nose," Tom said.

"Yes, he was born that way." Brady shrugged and lowered Cyrano, now fully ten weeks old, to the floor.

"And still you bought him?" Tom said, looking at Vince and pressing his fingertips together in a temple.

Cyrano appeared to have found a friend in Pugsly. His ears were forward, and his tail stood erect from his spine. He pranced back a little and then forward, sniffing all the while as though he intended to vacuum Pugsly's essence into his own being. Pugsly's mouth closed as his ears drew back. A low and barely audible growl emanated from his chest.

"There, see," Brady crooned while stroking Cyrano's back, "You two can be the best of friends. I want you to be." After the dinner, Brady, weary of making conversation with adults, retired to the "Barbie den" to relax with the doggies and watch TV. It was some time during this period that she fell asleep, but she woke up to the rhythmic vibration of the dogs. At first she thought it was a dream or confusion from her illness, but then she realized that the dogs were attempting to have sex. Pugsly was on the receiving end, and Cyrano had a look she had never seen before.

In her dreamlike state, she wondered if any of this mattered to Tom or Vince. Pugsly was a show dog, and they told her never to let him off his leash at the park because he had to stay in a controlled environment, which meant no sex with dogs not of his caliber or breed. But that had meant female dogs. Could dogs be gay? And if so, would this make Cyrano off-limits? Brady took another look at Pugsly's bobbing head, noting that his eyes rolled back while his mouth lolled open. She hated to invade their privacy, but still, she worried. Finally, she decided to check it out with Tom and Vince.

She wandered down the hallway, trying to find where the party had gone. She heard voices, laughter, and music drifting up from downstairs, and she walked toward it. Although the music was so loud she doubted they could hear her, something made her feel uneasy, so she stopped in the middle of the steps and banged on the wall. The voices stopped, and she could hear a scrambling of movement. Brady stepped back up three stairs.

Finally, she heard her father's voice. "Brady, I thought you were asleep. You were a few minutes ago. I checked." The statement sounded like a question.

"Yeah, I was, and I woke up. Anyway, I just wondered something."

There was a laugh that cut off, and she wasn't sure how to go forward. "Can I come down?" she asked.

"No, we'll come up." This time it was Michael.

"Okay," she said, and she turned toward the wall. And then, because she felt awkward and wanted this to be over, she closed her eyes and called down, "Can dogs be gay?"

"What?" Brady recognized Tom's voice. "Why are you asking, Brady?"

"Because Cyrano and Pugsly are, I'm pretty sure, having sex upstairs on the bed, and I was just wondering if this was a problem."

She heard a scuffle of feet and movement before she saw Tom bounding up the stairs in what appeared to be a green satin blanket.

"If that horny little phallic symbol hurts my dog, I'll kill him," Tom said, pushing by her. She scrambled after him to protect her canine progeny. Behind her she could hear several other feet.

"Don't hurt him. It's not like he can get Pugsly pregnant, I mean, right?" Brady yelled to Tom's back.

Tom didn't answer, and Brady ran behind him realizing that he was wearing a full-length green satin dress. She stopped and gaped but realized Tom would get to Cyrano before her, so she started again, double speed. As she pulled closer to Tom, she could see candelabra earrings swinging from his ears below a red wig. The earrings sent flecks of light careening along the walls as he ran. Bracelets clinked on his wrist as he held tightly to the skirt, revealing the largest pair of Kelly green satin pumps that Brady had ever seen. It was a beautiful dress, but he was a man.

"Where is he?" Tom asked, exasperated. She stopped and

gasped for breath, shocked at the sight Tom's made-up face—complete with false eyelashes. She felt a wave of nausea, but at the same time she struggled to keep from laughing.

Tom leaned in to her face and snarled again, "Where is he?"

Brady smelled liquor on his breath and moved back.

Tom moved closer, and she felt her back hit the wall. "Where?" His lacquered lips pulled back to reveal bleached white teeth. He held his hands as if to grab her shoulders but did not touch her.

She looked over his shoulder toward the pink room.

Tom followed her gaze and bolted toward the door.

"Don't hurt my dog!" Brady shoved off of the wall and raced after Tom just in time to hear a growl, an aggressive bark, and then a yelp.

"Stop, Tom! Do not touch her," Brady heard Michael's voice from down the hall.

Brady's bare feet dug into the Persian rug to push herself faster. "Please don't hurt my dog, please, please don't." As she rounded the corner and went through the door, she ducked her head, preparing for disaster. What she saw was just weird. Tom was seated against the wall on the floor, and his wig had been pushed off by his slide down the wall and had fallen into his lap. He was holding his dog in his arms with its face up against his own. His right shoe had fallen off of his foot and lay on its side in front of his knee, which bent and tucked underneath his body. His left knee was bent up to his chest, exposing his crotch, which was covered by a sparkly Kelly green covering. Brady wanted to run from the room but stared openmouthed. She saw the tiny brown form lying still on the floor. She rushed toward it. She stroked his side, but his eyes remained closed. She sat back on the floor, eyes blurred. Her hands clutched one another, "Please." She looked down at him and saw that he was breathing, and then he opened his eyes and lifted his head. She scooped him up, and he barked in her face and wagged his tail as though nothing had happened. Eager to get away from Tom, Brady struggled to stand and walked into the hall. She saw Dad and Michael walking toward her. They were both barefoot, and Richard's shirt was randomly buttoned.

"I want to go home," was all she said as she walked around her father, to the foyer, and out the door to the car. It was locked. She stood waiting and tried to erase the image of Tom splayed out on the floor from her mind. Whatever had been going on down those stairs with her father and Michael, she never wanted to know. She wanted to get in the car and drive away and never come back.

Dad had followed her to the door, and Brady felt him staring at her, but she did not want to talk.

"I'm going to get the key," he finally said, and he walked back into the house, slamming the front door behind him.

* * *

Richard had run up the stairs and left his jacket and shoes, and now he returned to the basement to collect them.

Vince met him on his way up, and clearing his throat he asked, "So, is the excitement over?"

"Yeah," Richard said, avoiding eye contact. "We're gonna take off."

"Too bad," Vince said, "it was just getting good."

Richard silently gathered their jackets and shoes, dropping one shoe from the jumble on his way up.

Vince bent to pick it up and asked, "Need some help?"

"No, I've got it, thanks." Richard took the shoe from him.

"It's not my fault your horny little dog tried to bugger mine." Vince centered himself in Richard's path, arms crossed over his chest.

"No one said it was." Richard stepped around Vince.

"We miss you guys," Vince said over Richard's shoulder. "Do you ever go out anymore? Or are you completely preoccupied with the lit-tel girl?"

"Pretty preoccupied, I guess," Richard said.

"Guess we're going to have to find new friends," Vince said, following closely.

"Guess so." Richard moved more quickly down the hall and headed out of the door to the car.

Vince reached forward and took hold of his arm, spinning

him around and sending shoes flying. As Richard bent to pick up the shoes, Vince leaned under his face and forced a deep kiss into his mouth.

Richard dropped the clothes and pushed Vince away from himself. He whipped around to assure himself that Brady and the dog were around the corner and out of sight.

"Stop it. Get away from me," Richard said.

"Oh come on, just a few minutes ago you seemed pretty open to my suggestions." Vince smiled, and it made his eyes narrow like a predator's.

"I was caught up in the moment, Vince. It was a mistake. I'm sorry." Richard snatched the clothes from the ground and sprinted toward the car, and Vince followed. Pulling the car door open, Richard threw the clothes in, almost hitting Brady with a shoe. Slamming the car door shut, Richard backed against it and whispered to Vince, "It is over. Go away."

"Fine, I'll go away, but you're not fooling me. You did want me." Vince said, pointing repeatedly to his chest. "I know the truth." Vince walked back to the house and slammed the door shut, leaving them in the dark.

Richard got in the car even though Michael was still in the house. He was not willing to go in and get him.

"I'm sorry," Richard said to Brady's image in the rearview mirror.

Brady appeared to be asleep, but she couldn't have been because there hadn't been enough time for her to fall asleep.

"Brady?" Richard tried again, even touching her this time.

She did not stir.

"Look, if you're not going to talk to me, there's nothing I can do. You saw something you can't understand, and I'm sorry," Richard said to her over the back of his seat.

Brady never responded. All he could do was wait. He was just nodding off when the dome light came on and Michael sat down in the driver's seat.

"Where were you?" Richard asked.

"Damage control," Michael said, starting the car and pulling away down the circular flagstone driveway.

"With Tom?" Richard asked.

Michael nodded.

"And we have more ahead of us," Richard said, nodding toward the backseat. "We were okay until the dogs woke up," he added.

"Who knew we had such a randy little pooch?" Michael said, grimacing as he pulled onto the freeway.

"You want a cigarette, you stud?" Richard said, looking at the dog in Brady's lap.

Cyrano jumped off of Brady's lap and began sniffing and whining on the floor of the car.

"What is he doing?" Richard asked, alarmed.

This comment awakened Brady, who answered, "He has to go to the bathroom. He needs to be let out." She looked at Michael in the rearview mirror.

"We're on the freeway; I can't stop now," Michael said.

"Well, he has to go, and if you don't, he's going to stain the carpet." They all heard the hiss of urine. "It's too late," Brady said, looking directly at Michael's image in the rearview mirror. "I'm sorry." Her tone did not sound contrite.

"Goddamn dog!" Michael said.

"Michael, knock it off. We've cleaned it off of other things; we'll get it out of your car," Richard said.

"That stupid dog ruins everything," Michael fumed, hitting the steering wheel with the palm of his right hand.

"It's not his fault," Brady said. "He just had to go. If you're planning to blame him for what happened with Pugsly, you can't. He was following his instincts the way everyone does." Her voice went very cold and calm as she added, "even you two." Her arms crossed over her chest and she threw one leg over the other, angling her body away from the front seat and toward the dark window. "At least he doesn't dress up and play games to do it."

Her words dripped with disdain and revulsion and hit Richard like a punch to an old bruise.

Finally, she asked in exasperation, "What were you doing down there?"

Michael stole a glance at Richard, who tried to answer, but Brady interrupted.

"You know, if someone were to ask me if I thought homosexuality was an abomination to God right now, I would say, yes!" Her voice rose on the word "yes," making both men flinch in front of her. Her voice gathered strength and volume, "You know, none of this is easy for me. But I kept thinking, being gay can't be bad because Michael took care of me when I was sick, and Dad helps me with my homework, and you guys care about what I eat. You used to drink—and there was a lot of *that* tonight, even if it wasn't you—and now you don't because you take care of each other. So that's all good. And I used to think we were a good family, but now, I don't know. Maybe you've been covering up the bad stuff, and now I'm seeing what everyone says about being gay. I told myself it was okay because I wanted to be in a family like everyone else. You made me feel good—better than before. And so I went along with the rest of it. Her voice broke, and her eyes burned with tears of fury. "But tonight I felt . . . grossed out . . . and ashamed." She breathed deeply and gathered strength. "That," she pointed in the direction from which they were driving, "cannot be normal."

Apparently too angry to find words, she kicked her feet forward into the back of Richard's seat. It jolted him. She kicked twice more, but instead of releasing her rage, it appeared to build. She unbuckled her seat belt, and both men turned toward her. Michael swerved and had to struggle to regain control of the car. Brady banged her head backward into the cushions of the seat again and again.

Richard unbuckled his seat belt to reach for her, but he was afraid with all of the flailing that he might wind up being kicked.

Brady began talking again, this time through clenched teeth: "And you make fun of my religion. You think I don't know, but I do. When we say grace, which, by the way, I've stopped asking that we do, have you noticed? You roll your eyes and laugh. You think I don't see, but I do, and I hate it." On her last word, she suddenly stopped banging her head on the seat, then she slid sideways, raised her legs, took aim, and thrust her feet forward directly into the window. Richard, unable to stop her, lowered his head and covered his face to ward off flying glass. But the window stood stubbornly unbroken. This appeared to enrage her, and she stopped talking all together, focusing all of her energy on slamming her feet into the window.

Richard knew it would eventually break, so, following the rhythm of her legs with his left hand, he gathered her ankles with one arm and reached forward with the other to press her legs into her chest. He leaned as much of his body as he could between the front seats in an effort to stop her. He was almost forced back, not by the power of her legs, but by the look of absolute rage on her face. He began to loose his grip, and he watched her grind her teeth and draw her limbs together for one last powerful thrust. Richard reached forward too late, and although Brady's feet didn't hit the window, he received the full force of her kick into his shoulder, twisting his back painfully between the seats. A gasp of agony escaped his mouth, and he struggled to straighten his back. He saw a look of satisfaction on Brady's face, which was replaced by remorse and concern.

Finally, he placed his hand firmly onto her chest and pressed her into the seat, arresting the motion. "Brady, stop, stop, stop," Richard said.

Finally she did, and she came to rest facing the back of the seat.

Richard gasped, "We are good people who do love you and each other. I believe that you saw something tonight that you were not ready to understand, and I am so, so sorry." He stroked her cheek as he spoke. He wished she would look at him, but she stared at the back of the seat, her breathing rapid and shallow.

"Whatever," she said.

Michael was steering onto their street, and Brady squirmed to an upright position.

"Please talk to me," Richard said as they in opened their doors and climbed out of the car.. "It will be hard to talk about this later," he implored her, taking hold of her arm.

"Fine by me," she said, rolling her eyes. There was something adult in the sarcasm of her response, and that grieved him.

She moved around and away from him , and she stared at his hand on her arm. "Is there anything we can explain about what you saw tonight that might make you feel more comfortable?"

Brady looked back him and said, "You want me to say everything is all right. That Tom being dressed as a woman with makeup and . . . whatever else was okay. Well, sorry, it isn't, it just isn't okay." Her lips started to tremble again. She looked down and asked, "Why are you barefoot?" Her question was an accusation.

Richard flashed on when he had taken off his shoes and hesitated.

"Uh-huh, that's what I thought," Brady said, nodding grimly.

Michael stood silently with a paper towel in his hand and waited for them to go into the house, allowing him to clean up the dog urine. Brady kicked the car door shut, and the sound of the door slamming reverberated back, passing through their bodies on its way.

Richard and Michael stood in silence. Richard wondered. How could he tell her that after a long period of helping with homework, packing lunches, serving balanced meals, going to bed and getting up early, attending church even, topped off with making love silently, clinging to the headboard to avoid waking her, that they had found themselves at a party with familiar friends and things had gotten a little out of control?

"Come on, let's go to bed. We'll deal with it in the morning," Michael said.

THE MORNING AFTER

Richard sat over his oatmeal and coffee with spoon in hand. He didn't want either. He'd awakened with a fist of dread in his gut. He needed to talk to Brady about last night and should talk to Michael before that conversation. He didn't want to do either of those. Go for a run?

"Are you reading that?" Michael asked and pointed at the *Los Angeles Times* Richard was holding in front of his face.

"Isn't it obvious?" Richard shook the paper.

"No, you are staring at it and sighing, but you're not reading. You never read the *LA Times*; you read the *New Yorker* on Sundays. I read the *LA Times*."

Richard looked at the paper with widened eyes and handed it to Michael, who opened it and began to read. Richard made no move to get another paper. He stared at the headlines that blocked Michael's face. "You're usually not even up at this hour."

Silence followed. Finally Michael spoke. "I couldn't sleep."

Richard drew a deep breath and exhaled, making the paper waver. He sat back and rested his chin in his hand, exhaling through his nose.

"What is it?" Michael lowered the paper, crushing it below his hands.

"What do you think it is? I don't know what to say to Brady. Is this really no big deal for you?" He shook his head, stood, and paced. "So far since she's been with us, she's wound up in the hospital—"

"Could have happened at the grandparents too," Michael interrupted.

"And now this . . . how is this going to look in court? What's Ryan going to think?" Richard looked up as he sensed movement.

Brady stood at the top of the stairs. "I'm going to invite Fiona over," she said, pulling out her phone and speed-dialing.

Richard looked at Michael. "Shouldn't we talk first?" he whispered.

Michael nodded and raised his eyebrows. He folded his hands over the paper.

"Brady, can we talk to you?" Richard asked, hating the wheedling tone of his voice.

"Hi, Mrs. Sanchez," Brady's voice was jarring. "Is Fiona there?" She paused. "Wow, really? She usually gets up early to watch cartoons. Is she still sick?" Pause. "Okay, great, have her call me. I'm not going anywhere today." Although she was talking to Mrs. Sanchez, she said it loudly, as if telling the two men that no matter what they had planned, she was busy.

Brady hung up, noted the time, and sighed heavily before going back into her room and shutting the door firmly.

Richard and Michael exchanged glances. "Now's the time," Richard said.

"Okay, what are you going to say to make this all better?" Michael asked, his eyebrows nearly meeting his hairline.

"You act like this is my problem—just mine," Richard said. He leaned toward Michael, stabbing at his own chest with his index finger.

"I never promised to become something I am not," Michael said. We were with friends. We are gay. They were drunk. We were not. We didn't do anything wrong, and I'm not apologizing for anything.

Richard sat down at the table. "That's not what I'm suggesting."

"Okay, what are you suggesting?"

Richard rested his chin in his hand. "I wish it hadn't happened."

"I don't." Michael stood and began gathering the paper. "It was bound to happen in one way or another, and I don't want to set the expectation that I am willing to have sex holding my breath for the rest of my life."

Richard crossed his legs and turned away from Michael. *No ally here*, he thought. *You're on your own.* He uncrossed his legs and used the inertia to propel himself out of the chair. He felt shaky, but he kept going all the way up the stairs to Brady's bedroom. He knocked softly. There was no response, so he knocked harder. He was about to knock a third time when he heard Brady's voice.

"The door is unlocked. Just open it," she said.

He hated the irritation in her voice but pushed himself into the room without a word.

Her bed was unmade, and she was lying on her side among the snarled bedding and reading *Divergent*. She didn't look up.

Richard stood awkwardly between her bed and the door. He walked slowly and sat on the bed, careful not to jar her book. She continued to read.

He cleared his throat, "Brady, I—"

"I don't want to talk about last night, if that's what you're going say," she said to the pages.

"I wasn't going to say that," Richard said, holding a warning finger up. "What happened when you called Fiona?"

"She was asleep." Brady shrugged.

"She'll call back," Richard stated.

Brady shrugged again but glanced at her phone. "Can I call again? Maybe her mother forgot to give her the message." She looked at Richard for the first time since he came in.

"Why don't we take Cyrano for a walk? And maybe when we get back, she will have called." Cyrano's ears went up at the sound of his name, and he walked to the door.

Richard pointed at the dog. "Look how smart he is! He knows what I'm talking about."

Brady smiled begrudgingly and looked at the phone one more time before slipping it into her jeans pocket. She looked at Cyrano and smiled broadly. He pattered back to her and put two paws on the bed, darting his nose at her face. She laughed.

The three headed out of the door. They walked down the hill to a street that led to the dog park where Cyrano could be off his leash and, while not running with the big dogs, he could at least run with the little ones. Brady smiled at his excitement as they walked closer to the enclosure.

"He's so excited to see the other dogs. Maybe we should buy him a friend," Brady said, checking Richard's face for agreement.

"Going to the dog park is good," he said, nodding in a way that said that was the end of discussion.

Brady threw the ball, and a half dozen assorted dogs ran after it, winding up in a confusing jumble of snouts and tails. The ball became hopelessly lost in the process. She looked at Richard and shrugged, saying, "I guess I'll just let him play."

A van rattled by and Brady's head shot up. Richard recognized Fiona in the front seat. Brady smiled immediately, waved enthusiastically, and yelled, "Fiona!"

Richard could sense her desperate need for Fiona to come and make life normal again. Richard joined her in waving, even yelling Fiona's name.

The van did not stop. It didn't even slow as it disappeared around the corner. Richard looked at Brady, who was no longer waving. Her shoulders were bowed and her arms were drooping, but the worst was the despair on her face. He wanted to run after the van and demand that Fiona get out and play. He crouched down next to Brady and tried to explain. "They probably had errands to run."

"No, they were going home," Brady said, eyes filling. "She didn't even wave."

"Maybe she didn't see you. The car was going fast," Richard said.

"I don't get it. She said I was her best friend just before she got sick. We did everything together. What is wrong?" Brady said.

"Brady, it's probably nothing. Give it some time, and she'll call you back. I know she will. Hey, look at your dog!" Cyrano was running pell-mell up and down the yard at the front of the pack of other dogs.

"He looks like a dog-food commercial," Brady said. "He looks so proud," she laughed, adding, "crooked nose and all. He's the leader of the pack."

"Let's go home, shall we?" Richard asked, and then he seized the opportunity to say, "Brady, we have to talk about what happened."

Brady raised her hand to stop him.

"No, we have to deal with this. I know you hate it and it makes you feel uncomfortable. But we can't just let it go," he said.

She raised her hands to put them over her ears.

"Fine," he continued. "I am talking to the lawyer about it because I think it could raise some legal problems."

"I'm not going to talk to anyone about it, so no one will know that it happened. You don't have to worry about it coming out in court or me saying anything to a psychologist or a social worker because I am not going to talk about it, ever," Brady said, underscoring the comment with the slash of her hand from left to right, palm down.

Richard stared at her. "Yeah, I wish it could work that way. Just don't talk about stuff that bothers you and make it disappear."

Brady was listening to him.

"But it doesn't work that way. Trust me. I've done that with being gay. I pretended not to be gay; I even married a woman and had a baby." He flourished his hand at Brady as if to say, *Voila*. "It may have fooled some people, but it didn't change the fact that I knew I was gay. It made it worse for me. Just as it will for you. You saw something that bothered you, pretending it didn't happen will not solve the problem. It will backfire."

Brady looked away from him and hugged her body tightly with her arms, gripping at the elbows.

Richard held his breath and waited.

"Does it have to be now?" Brady looked so tired as she said this.

"It has to be soon. And it has to be discussed with Ryan. You want to start there?"

Brady shrugged one shoulder. "When?"

"As soon as I can set it up."

"Okay." She began to walk, and Richard had to catch up.

As they walked in the door, Brady checked her messages; there were none. Richard called his lawyer.

PETITION

Ninety seconds into the call Ryan stood up and interrupted. "Christ, Richard, how's this going to look to a judge?" He ran his hand over his face. "Are you all at home? Seriously, I need to talk to all three of you."

He grabbed his coat and notes and calculated the time he could afford to spend with them and still pick up Stephanie.

Seven minutes later, Ryan knocked on their door and let himself in.

"I need to make this quick," he said to Richard, and then he looked beyond him to Michael, who was in the kitchen starting dinner. "Where's Brady?"

"I'll get her. She's in her room," Richard said.

Ryan crossed his legs and twitched his foot. *Why wasn't Brady already down here?* He turned his attention to Michael. "So you had yourselves an evening."

Michael nodded as he chopped the broccoli and then the cauliflower. "It sounds terrible, but it wasn't. Our friend Tom does some drag cabaret stuff for entertainment, and Brady saw him in costume. That really is all that happened, but because she won't talk to us, we can't help her to understand."

Ryan studied Michael before saying, "Richard said he'd taken his shirt and shoes off."

Michael nodded. "He had."

"He said you had as well."

"Right, yes, that is true," Michael said.

"Why was that if you were just listening to music?" Ryan asked.

Michael swallowed. "Okay, Tom's cabaret character is a fairy godmother who grants wishes, and this particular evening he was granting wishes for Vince."

"Who's Vince?" Ryan asked.

"Tom's boyfriend," Michael said. "His much-younger boyfriend."

Ryan stared at Michael and asked in a lower tone, "So what were Vince's wishes?"

Michael gritted his teeth in a tight smile and tilted his head back. "Vince has a thing for Richard, and he wanted him, you know?"

"No . . . I don't," Ryan said.

"Vince wanted to have sex with Richard. Richard didn't want to," Michael said, touching his forehead.

"So why was *your* shirt off?" Ryan asked. His tone was flat.

"We were doing other—more acceptable—things instead."

"Such as?" Ryan was surprised to find himself titillated and realized he was leaning forward. He swallowed, and it embarrassed him to find his throat was dry.

"Back rubs," Michael said. "I was rubbing Richard's back."

"And Tom and Vince?"

"Tom was singing, and Vince was rubbing my back," Michael said, clearing his throat.

"And then what happened?" Ryan asked.

"And then we heard Brady. Richard had checked, and she was sound asleep, according to him. We thought she'd sleep until morning. She's been sick, you know? But I guess the dogs woke her up because she said something about the dogs having sex. Then Tom was worried that his dog was going to get hurt, and he went running up the stairs. I tried to stop him. If she hadn't seen him, you would not be here right now." Michael pinned Ryan with a scolding look. "She really did not see anything."

Movement drew Ryan's attention to the top of the stairs, where he saw Brady, her arms crossed, jaw set, and eyebrows clenched together. Exhaling noisily, she started down the stairs. Ryan could hear each deliberate step become louder than the next.

Ryan closed his eyes. He didn't have time to deal with adolescent angst tonight. Richard had led the way down and settled in a wingback chair.

Brady stood with her arms still crossed. She did not greet Ryan or even look in his direction.

"Let's go to the backyard." Ryan stood and gestured at the raised wooden planters with tidy rows of green lettuce that were visible through the glass sliders. He walked to the door and opened it. "Come on, you can do this," Ryan said, raising his voice and jerking his head toward the door.

Richard started forward.

"I've got this, Richard," Ryan said. "I need to talk to Brady alone."

Brady walked, keeping her eyes forward, and lowered herself onto the bench, and Ryan joined her. The warmth of the bench seeped through Ryan's jeans, and he settled in more deeply and enjoyed the brilliant pink blossoms that bordered the garden. Unsure of where to begin, he started slowly. "I need to talk to you about what happened at the dinner party."

"Yes, I know," Brady said.

"I'm told you don't want to talk to anyone about this."

"Yep," Brady said, staring straight ahead. "And after this I still don't want to talk to any one about this. Ever."

"I can't promise you that," Ryan said.

Brady stood and walked to the slider. She began to open it.

"If you walk through that door, I will no longer be your lawyer," Ryan said.

Brady stared at him and stood with her hips cocked, as though ready to bolt.

Ryan knew she was calculating how serious he was, and he held her gaze until she lowered her eyes.

"Sit down, Brady. This is important. The law says that there's no problem with placing children in same-sex families as long as sex is not exhibited, seen by the child. I feel that that line may have been crossed in your case. It is important that you be honest with me. Brady, what did you see in the basement?"

And she told him in agonizing detail, which, when repeated in her soft, young voice seemed even more lascivious.

Ryan forced himself not to react even when Brady described the G-string and he could feel his stomach rising. "What made you stop on the stairs?" Ryan asked.

"That's a rule in our house." She cocked her head to one side. "They knock on my door. I knock on theirs. But I also make noise before I enter any room, like if there isn't a door but I feel like they need warning."

"And why is that?" Ryan asked.

"It keeps us from getting embarrassed." Brady shrugged. "Half the time they're just reading the paper, but they still jump away from each other. I don't want to see . . . any of it. And they don't want me to."

"They've said that?" Ryan asked.

Brady nodded. "That's why they told me to knock. Making noise before I come into a room—I figured that out for myself."

A memory flashed into Ryan's mind of walking in on his own parents in the middle of the night and how the experience made him more cautious in the future. Brady's family was no different from his own, and his experience had not been traumatic, just embarrassing. Still, no one dressed in drag at his parents' parties or coupled up. Why, in the middle of a sensitive custody battle, would Richard and Michael take such a gamble? What if these men weren't the cleaned-up, well-meaning gay men who simply wanted to raise this little girl?

He could feel her staring at him. "I don't know, Brady. I'm not sure this is a better home for you than your grandparents."

"I was the one who was there and saw it all. I'm okay with it, so you should be okay too," Brady said.

"Why do you want to stay here?" Ryan asked.

Brady thought before she answered. "I feel like I belong here. I fit in, and I never have before." She pulled her foot up on the bench and rested her cheek on her knee. "I'm happier here. I need to stay here." She stroked the top of her red sneaker and raised her eyes to his.

Ryan wanted to agree with Brady. But what if she had come down five minutes later, or five steps farther? What would she have seen then? Maybe Richard was saying no to Vince in order to be a responsible father, but maybe he had not said no at all. Maybe her voice had been the only thing that stopped them.

Brady and Ryan walked into the house together. Michael stood in the kitchen stirring the sauté pan that sizzled with something savory. Richard looked up from where he was reading. The room was lit by the amber glow of the setting sun.

Ryan's stomach growled, and he looked at his watch. He opened his mouth, unsure of what he was going to say. "I don't know if I'm willing to represent you if I'm not sure that this is the best home for her. I'm sorry, I need to think about it, and I'll call you in the morning." Ryan's hands flopped at his sides as he spoke, so he shoved them into the pockets of his trench coat.

Ryan felt everyone staring at him and wanted it over. He walked to the door and pulled it open. The cool night air blew in, and he stared out into the dark. He tried to will himself through the door but couldn't.

"I can't go," he said without turning, "because if I do, I'll never be back." He turned back to face them, closing the door as he did so.

"I've cared more about you people than any other client. I want you to be a family because I think you'll be good for each other. But this has shaken me." He turned to face Richard and Michael. "I will never forgive myself if something happens to Brady." For just a moment, he turned slightly toward the door again as if to leave. He watched Brady set the table for the dinner as Michael cooked.

He groaned, "Okay, I'll stay on your case, but you have to meet me halfway. No more borderline parties. For any judgment calls, err on the conservative side. And if you two have trouble with each other, get counseling, talk to each other, and never, ever send her out of the house. This is her home, and you are fighting to keep her. Before you act, always think how it will look to a judge."

The stillness in the room was broken by the oven timer. "So would you like to stay for dinner?" Michael asked.

"Oh, shit!" Ryan said. He glanced sheepishly at Brady and covered his mouth. "Sorry, but I really have to leave. I should have been at my parents' ten minutes ago, and I still have to pick Stephanie up." He pulled his phone out of his pocket and rushed to the door, which he struggled to open while juggling his phone and briefcase.

Brady ran up and opened it for him.

"Goodbye, see you later," Ryan said over his shoulder, and he disappeared into the night.

* * *

"Who's Stephanie?" Brady asked as the door slammed behind Ryan.

Richard spread his palms out to show he had no idea. He added, "Whoever she is, she's meeting his parents tonight. Maybe he's going to marry her?"

Brady felt a stab of jealousy because she had a crush on Ryan. And then she thought, maybe she wasn't a lesbian after all.

BACK TO SCHOOL

During the afternoon, Brady had called Fiona again, this time to find out what homework she had missed while she was sick, but Fiona had not called back. Brady couldn't believe that Fiona would be so mean. After all, she had collected all of Fiona's homework when she was sick. Although it embarrassed Brady, she called again after dinner, but when she asked for Fiona, her mom said, "I have to check."

Check to see if Fiona was there? Their house wasn't big enough to not know if someone was there. But Mrs. Sanchez returned with the statement that Fiona was asleep again.

"Oh, it's okay," Brady said, "I'll get the homework from Mrs. Patterson. It's no problem." But it was a problem, and Brady went off to sleep imagining just how she would explain to Fiona that friends don't treat each other like this.

Because Brady had not spoken to Fiona directly, she didn't know if she would meet her at the corner or not. But as Brady reached the corner, she could just see Fiona's retreating figure and recognize her pink plaid backpack bouncing against her teal blue windbreaker.

"Hey, Fiona!" Brady shouted. But Fiona continued away from her, not seeming to hear. Brady shouted more loudly, "Fiona! Fiona! Feeeoohhhnah!" Fiona seemed to speed up. Brady ran faster, reaching the school as Fiona disappeared around the building. Brady kept going, rounding the building as Fiona disappeared around the next corner. Unable to keep running, Brady stopped to catch her breath and resettle her backpack, and then she walked into the classroom.

"Why, hello there!" Mrs. Patterson said. "I missed you. I heard you were in the hospital." Her eyes widened.

"Yes," Brady said, and she told her of the almost-near-death experience with as many dramatic details as she could fit in before taking her seat next to Fiona.

Fiona refused to look at her, and throughout the day, if Brady spoke to her, she ignored her. During free write, Brady wrote letters to Fiona filled with things she would say if Fiona would listen.

Any hopes Brady had that Fiona might have lunch with her were destroyed when Fiona ran out of the classroom so fast Brady couldn't keep up. Brady walked and stood alone in the milk line, where she could see Fiona at the front.

"Missing your lesbian friend?" Allan Mitchell hissed from behind her in line so close that Brady could feel his breath on her cheek.

"What?" Brady asked.

"You heard me. Missing your lesbian friend?" He jabbed his hand in Fiona's direction and kept going. "She was sick, and then you got sick. You caught it from her. You know you did." With this said, he stepped out of line, allowing her to see a group of boys, all pretending to suppress laughter. Zach was in the center and found the comment so hysterical that he pretended to fall to the floor and that had to be helped up by his friends.

Brady locked eyes with him. "You're going to get it because you've already been warned not to say stuff like that to me."

Zach sobered up. "Hey, it wasn't me. It was Allan." And he stared back at her with unblinking hostility that made her lower her eyes.

As if led by a silent signal, the boys disappeared, leaving Brady standing alone. She now understood why Fiona was leaving her out. The boys must have bullied her too. Worst of all, Zach had put into words Brady's worst fear. Was she a lesbian? Did she catch it from her father? Brady turned toward the classroom and saw Mrs. Patterson locking the door. Brady ran toward her and past the group of boys, who had reconvened and generated a wall of laughter as she passed. Brady ran up to Mrs. Patterson, who looked impatient.

"Oh Brady, I would think you would want some time to play after being sick for so long. I need to go and have my own lunch and get some fresh air." She walked past Brady.

Brady looked at the bag lunch in her hand and couldn't remember, didn't care, about the contents. She could see the whole day telescoping out in front of her. She found herself longing to be sick again so that she could avoid being in school where people jeered and her best friend rejected her. If Mrs. Patterson noticed any of this, she didn't seem to care, and that, in Brady's mind, made her as bad as Fiona.

The next day when Brady reached the corner where she used to meet Fiona, she didn't even look for her. She was staring at her shoe tops as she walked when she heard the rattling of Fiona's mom's van. It screeched to a stop and backed up. Fiona's mom motioned for Brady to open the door, but Brady could see Fiona's bowed head from where she sat in the front passenger seat. She stood still, but Fiona's mom motioned again, this time impatiently. Brady opened the van door.

"Climb in." Mrs. Sanchez waved her in.

Brady climbed in and buckled up.

"I was sorry to hear you were sick, Brady," Mrs. Sanchez said.

"Yeah, I wound up in the hospital," Brady said.

"Was it scary?" Fiona's mom asked.

Brady shrugged and stared at her hands in her lap. The three were silent for the rest of the trip.

As they pulled in front of the school, Fiona's mom seemed relieved to have them go.

Freed from the van, Fiona rushed to the classroom well ahead of Brady.

Brady didn't even try to keep up.

When time for recess came, Brady watched to see if Fiona would want to play. But Fiona purposely walked around her desk to get a handball from Mrs. Patterson. *And who is she going to play handball with anyway?* Brady wondered.

Brady walked out and sat against the wall. Fiona was standing in one of the handball courts with a soft blue rubber ball in her hand, occasionally bouncing it against the backboard. She turned and walked toward Brady.

Brady felt her heart speed up, and she wanted to run and hug Fiona. This scared her.

As Fiona came nearer, Brady said, "I thought you didn't like me anymore." "I guess I'm tired of playing by myself," Fiona said. Fiona held out the ball on her flattened palm.

Brady wanted nothing more than to snatch it from her and run to the handball court. But Fiona had been mean. Brady needed to know why before she could be her friend again.

"What did I do to make you leave me out?" Brady asked.

Fiona pulled the ball back. "They say you're a lesbian and you caught the kissing disease from me."

"What? I had strep throat. So did you. What's the kissing disease?" Brady asked.

"Don't you know anything?" Fiona asked. "It's mono," she said, rolling her eyes.

"What's mono?" Brady asked.

"You get it from kissing," Fiona said, shrugging.

"Who do you have to kiss to get the disease?" Brady asked. She knew that she hadn't kissed anyone except her fathers and her dog.

"I don't know. Someone with the disease, I guess. They're saying we got it," Fiona paused, the corners of her mouth drawing down, "from kissing." The two girls stared at each other in horror.

"But we haven't," Brady said.

"I know, but they say we did, and I don't want them to say

that I am gay like they do about you," Fiona said. She shot Brady a guilty glance and then looked away.

"I'm not gay," Brady said, hoping she sounded more sure than she was.

"Well, your dad is," Fiona said.

Fiona's words felt like a series of punches to Brady, and she gasped. Brady had told Fiona that her mother died and that Michael was her dad's roommate. Fiona must have figured it out for herself.

"That doesn't make me gay," Brady said. "My dad said nobody knows what causes people to be gay or straight. People just are what they are."

"I don't know, I look just like my mom, and my mom says it's because I inherited her genes. So couldn't you be just like your dad?" Fiona asked.

"No," Brady said.

"Why not?" Fiona asked.

Brady didn't know, so she lashed out. "Why do you want to play with me then? Aren't you afraid they'll call you a lesbian?" Brady said, digging the heels of her sneakers into the blacktop and pushing her back against the wall.

Fiona lowered her gaze, wagged her head, and shrugged. "I know you're not," she said.

Brady stood as her voice rose. "Yeah, and you knew we didn't have mono either, but you didn't say anything." She crossed her arms and turned her back on Fiona. "Why didn't you say anything? Why did you leave me out? That made stupid Zach think he was right." Brady could feel herself starting to cry. She stopped talking.

"Look, I'm sorry. I'm tired of being alone too," Fiona said.

"I don't know," Brady said, looking away.

"You can sit there and be sad and mad, or you can just come and play with me," Fiona said, looking at Brady sideways. Fiona's hands were jammed in her jeans pockets, the ball barely held by three fingers of one hand.

It occurred to Brady that Fiona had just been protecting herself. "Let's go, they're going to ring the bell soon," Brady said, snatching the ball from Fiona.

Fiona smiled and raced Brady to the court, where they were able to play a satisfying five minutes.

And then the boys came back. Allan was in the lead with a dodge ball, which didn't belong on the handball court. And Zach was right behind him. They didn't say anything to the girls. They took over the court, throwing the large ball at each other and making it impossible for the girls to play. Allan, in an effort to dodge the ball, backed right into Fiona, knocking her to the ground.

"Oh, I'm sorry, did I hurt you?" Allan's voice sounded concerned, but his face carried another message and he finished with, "Am I ruining your little lesbian game with your little lesbian friend?"

Fiona got up and, staring at the tarmac, muttered, "No, I'm okay," as she moved off to the side of the court.

Brady looked at the boys. They seemed so big and mean, and she felt her stomach quiver. She looked to Fiona for support, but Fiona was sitting in the shade against the wall.

Brady watched the boys bouncing the dodge balls wildly back and forth between the two courts. Brady joined Fiona on the ground in the shade, but her chest felt tight, and she squeezed the little blue ball over and over as though it were the cause of her problem. This wasn't fair. When Fiona was given the handball, she was given the court. That was the school rule. Those boys shouldn't be allowed to just take whatever they want and make nice people step out of the way. Why didn't Fiona stand up for herself?

Brady stood up with one fist crushing the ball and the other holding tightly to the bottom of her sweatshirt. Her heart was booming in her chest, and she ground her teeth. Images flashed through her mind: the jeering boys, Fiona leaving her out, Casey's sidelong smirks, the notes in her math book, her feet kicking against the car window. She began to run. Zach was two courts away from her, and as she pushed herself forward, she went even faster.

When Brady was a foot from Zach, Tyler yelled, "Hey, what's she doing?" Zach turned, no longer smiling, but at that point Brady was in the air, her weight hitting his body in the chest and sending both of them crashing to the ground. He looked up at her startled and afraid. Pulling her arm back and swinging with all her might, she hit his face so hard that the back of his head smashed against the blacktop. Her knuckles scraped against his teeth, and she looked down and realized her jeans were torn at the knees and blood was soaking into the denim.

Rolling off of Zach, Brady sat up gasping and pointed at him with her bloody index finger. "You do not get to take whatever you want from other people. You can't make fun of me anymore because I don't care what you say. You're just a stupid bully. I'm not afraid of you. So get away from me."

Zach was struggling to stand, but she shoved him in the chest and knocked him back down.

Standing over him she ranted, "Leave me and Fiona alone. We didn't do anything to you, so leave us alone."

"What is going on here?" asked Mrs. Simpson, the noon aide.

"I don't know," Zach said, eyes tearing up. "We were just playing, and she jumped me."

"That is not true!" Brady said, shoving him in the chest with both hands.

Mrs. Simpson grabbed her arm and pulled her back. "Well, you're both coming with me now."

SOLOMON

B rady was eager to tell the truth to Principal Collins, who looked liked a short, energetic version of Groucho Marx, a funny guy her grandfather liked to watch in old movies. She pointed at Zach. "He's been spreading rumors that Fiona and I caught mono from each other. He said we were lesbians and we caught it by kissing." She drew her hand back and covered her mouth. Afraid to look at Zach any longer, she turned to Mr. Collins and said, "Ask Fiona. She knows. She stopped being friends with me because she was embarrassed too."

He called Fiona in and asked if this were true.

Fiona nodded. "Brady stood up for me out there. The boys were breaking the rules. I was letting them because I was afraid," Fiona said, lowering her eyes.

Seeing Fiona look so sad made Brady's heart ache, and she reached for her friend's hand. Zach shifted next to her, and she pulled back.

She heard Zach's dad shouting as he walked though the office door.

Mr. Collins sent Fiona back to class and sent Brady out to the hall. He stood in front of her as he waved Zach's dad into his office.

Brady could hear Zach's dad shouting at his own son while she sat smiling at the tops of her shoes. She wondered if the police should be called. Mr. Webster sounded like he was going to beat up someone.

When her dad came in, he couldn't have been more apologetic, and Brady hated him for it.

"I cannot believe that you are talking about my daughter, Brady Lawson. You must have the wrong kid," her dad said to the school secretary.

"How do you think she scraped her knuckles?" Mrs. Bretzen asked, pointing at Brady.

Brady held up her scraped hand but ducked her head because she couldn't keep herself from smiling.

Dad examined Brady's hands, and his jaw loosened. "Brady, what happened?"

Brady began to retell her story, and having Zach and Allan there increased her satisfaction. She could feel Dad tense next to her when she described Zach calling her a lesbian.

Mr. Collins asked, "Did you tell Mrs. Patterson?"

Brady nodded.

Mr. Collins called Mrs. Patterson to his office, and she said that she had warned Zach that he would be suspended if he kept harassing Brady.

Everyone looked at Zach, who shrugged. "I did stop. I can't help it if other kids do it."

"You told us what to do and what to say, Zach," Allan said. "I didn't know what a lesbian was until he told me," he said, appealing to the principal.

"I want to let Mrs. Patterson go. Unless there is anything else you would like to say?" Mr. Collins said to Mrs. Patterson.

Mrs. Patterson nodded and turned to Brady. "It made me sad that you did not tell me that the harassment had started again. I can't help you if you don't tell me something's wrong."

Brady felt her stomach tighten and clenched her teeth. "I'm sorry," she said, flicking her eyes back to Mr. Collins and thinking, *Mrs. Patterson should have known.*

When all witnesses, bystanders, and persons of interest had left the scene, Mr. Collins shut the door first with Zach and his dad. When Zach left, he was crying and his dad's face was red. Zach handed Brady a letter of apology, which she read.

The letter said, "I'm sorry I told other kids to make fun of you and call you names. I'm sorry I did it myself. I know it made you feel bad. I think you're smart."

As Brady read most of the letter, she thought, *That's just Zach saying, "I'm sorry I got caught,"* but the last words got her. Did Zach really mean that he thought she was smart? Did other kids think so too? Thinking about this made her smile and squirm in her seat.

Mr. Collins called her and her father to his office.

"We understand that Zach and his friends were harassing you, but the solution is to go for help and not to hit others," Mr. Collins said.

"She did go for help," Richard said, eyes narrowing.

Brady lowered her head.

"Yes, but she needs to go to an adult every time. It is never okay to hit another person. We have a no-tolerance policy on fighting," Mr. Collins said. "The whole school is aware of and talking about your daughter's fight. What do you think they will learn if she gets away with no consequences?"

Dad stood up. "What are you saying? What consequences?"

Mr. Collins held up his hands and said, "First, understand that Zach is being suspended for a week, and Allan for three days. If anything like this happens again, Zach will be expelled and not allowed to come back to our district."

Dad nodded and stared unblinking at Mr. Collins.

Mr. Collins took a deep breath and exhaled loudly. "Because Brady chose to hit Zach rather than go for help, I have to suspend her for one day."

"No, no you don't. This was self-defense," Dad said.

Mr. Collins looked at Richard with raised eyebrows and an open mouth. "You understand that your daughter ran across two handball courts before jumping into the air and landing on Zach?"

Dad nodded.

"You know that she landed on top of him, making both of them fall to the ground?"

Dad nodded more vigorously.

The principal shifted slightly in his seat before adding, "You also understand that while your daughter was on top of Zach, she balled up her fist and slugged him in the face—twice?"

Dad's eyes were bright but unfocused as he leaned toward Mr. Collins.

"And how do you see that as self-defense?" Mr. Collins squinted one eye in concentration.

"It was self-defense because the boy had been systematically teasing Brady and recruiting others to join in the harassment specifically because they felt she might be gay. If one of your students called a child a nigger, spic, dego, or kike, you would consider it racism, right?"

Mr. Collins grimaced at the words before answering, "Of course."

"They substituted *lesbian* for *nigger*, but the damage is the same. Repeated name-calling of a vulnerable student for being gay, whether or not it is true, is not that different from racism."

Mr. Collins nodded. "But even in cases like those, students are suspended for fighting. We want students to go for help and never fight. That's what Zero Tolerance means. We don't want a school where kids throw punches without consequences. Kids can't learn if they're not safe."

Dad sat back in his chair. "Okay, one day. But unless you want a very expensive lawsuit, you need to get a muzzle on that Zach kid."

"Absolutely. It won't happen again," Mr. Collins said and stood up.

Dad and Brady gave Fiona a ride home, and they stopped for hamburgers at Tomboy's Famous Chili Burgers on Manhattan Beach Boulevard, where Brady and Fiona had cheeseburgers with ketchup and no lettuce and both French fries and onion rings. The two of them giggled over jokes only they understood, which made them even happier. And Dad, despite the fact that the principal had said not to, began to call Brady "Slugger."

PRAYERS AND EPIPHANIES

The night before the hearing, Richard awakened raw with fear. Unable to get back to sleep, he stared around the unfamiliar room illuminated by the face of the clock radio. What if they lost Brady to the grandparents? Richard imagined them returning without her. He pictured her room without her in it. It was a definite possibility.

He heard a knock at the door that got louder quickly. "What is it?" he asked.

"I can't sleep," Brady said through the door.

Richard threw back the covers and opened the door.

"Sorry," she said, clutching one hand with the other.

"Okay," he whispered to avoid waking Michael, and he motioned for her to go back to her room as he followed her.

She climbed in under the covers, and he slid in behind her, pulling her close to him, wrapping his arms around her. He could feel her heart beating.

"I'm worried," Brady said.

He was scared too and prayed to find the right words to comfort her. "Me too, but look how far we've come. Three months ago you thought I was dead, and I didn't know anything about you. Now we're a family with Michael, and no one can take that away from us."

She didn't say anything for several minutes, and Richard thought she might have fallen asleep. But he heard her gasp and then sob.

"I'm sorry," he said, stroking her hair. "I know it's scary because it's so uncertain. And it could be that you will move back with your grandparents, but you will still come and see us and be in our lives. We will always be a family no matter whether we're together or not."

Brady sat up and turned toward him, rubbing tears from her cheeks and sniffing.

"Will I have to go back to Valley Christian?"

"Brady, we filed a complaint against that school. There is no way your grandparents, the judge, or anyone is going to ask you to go back there even if you do go back to Oregon. I've heard Ryan say it, and I've said it. We just have to be prepared for whatever decision the judge makes. And you now your job is to sleep. Tomorrow is big, and you want to be rested."

"If I go, who will take care of Cyrano?"

"I will, or maybe we'll send him with you," Richard said.

"Grandma doesn't like dogs," Brady said.

"Brady, I know this is hard, but we can't decide all of it tonight. You're going to have to have faith. We could pray," Richard said.

Brady nodded.

Richard began, "Dear God, please be with us tonight so we can get some rest and again tomorrow so that we say what needs to be said to make people understand that our family needs to stay just the way that it is. Please give us strength and courage to get through tomorrow. Help us to let go and trust you to take care of us and to help us through this situation."

Brady jumped in with great passion. "And please bless Mr. Stephens with the right words for the judge. And please make Grandfather understand that everything is good here and he doesn't need to worry about me anymore."

Richard realized Brady was staring at him. "You and I need to work together to let your grandfather relax and let go of your mother. He feels like he did a bad job raising her, and he's worried that he's letting it happen again. He's not trying to keep you away from me. He's trying to protect you by hanging onto you."

Brady leaned forward, kissed her father good night, and lowered her head to the pillow. She rolled to her side and, tucking her hand under her chin, went off to sleep.

Richard stared at her enviously before kissing her on the forehead and returning to his bed.

THE HEARING

Brady pulled on shoes and the red dress that had been chosen by Michael because it was "power red" and would earn her respect. Her hair, which had started to regain a little curl, framed her face nicely with just a little brushing and was held in place by a shiny black headband. The two men dressed carefully and conservatively, as though coloring within the lines, and wore dark suits. Brady and Richard seemed to be in a race to get out of the door. Michael, who was accustomed to being the taskmaster, was almost left in their wake.

When they got to the courthouse, they went through a routine similar to boarding a plane: passing through metal detectors and finding the door, instead of a gate, that led to their hearing. And then they waited. Brady tried to read but had trouble concentrating. Richard and Michael sat next to her with *The New York Times*.

Gradually the cast of characters arrived, some familiar to Brady, some new, and she was pleased to see Ryan, who walked right up to her, pulled her face to his, and said, "Break a leg, sweetheart!"

"Hi, Grandma, hi, Grandpa," she called, and she ran to her grandparents. The familiar smell of her grandmother's soap made

Brady feel homesick. Brady recognized Grandpa's suit that he wore for church, but Grandma had on a navy blue skirt and a white gauzy blouse under her London Fog raincoat. Brady knew Grandma hated to wear panty hose, but she had them on along with navy blue pumps.

"You look beautiful, Grandma," Brady said.

Brady watched Grandma smile and blush in a way she had never seen before. As Brady felt her grandmother's cheek against hers, she grabbed hold and sank her face into her shoulder. But when she saw her grandfather standing off to the side like a shy kid, Brady teared up. He was in a raincoat too. She had been so busy caring about her dog, her dad, and herself that she had not thought about what this was like for her grandparents.

Brady walked over and took her grandfather's hand, staring up at him while he bent and kissed her forehead. He stroked her cheek, and she wanted to tell him—tell them both—that she was okay, well loved, that she had a dog and a friend and loved her new school. There was so much she wanted to say that it all bottled and stopped in her throat. She was happy without them. She was happier.

"What a very lovely dress, Brady," her grandmother said, stroking her sleeve. Brady nodded, unable to speak. Her grandmother noticed Brady's tears and handed her a tissue from her handbag, and pulling her close, she said, "It's going to be fine."

Brady wondered if it was going to be fine. With so many people wanting different things, not everyone was going to get what they wanted.

Looking through the door, Brady saw Judge Robinson, a tiny woman with bright red lipstick and dimples that showed when she laughed. Ryan told them it was good that they got Judge Robinson because she put kids in families with their biological parents more than other judges.

Brady tried to find comfort by reminding herself they had a plan if the action in the courtroom became too much for her. She could lift her left hand, and either Richard or Michael would take her out of the courtroom. Ryan had practiced the worst questions with her. He would question her about one thing and then lean in and say, "Does it bother you that your father sleeps with a man?" And she was to say, "Are you asking about Michael? He is my father too, and he takes good care of me."

They were called to order by the clerk, and everyone sat down. Ryan walked to the front of the court in a black suit that made him look like a model and began, "Your Honor, I am representing Richard Lawson, who is filing for custody of his daughter, Brady Lawson, because he is ready to be a parent." And he described how happy Brady had been at school and that they had a good routine that kept her fed and helped her get her homework done.

Then he talked about how kids were mean at Valley Christian and that it made her grades go down. And that she had to call her dad in California to get help for problems in Oregon. He was saying Brady didn't trust Grandma and Grandpa. That wasn't true. She lowered her head and hunched her shoulders. She pictured her grandpa as he had looked earlier, lonely and left out. She covered her ears. Ryan finished with something about her never being able to grow up at her grandparents and be successful. She couldn't stand to look at them. She wished she could tell them it wasn't like that. It wasn't their fault.

Ryan continued, saying that she had been bullied in California but because she was able to talk to Dad and Michael, they actually helped, and the bullies were stopped. Brady felt movement next to her and saw Richard smile at Michael over her head.

Ryan's voice got deeper. "Although we are not asking for joint custody, in her father's house she will be encouraged to visit and be visited by her grandparents, but she will also benefit from a relationship with her father and freedom from harassment. The law is set up to protect the needs of the child, but we believe that with close inspection, you will realize that everybody's needs are fulfilled by granting custody to Brady's father but encouraging scheduled visits with the grandparents. Thank you." Ryan sat down.

Mr. Cory, her grandparents' lawyer, stood up. He looked like Abraham Lincoln, tall and thin. His hair was black and slicked back, and he wore a black suit. His voice was gravelly deep, his movements smooth as a dancer's, and he punctuated his speech with a sweep of his arms.

Mr. Cory talked about how Grandma and Grandpa had been Brady's parents since Mom died in the car accident. They tried to find Dad but couldn't. They paid for everything, including piano and dancing. (Both of which she hated.) They went to her recitals, which Grandpa hated, although he never said so. She found his playbill once, and he had ticked each kid's name off as they performed. She asked him about it, and he said it seemed to make it go faster. Mr. Cory got louder when he pointed out that they paid for Valley Christian, a *private* school.

Dad muttered under his breath, "And didn't that turn out to be a good investment?"

Mr. Cory went on to say that Richard had given up his right to be Brady's dad because he let her grandparents raise her. And he tried to stop them from having her by not putting her on the plane that time in California. Mr. Cory said he "refused to send her back to Oregon on the mutually agreed-upon flight." He made it sound like Dad did it on purpose. Brady remembered how wonderful it felt to know she didn't have to go back to Casey and the rest of the kids at school. That she could stay with Dad and be happy. Mr. Cory was making everything sound so bad.

She looked at Dad, who shrugged and whispered, "Would we have been better parents to send you back for more torture?" Brady turned back to Mr. Cory, feeling worse.

Mr. Cory continued, "The law says that the parent working in the best needs of the child will support her 'physical, emotional, and *religious needs*.' Brady's religious needs make placement with her father inappropriate. Brady's Christian faith is very important to her, and the two men, Richard Lawson and Michael Elson, maintain a homosexual relationship, which is considered a sin in the religion Brady observes. The conflict between her beliefs and her life would cause a crisis of faith and lead to detrimental consequences for her, including but not limited to confusion, depression, and self-destructive behavior. We ask that the court truly consider the best interests of this particular child before placing her in a home that is hostile to her faith, which is integral to her upbringing." Mr. Cory sat down.

Above her, Brady heard Dad exhale loudly, but she did not look at him. Her scalp prickled. They were saying she couldn't stay with Dad and Michael because she was Christian. She shook her head and whispered, "No."

Dad was called to the stand and sworn in. He talked about Mrs. Patterson and how well Brady did in school even though she had started late in the year. He told the judge about how Brady had Fiona as a friend, and how he and Michael had done homework with Brady every night, and how they had packed her lunches, and read aloud with her, and had gotten her to school on time. It all sounded so good that she felt homesick.

Ryan's voice became soft, and he leaned in to talk to Dad. He asked Richard about being homeless and winding up in the emergency room. Her dad looked down as he told of having his stomach pumped and being strapped down because he was fighting the doctors. This was new to Brady and caused her to duck her head and squeeze her hands together. His voice was hard to hear. But then Ryan guided Dad into getting better and wanting to reunite with her.

Ryan sat down, and Mr. Cory approached Richard. "How many times have you been to the hospital for alcohol-related problems—not just the emergency room?"

Brady lowered her chin to her chest.

Dad was silent.

Mr. Cory asked, "Hard to remember?"

Brady raised her head.

Dad shrugged.

"You need to speak, Mr. Lawson," Judge Robinson said.

"I remember being in the hospital two or three times." He grimaced. "I think."

Mr. Cory raised his index finger straight up as he consulted a paper. "Twice that, Mr. Lawson. Six times you were hospitalized. The last one was just over three years ago."

Brady leaned her head forward, allowing her hair to cover her hands and fingers, which were poked deeply in her ears. She didn't like to think about Dad the way he was before her and before Michael.

Mr. Cory turned to Judge Robinson. "So we have a pattern of alcohol abuse for at least seven years that was so destructive it required hospitalization." Here, he paused and turned back to Richard. "When would you say you had your first drink, Mr. Lawson?"

Mr. Cory stood over Dad as he waited for the answer.

Brady moaned softly, but with her ears plugged it echoed in her head.

Mr. Cory shuffled his feet impatiently. "I can tell you that you were arrested for public intoxication when you were fourteen. Does that help?" He flicked a look at Richard but continued, his speech picking up speed. "So where does that put us now, let's, see at about twenty-three years of drinking, Mr. Lawson. And we're supposed to be bowled over by the changed man you have become in the past three years? And you want Brady, who has been doing beautifully at her grandparents, a straight-A student at a well-respected college prep school, to be placed in your home. All based on three short years of sobriety?" Mr. Cory stood back so the room could see him, holding his palms out, his head cocked to one side and his mouthed agape.

Brady looked down at her hands so tightly gripped on one another they seemed to be one fist. "It is not like that," she whispered, and she forced herself to look at her father, whose face was growing redder and whose mouth was open. She could hear him breathing heavily.

He opened his mouth to speak, but Mr. Cory cut him off.

"In addition to that, you already forfeited your natural parent status when you were out of contact and sent almost no money for ten years. This includes the medical expenses for the birth, which were paid by Mr. and Mrs. Nordland. We are all here to do what is in the best interests of the child, and I am wondering, why do you still think being placed in your home is in her best interests, Mr. Lawson?"

"Yes, because it's different now," Dad said.

"How is it different now, Mr. Lawson?"

"I am different now. I am sober and in a strong relationship with another sober man."

Mr. Cory interrupted and pointed to Michael. "The strong relationship would be with Michael Elson?"

"Yes." Dad looked at Michael and swallowed hard.

Michael nodded back. "You're okay," he mouthed to Richard.

"What do you do for a living, Mr. Lawson?"

"I write."

"What have you published?"

"Several short stories and some book reviews."

"How much does that pay?"

"Not that much, but it's getting better." Richard squirmed in his seat.

"How much annually, would you estimate?"

"$2,000."

"Annually, or a piece, Mr. Lawson?"

Richard ducked his head and said, "Annually, for now."

"So, let's just say that you and Mr. Elson were no longer an item. What would you do to support your daughter, since $2,000 a year won't make it?"

Brady's head was so far down it brushed her legs. This was awful, and they'd just started.

Ryan stood and said, "Objection, Mr. Cory is using a hypothetical situation. Is his salary hurting Brady now?"

Judge Robinson nodded before she said, "Sustained."

Mr. Cory turned to Ryan and sneered, "But that's just it. They are not married right now. If they break up—" Mr. Cory leaned toward the judge— "and statistics say they will, Mr. Elson has no obligation to support Mr. Lawson's child. I know these little details are unpleasant, but someone needs to think them through."

Ryan stood up, saying, "Another hypothetical situation, Mr. Cory?"

Judge Robinson rose in her seat. "Do you have an objection, Mr. Stephens? Do not argue with each other in my courtroom," she said, tapping a pencil on the pages in front of her.

Ryan put his hand over his mouth. "Forgive me, Your Honor. But Mr. Lawson and Mr. Elson were registered as domestic partners in April—something Mr. Cory is well aware of. Mr. Elson plans to adopt Brady, in which case he will be legally bound to support her whether they break up or not."

Judge Robinson nodded and started to speak.

Mr. Cory interrupted, "A future adoption isn't hypothetical?" He held his hands out to sides.

Ryan rounded to face him. "The plans are in place, court dates are set, paperwork filled out. It is different from a breakup you're making up."

"Stop and approach the bench." Judge Robinson was now standing, but even so, Brady could only see down to her chest.

Brady couldn't hear, but she could see Judge Robinson's face. She looked like a mad teacher.

"I get it, I'm truly sorry," Ryan said, resting his hand on his chest.

Mr. Cory nodded, put his palms together, and bowed his head.

"The next outburst from either of you will earn you a $2,000 fine for contempt of court." Judge Robinson waved them away with her robed arm.

"Mr. Cory, you may begin again." Judge Robinson settled hard against the back of her chair, arms tightly folded over her chest. Her mouth was a straight line.

Mr. Cory began, "Placing Brady in her father's home may feel good, but it is definitely *not* in her best interests."

Brady looked up and wondered how Mr. Cory knew what was in her best interests. He had never talked to her.

"Prior to March of this year, how often did you see your daughter?" Mr. Cory asked.

"Never."

"Were you there when she was born?"

"No."

Brady wrapped her arms tightly around her stomach and stared at the tops of her shoes. She wanted to leave but did not want to draw attention to herself.

"Were you with your wife during her pregnancy?"

"I was there for most of it."

"And then what happened?"

"I found it necessary to leave."

"You found it *necessary* to leave?" Mr. Cory's mouth opened.

What did that mean? Brady looked at Michael with a furrowed brow.

He looked at her, sighed, and patted her leg.

Brady turned away from Michael, her lips pressed together like a clenched fist.

"Yes," Dad answered.

"Why was that, Mr. Lawson?"

"I wanted to be responsible for my child by marrying her mother. I found that I couldn't do it."

"Why not?"

Dad stared at Mr. Corey. "The day-to-day tension of pretending to be straight—I just couldn't do it after a while." Dad's voice shook.

"I see; that *would* be difficult. So you came out to your wife and divorced and paid child support ever since. Right, Mr. Lawson?"

Brady didn't understand what Mr. Cory was saying, but she hated the way he was saying it. It sounded like the bullies at school.

"No, I just took off," Dad said.

"Took off?" Mr. Cory asked, angling sideways so everyone in the room could see that his head was cocked and brows were furrowed.

Brady drove her nails into her upper arms and forced herself to look at Dad. He looked ashamed, and she wanted to disappear. She didn't want to hear this part of the story, when her Dad didn't want her.

"Yes, I abandoned my wife and unborn child." He sped up. "I drank myself into a stupor every night because of it. I'm ashamed of it, and I cannot—will not—defend it. I'm sorry for my behavior, but I am different now, and I am a good parent to Brady. I love her. Michael and I are very secure."

Brady watched Dad look at Michael, who nodded back.

"We both love her very much." Dad moved his gaze to Brady and cleared his throat.

Brady swallowed hard and blinked back tears but did not look down.

"Well that's very stirring. And all of that is based on how much time?" Mr. Cory asked.

Michael growled under his breath, but Brady heard it.

"She's lived with us for three months. A lot can and has happened in three months."

"Yes, it can, can't it, Mr. Lawson? But still, three months in comparison to ten years of life?" Mr. Cory cocked his head as he gazed at Richard for an uncomfortably long time. "Did you know that your wife had died during that period?" Mr. Cory asked, rushing the words together.

Brady saw Dad begin to roll his eyes and stop. Ryan had told them not to.

"Yes, the Nordlands sent me a letter saying that she had died and that they were taking care of Brady." Dad gestured at Frank and Kathleen.

"Did you call or write back?"

"No."

"Why not?"

"I didn't think they wanted to hear from me."

"It never occurred to you that your daughter was basically an orphan and the one parent who had cared for her all of her life was suddenly dead, and that she might benefit from being with her father?"

"I wasn't in a position to help anyone."

"And why was that?"

"I was drinking too much."

"Alcohol?"

Ryan interrupted. "Your Honor, I object to Mr. Cory's belaboring the point. The court knows Mr. Lawson was an alcoholic. Let's move on."

"Yes, Mr. Cory, I remind you to stick to present damages, please," Judge Robinson said.

Mr. Cory pursed his lips and tipped his head to the side. "Did you send any money, Mr. Lawson?"

"Two checks, for a total of $880."

"Really? In ten years?"

"Your Honor, Mr. Cory already established Mr. Lawson's income at $2,000. Why are we beating this dead horse?"

Mr. Cory walked to the judge's bench and put a file in front of her. "Here are receipts showing a pattern of how much money was spent by the grandparents to raise Brady." He turned and showed the receipts to Richard. "You'll notice it totals over $70,000. That's what being a parent costs, Mr. Lawson, and that is what my clients are asking that you pay for their part in raising your daughter."

Brady hunched in a tight ball and longed to disappear. She was expensive.

"How soon after your wife's death did you hear that she had died?"

"Years after, two, I think."

"Why did it take so long?"

"I was out of contact." Brady shot a look at Dad. His eyes made him look dead inside.

"Right, because you were a homeless alcoholic?"

Brady lowered her head so fast she felt Michael look at her.

Ryan rose. "Objection, Your Honor, the court knows my client was homeless. You aren't establishing anything. You're trying to break him, and you're wasting our time."

Judge Robinson nodded and said, "You have made your point, both of you. Do move on and show some sensitivity for all of the people in the room."

Brady wanted to raise her left hand and ask to go out with Michael, but she didn't want Richard to be alone. She leaned so close to her knees she could kiss them and drove her nails even deeper into her arms. The pain distracted her.

"I am trying to demonstrate that Mr. Lawson was unable to provide for Brady for all but three months, *three months*, of her life. I know it's painful, but it is our job to expose these realities"— Cory directed these words at Ryan—"so that when this case is over, Brady will not be alone when her father relapses."

Relapse? Brady had learned the word after going to an AA meeting with Dad. He said he would never drink again. He never wanted to go back to the way he was. Mr. Cory made it sound like it was definitely going to happen. Brady's stomach tightened, and she knew she was afraid.

Ryan stood up. "Your Honor, it is a hypothetical situation as to whether or not Mr. Lawson relapses."

"Sustained," Judge Robinson nodded, allowing him to continue.

"Mr. Lawson is sober, is in a strong, long-term relationship, and is very much involved in parenting Brady. Now is what matters."

"Stick to present concerns, Mr. Cory, without exception," Judge Robinson said.

Mr. Cory sighed and nodded. "Your Honor, I will comply, but I do still argue that Mr. Lawson gave up his right to parent when he knew for at least two years that Brady's mother was dead and that her grandparents were raising her and he still allowed it to continue." Cory flourished his arms like he was posing for a picture and sat down.

Ryan spoke directly to the judge. "Your Honor, in order for Mr. Lawson to give his right to parent Brady to the Nordland's, he had to actually agree to it. He was truly out of contact, so he could not have agreed to it. Giving no answer to a question that was never asked does not mean he was saying, 'I don't want to parent my daughter; you do it.' But now he is spending his money to travel here so that he can become a legal parent to his child and have her in his life and raise her. That is all that matters."

"Did your client attempt to contact Mr. Lawson?" Judge Robinson asked Mr. Cory.

"They absolutely did, your Honor." Mr. Cory squared his shoulders as he answered. "They wrote to the rehab center from which his first letter had come. This was the response." Mr. Cory read from a paper. "Privacy laws prohibit us from either confirming or denying the presence of any person at our facility." Mr. Cory lowered the paper and stepped toward Judge Robinson. "My clients even went beyond this and ran ads in both the *Los Angeles Times* and *The Oregonian*.. They did all of these good faith efforts in the slim hope that Mr. Lawson, in his addled, homeless state would get a newspaper and read it. Above and beyond expectations, I think you'll agree." Mr Cory raised his eyebrows and tilted his head toward Judge Robinson.

The judge pursed her lips, but nodded.

"Did they attempt to find Mr. Lawson, after there was no response to the ad?"

Mr. Cory's mouth was open, and his arms were extended with palms open. "Their daughter was dead. And in their grief, the grandparents wanted to do the right thing for their granddaughter. The father had been gone since two months *before* Brady was born. They never expected to see him again. They felt he was dead."

Judge Robinson leaned forward. "Nonetheless, Mr. Cory, here he is, ready to raise his daughter. Your clients needed to have moved to end his rights when they took it upon themselves to raise her as their child. No, Mr. Lawson's parental presumption stands."

Ryan looked over his shoulder at the three of them and squeezed his hands into a contained fist pump.

"What's all this mean?" Brady asked Michael.

"It means the judge believes your dad is doing what is right by you just because he is your dad," Michael said.

Mr. Cory dropped into his chair, shaking his head, and began writing furiously.

"Mr. Cory, you may call your witness," Judge Robinson said.

Mr. Cory nodded, stood, and said, "I'd like to call Frank Nordland to the stand."

Brady watched Grandpa walk forward, his hands pulling the tabs on his suit jacket pockets. Frank had told her long ago that when he was a boy, he had been taught never to put his hands in his pockets, so he settled for this halfway measure instead.

Mr. Cory pivoted and addressed Frank. "Mr. Stephens is going to say that Brady was bullied at Valley Christian so badly she couldn't return from California. Where will she go to school when she returns to Oregon?" Mr. Cory asked Frank.

"We've found a neighborhood school for the time being until we can find one more to our liking."

Brady's stomach tightened, and she watched Judge Robinson raise her head to look at Frank.

"More to your liking?" Mr. Cory asked.

"We like Christian schools, where God and morality are included in the curriculum."

"Aren't you worried that the problems with harassment due to having a gay father might continue in another Christian school?" Mr. Cory asked.

"No, that was a problem that was created by her father, and it will go away when the kids aren't so aware of the situation. I will see that it goes away if she lives with me."

Judge Robinson said, "Her father will still be gay whether she lives with you or not."

"Okay?" Frank shrugged.

"How will you make the teasing go away, Mr. Nordland?" Judge Robinson asked.

"I'll post a guard if I need to. I think the problem will go away when she leaves her father's house," Frank said.

Brady sat up straight and shook her head.

Mr. Cory said to Judge Robinson, "We have reason to believe that the teasing was not as extreme as it was made to seem. We feel instead that it was inflamed by the father through email in order to make a better case for himself and get Brady moved to his house in California."

Judge Robinson stared at Mr. Cory for several seconds before making a note.

"What's all that mean?" Brady asked Michael in a whisper.

"They're saying you and your dad sort of made up, or made worse, the harassment at Valley Christian so he could get custody of you," Michael said.

"I did not make it up," Brady said to Michael loudly enough to make Judge Robinson turn to look at her along with Frank and Mr. Cory.

Michael shushed her.

Frank raised his eyebrows and looked over her head at Kathleen.

Brady had pulled her legs under her body to see better, and now she pulled them out from under her. The chair rattled as her bottom hit the seat.

"Brady," Judge Robinson said, "If Mr. Stephens would like to talk to me about your speaking, he may, but you have to be sworn in as a witness."

Brady wrapped her arms tightly around her body and lowered her chin to her chest as her face grew hot.

"Your witness," Mr. Cory said.

Ryan said, "Mr. Cory is trying to show that your son-in-law did two things: chose not to parent Brady and encouraged you and your wife to be Brady's parents. Do you think this is true?"

"Yes, I do," Grandpa said.

"Does that seem fair to Richard?" Ryan asked, looking up from the papers and cocking his head to the side. "I mean, he left before the baby was born."

"He knew he had a baby coming, and he took off. That's choosing not to parent. Richard knew we had Brady, and he didn't come and get her. That's allowing us to parent her. Yeah, it seems fair to me."

"Richard Lawson knew you and Kathleen had Brady?"

"Not at first, but after a while, yes."

"How did he find out?"

"He wrote to us when she was about seven. He was writing a letter as an exercise in some rehab program and sent it," Grandpa said.

"How long had Brady been in your custody at the time that Richard wrote to you?" Ryan asked.

"Two years."

"At the time of your daughter's death, why didn't you try to find Mr. Lawson?"

Frank cleared his throat and straightened in his seat. "We posted ads in papers California and Oregon. When he didn't answer, we thought he was dead."

"Why is it that you and your wife never adopted your granddaughter?" Ryan asked.

Frank swallowed and cleared his throat. "I guess it didn't seem necessary. Richard was gone and nowhere to be found, it cost a lot of money to adopt, and life just moved on. It didn't seem like he was going to show up. She was our daughter and in our house. Adoption looked unnecessary and expensive. Things seemed fine without it."

"You brought up expenses. Did it occur to you that you could get child support from Richard?" Ryan asked.

"It has now, and we've sued for it."

"But back then?"

Frank stared at Ryan and blinked repeatedly. "Richard was a hopeless drunk. Didn't seem likely that he'd have any money. And we couldn't find him even if he did."

"How'd you know he was a hopeless drunk?" Ryan asked.

"He was in and out of rehab." Mr. Nordland shrugged.

"But you didn't know that until Brady was seven. Two years *after* you decided not to adopt, you heard from Richard and found out he was in rehab, right?"

"Correct," Mr. Nordland said.

"In California, right?"

Mr. Nordland hesitated, "Yes, one was in California."

"Wouldn't that have been a place to start? Where did you start?"

Frank's head was bowed and his eyes distant. "We ran ads. I've told you. He didn't answer."

"I'm just thinking: some families hire private investigators to find missing fathers so they can avoid what we're going through right now. Did you ever think of doing that, Mr. Nordland?" Ryan asked, skewering Frank with his gaze.

Frank stared straight ahead at nothing and started to speak several times but stopped and started over.

Judge Robinson furrowed her brow and leaned toward Frank.

Frank moved his hands in small gestures as if to coax words from his mouth. "I did hire a private investigator," he said, clearing his throat.

Mr. Cory jumped to his feet, hand extended as though hailing a cab. "Objection, Your Honor. This is new information. I need some time to counsel my client." He lowered his hand to his chest, where he smoothed his lapel as if to soothe himself.

"Mr. Cory, you may have your break," Judge Robinson said.

Frank left the witness stand and huddled with Mr. Cory and Kathleen.

Brady's attention ricocheted between people. She knew people were not angry but nervous. She wasn't sure why.

Finally Mr. Cory walked away, his hands at his sides, palms open. Frank took the stand again.

Ryan asked, "So you hired an investigator."

"I did." Frank answered and then he stopped.

Ryan opened his palms to Frank, beseeching him to continue. "What did you find out?"

"I found him." Frank stated, leaning back in his chair and raising his chin.

"You found Richard Lawson?" Ryan's jaw dropped, and he exchanged looks with Judge Robinson.

"I did."

Dad smoothed his brow and closed his eyes next to Brady. She watched him shake his head. *He doesn't remember*, she thought.

"Where was he?"

"In California."

"Where in California?"

"Los Angeles area. He was living under a freeway overpass," Frank said.

Richard closed his eyes and started to slump but straightened his shoulders instead.

Michael sighed and lowered his shoulders, looking sidelong at Brady.

Brady could feel his eyes on her as she stared at her hands squeezed together in her lap.

Frank blinked deeply and then looked evenly at Ryan. "He seemed to be living with a few other people. There was a blue plastic tarp on the ground with blankets and sleeping bags. The place smelled like garbage and sewage. I parked the car, and I got out. I remember having trouble getting across the ditch because it was deep and there was water running through it, but I couldn't see any other way. I came up the bank on the other side and started toward the group. The investigator had given me a picture of Richard, and I recognized him. It was weird. The people must have seen me coming, but they didn't look at me, just milled around doing nothing that I could see. I started toward Richard with the papers to be signed on a clipboard. I tried to get his attention. I got about six feet away from him and began to tell him who I was, but he never responded. And then I got this feeling that the rest of the group was starting to organize. They didn't say anything, but they started standing up and facing me. Richard never answered me even though he looked right at me. He acted strange, like he couldn't see me or anything. It was like he was somewhere else. I got scared. He was so out of it. I thought about Brady." Frank coughed and his faced reddened. "I did not want that man to know anything about Brady or my wife. During the time I was there he didn't say one intelligible word. He sat and muttered to himself. I don't think he would have understood anything that I said. So in the end I left with the papers unsigned."

Brady stared at her feet with her head bowed, but nothing could stop her from hearing. Dad really was like those homeless people you drive by and never think about. Did he beg for money? Could she ever feel the same about him?

Frank looked at Judge Robinson before he continued. "One thing I can tell you is the man I saw under the freeway that day is not the one over there." Mr. Nordland nodded at Richard, smiled just slightly, and acknowledged, "You're better now."

Brady raised her head quickly and looked at Dad. He straightened up, nodded, and smiled.

Above her head Brady heard Michael make a soft sound like the one he makes during sad movies.

Ryan said, "Yes, and all of that potential for transformation was in place even when you saw him under the freeway. Do you know where he did get well two years later?"

"No," Frank said. All eyes but Dad's turned to Ryan. Richard was watching Frank. His face was red and sweaty. He rested his hand on the table in front of him and breathed deeply. Richard looked around the court, but no one else seemed to notice.

"Your witness," Ryan said, and he sat down.

Mr. Cory stood but did not move from the table, "Based on how Richard looked, do you think he would have understood that he was signing away his parental rights for a child he had never met?"

"Objection, Your Honor, Mr. Nordland is not a psychiatrist, and this was five years ago. He's not qualified to assess Mr. Lawson's mental acuity even if he could remember," Ryan said.

Mr. Cory stepped around the table and walked toward Judge Robinson. "Let me put it another way, Your Honor." Turning to Frank, Mr. Cory said, "Mr. Nordland, what were you afraid Richard might do five years ago under the freeway in the homeless settlement with the other homeless?" Mr. Cory asked.

"Mostly I was afraid he might suddenly take it into his head to be a parent and she'd end up down there with him under the freeway." Frank's voice shook.

"You wanted to protect her?" Mr. Cory prompted, appearing not to notice.

"Yes." Frank pushed to the edge of his chair and nearly stood. "I did not want anything bad to happen to Brady. We love her," Mr. Nordland said, gripping the stand in front of him.

Mr. Cory looked at Judge Robinson. "If Frank had forced himself to wade through the stench of urine and vomit to talk to the incoherent, disoriented Mr. Lawson in hopes of having him sign to end his parental rights, it's my guess it wouldn't have stood up in court anyway. Mr. Lawson was not competent," Mr. Cory pointed at Richard and paused, "to sign such a sensitive document any more than he was ready to raise a child." Mr. Cory dropped his hand and faced the judge. "And the next question that we must think about is what would it take for him to regress to that state again—a break-up with Michael Elson, Richard's sole source of financial support? That's already happened." Mr. Cory sat down.

Ryan stood to say, "Objection, Your Honor. Every parent who comes in to fight for custody wants to keep the child. It's our job to make sure the child enjoys the benefit of all who have the right to parent her. Mr. Nordland may love his granddaughter, but that does not give him the right to keep her father away from her. Which is exactly what he has done by not telling us he saw Richard years ago," Ryan said.

Judge Robinson started to answer, but Mr. Cory rushed to explain: "What we know for sure is that Brady was in a stable home with her grandparents who never lived under a freeway and muttered to themselves. Are you really so sure of your client, Mr. Stephens? The stakes are very high for Brady. The point is that whether

Mr. Nordland had the papers signed or not, it wouldn't have made any difference. This isn't the shocking news Mr. Stephens was hoping for. No more questions."

"You may step down, Mr. Nordland," Judge Robinson said.

Brady watched Grandpa walk back to Grandma, who reached up and took his hand. He looked as tired as he did after a full harvest day on the ranch. He sat down and stared straight ahead.

BRADY TAKES THE STAND

B rady pulled on Ryan's sleeve and whispered, "I want to go now." He nodded, and Michael rose to walk out with her. She sat still. "No, I want to go there." She pointed to the chair Grandpa had just left.

"I have to talk to the Judge first," Ryan said.

"She already said I could, remember?" Brady said, voice rising.

"Judge Robinson?" Ryan said walking toward her.

"Yes, Mr. Stephens?"

"Brady wants you to hear her testimony."

"I'm picking that up," Judge Robinson said, peering over Ryan at Brady. She spoke to Brady. "I don't usually allow children to testify, but you seem insistent."

Brady straightened up and smiled at Michael, bouncing a little in her seat.

"Please remember that she is a child," Judge Robinson said, looking at Mr. Cory with raised eyebrows.

Mr. Cory nodded.

Judge Robinson looked away and rubbed the back of her neck.

The judge doesn't like Mr. Cory, Brady thought, and a tickle of pleasure went through her body.

Ryan called Brady to the stand, and she almost ran up there. The clerk swore her in, which was nowhere near as fun as she had imagined because she was so nervous.

Ryan was different with her than he had been with her dad. He settled a yellow pad on the barrier in front of her and leaned heavily on it, bringing his face close.

"This has been quite an experience hasn't it?"

"Yes."

"Not too bad, I hope."

"It's okay." She shrugged.

"How do you want it to turn out, Brady?"

Her throat tightened, and she closed her eyes to avoid seeing her grandparents. "I want to stay with my dad and Michael."

Ryan looked at Judge Robinson, who was writing.

"That's what the social worker said you wanted, and you know what else?"

"What?"

"It's what she recommended." He picked up a thick packet of papers with words typed on them. "Do you know what this is?"

Brady peered closely at the papers. "A . . . something from the county." She smiled and tilted her head to the side.

Ryan grinned. "It is the report from the social worker. Could you read this for us in a loud, clear voice so everyone can hear?"

"It says, 'Brady is thriving in this house with her father and his partner and is happily making plans for the future in regard to schools, public or private—both are possibilities. The only discomfort I observed came when the school in Oregon was mentioned. Brady seems unusually distressed at the prospect of returning to Valley Christian. Brady is well placed with her father and Michael Elson, and it appears to be the most nurturing environment for her at this time.'"

"Do you know what *nurturing* means?" Ryan asked.

Brady shook her head.

"Your fathers' house is a place that helps you grow on the inside as well as the outside." He turned to the judge. "Who could ask for more than that at this point in Brady's life?"

Judge Robinson looked at him, smiled, and wrote on the paper in front of her.

Ryan turned back to Brady. "Brady, let me ask you something else. I'd hoped to avoid this, so I'm gambling on your being brave." He walked back and picked up a box from the table behind him but kept his eyes on her. "Ready?" he asked.

She recognized it and pushed back in her chair, smile fading. "Do you recognize this?"

Her mouth opened; she breathed in sharply, lowered her eyes, and pulled in her shoulders. "Yes. How did you get that?"

"Remember when we first talked?"

Brady nodded.

"You told me about the box," Ryan said. "I asked your grandparents to send it to me. I need you to tell everyone what it is." He held her gaze.

She swallowed hard. *Did we have to start here?* "It's a shoe box that I put the notes in that were left in my math book," Brady said.

"Who are the notes from?" Ryan asked.

Brady lowered her head and stared at her knees. She no longer wanted to speak. *What do I do?*

She felt Ryan's hand on her shoulder but couldn't look at him.

Ryan squeezed her shoulder. "Hey," he whispered, "just answer the question, and it will be over."

Brady forced her head up and looked at him, eyes filled. She heard Judge Robinson exhale and put her pencil down.

"The kids at school," Brady said.

"What school?" Ryan asked, dropping his hand from her shoulder to her elbow.

Her head went lower, "Valley Christian."

"What kids?" Ryan asked.

"The kids who didn't like me, I guess," Brady said, shrugging and looking over his shoulder at the door.

"The kids who didn't like you?" Ryan said, looking at Judge Robinson. "How did you know they didn't like you?" he asked, and he tried to take hold of her hand, but she pulled from him and hugged her own body. "Hang in there, Tiger. Judge needs to hear it from you."

Brady looked over his shoulder.

Ryan followed her gaze to her fathers and moved out of the way. Dad gave her a thumbs-up, and Michael nodded.

Brady rocked herself slightly before speaking. "Well, not too many people who like you will tell you you're going to hell," she lowered her voice, "because of your father." Her back stiffened and her heart pounded as anger shot through her. Better to be mad than scared.

"One of the notes said that you were going to hell because of your dad?" Ryan asked.

Brady nodded.

"Why do you think the kids wrote that?"

Brady lowered her eyes back down to her hands. "Because he's gay." She folded her hands one over the other and looked steadily at Ryan.

Ryan turned and shook the box like a viper's rattle at Mr. Cory.

"So, not something made up by some gay father but a very real threat. This is the meanest, most evil thing one so-called Christian can do to another, using faith and God to hurt another believer." He handed the box to the judge, who opened one note to read. Ryan continued, "And when, during her visit to California, Brady told her father about the harassment, Mr. Lawson did what any father would do. He rushed to protect his daughter. He refused to put her on a plane and return her to her grandparents, to whom she had not been able to say, 'Help me, I'm being bullied to the point,'" He turned away from Brady to add, "of being hospitalized for an attempted suicide. And" he turned to the judge and kept his voice soft, "it was only an attempt because Richard figured out something was wrong during a phone call with Brady. He is the one who alerted the grandmother and made sure Brady got life saving medical help." He stepped back and raised his voice. "And since she couldn't tell her grandparents she was having trouble at school, she felt she would be sent back to that school where she wasn't safe and where the last thing she could do was learn. In keeping her off the plane back to Oregon, Richard Lawson was not trying to deny contact between Brady and her grandparents; he was just trying to do what good fathers do: protect his daughter."

"Objection, Your Honor," Mr. Cory said. "Neither the grandparents nor the school can be held responsible for bullying when Brady never told them about it."

"Sustained," Judge Robinson said.

"Brady, when you first complained to the principal, were you getting the notes in your math book?" Ryan asked, and Brady shook her head.

"No," Brady said. "They started after I told the principal."

"Let me make it clear," Ryan said. "You complained to your principal because kids, especially your very good friends, were leaving you out and forcing you to eat lunch alone."

"Yes," Brady said.

"And what did you expect to happen?"

"I expected it to stop. I expected them to be friends with me again."

"And is that what happened?"

Brady nodded at the shoe box.

"We need you to say it out loud so it goes in the record," Ryan said.

Images of jeering faces flashed into Brady's mind, and she blinked her eyes deeply to erase them. "No, it got worse," she said.

"Describe how it got worse," Ryan said, leaning forward and softening his voice.

Brady drew in a deep breath. "They sat with me, but they didn't talk to me. They'd talk to each other, but if I talked, they'd act like they didn't hear me." With these words said, Brady's mouth caved and, leaning down, she brushed tears off her cheeks.

Ryan leaned close to Brady's ear and whispered, "This is so much better if it comes from you, but I can tell the story for you if you'd like. What do you want to do, Brady?"

Brady rested her elbows on the stand and covered her face. She wanted the whole thing over, but the truth was, she could not form words, not even to tell Ryan she needed to stop. She raised her left hand.

"She needs a break," Richard said, standing and walking toward Brady. "We need to stop now."

The judge granted them five minutes.

Brady ran to Richard, who scooped her up and pulled her close. She buried her face in his neck while he carried her out of the room.

As they walked past her grandparents, Brady felt Grandpa's eyes on them until they passed through the door.

Brady sat on the bench next her father and cried until she was too exhausted to go on. She felt Ryan sit down next to her.

He wrapped one thumb and finger around her left ankle and tugged gently, asking, "How's it going?"

She forced her swollen eyelids up. "Okay, I guess." It sounded like she said, "Ohcaw, ah bess."

Ryan rolled his eyes. "Yeah, looks like a real party." He grimaced as he looked at her. "Okay, you make the call. Can you go back in there?"

Brady hesitated and felt Dad move his arms around her, pulling her close. She eased into his body and let her head fall against his shoulder. It felt so good to close her eyes.

"Remember how you told your dad about the kids teasing you in Oregon but not your grandfather?" Ryan asked, and Brady nodded. "This is an important point, Brady, and it makes sense to bring it out now. So you ready to fight the good fight, Slugger?" Ryan asked, raising one fist toward her.

"Yes." She smiled and raised a closed fist to meet his. They banged them together and smiled. Ryan stood and walked to the courtroom while she slid off the bench and marched behind him and to the witness chair.

"You were living with your grandfather and grandmother at the time that the kids were being so mean. Why didn't you tell your grandparents things were bad at school?"

"Because they wouldn't have understood."

"Okay, what wouldn't they have understood?"

"They would have thought it was Dad's fault."

"What makes you think so?"

"I'm pretty sure they believe the same things that the kids at school were saying."

"And what exactly is that?"

"That homosexuality is an abomination to God."

"*Abomination* is a big word. What's it mean?"

"Something really bad that God doesn't like."

"Okay, do you believe that?"

"No," Brady said, and she looked sharply at Ryan.

"Why not?"

"Because he's my dad and Michael takes care of me and they take care of each other. And I just don't believe that God would have a problem with that. They're good to me . . . and. . . ."

"How do they take care of you?"

"Michael cares *a lot* about what I eat." Brady's emphasis caused a small chuckle from Michael.

Brady noticed Judge Robinson picking up her pencil and writing.

"And Dad makes sure my homework is done, but it's more than that. They listen to me and ask questions, and they show me that they really care. They take me and my friend places."

"Where do you go?"

"Different places, to the movies, the park and bowling. And they play with me, and read to me.

"Yeah, that's come up, and you're a pretty good reader, right?"

Brady nodded.

"You need to speak, please." Ryan sounded annoyed.

Brady, anxious to please, almost shouted. "Yes, I am a good reader."

The judge smiled and raised her eyebrows.

"Then why do you like them to read to you?"

"I like the way it feels at the end of the day, all snuggled up on the couch."

Ryan smiled before he continued. "Do they tell you that they love you?"

"Every day my dad says it when I leave for school. And if he forgets, he texts it to me as I walk into school. And either one of them will say it to me at night when I go to sleep. Usually it's my dad because he prays with me."

"He prays with you?" Ryan asked, leaning closer.

"Yes," Brady said.

"Did he pray when you first came to his house?"

"No, I don't think he had much faith then, but he does now."

"Interesting. Do you think you had anything to do with your dad's return to faith?"

"Kind of, maybe," Brady said. She looked into her dad's eyes. He smiled, and his eyes were wet with the kind of tears that didn't look sad.

* * *

Mr. Cory smiled when he came up to Brady. She smiled back but then noticed that his jaw was set and didn't match the rest of his face.

"That was sweet," he said, but his eyes narrowed and looked scary.

Brady squeezed the arms of the chair.

"No, really, it all sounds so cozy and warm," Mr. Cory said. "You all have this great routine with reading and praying at night. And earlier Mr. Stephens mentioned that your routine included making lunches the night before and doing homework and being on time to school. But you know, I've been talking to your teacher, Mrs. Patterson, and she says there was a period when you were consistently late, and the school secretary said your dad starting writing down that it was 'An act of God' that made you late."

Mr. Cory paused.

Brady looked down.

"She also said that one time you hadn't been picked up even by the time she left at four thirty."

Brady looked with alarm at Ryan and her two fathers behind him, but Mr. Cory moved to block her view.

"Why were you late during that period?"

"We were coming from Tom and Vince's," Brady said.

"Who are Tom and Vince?"

"Friends of my dad."

"Where do they live?"

"I don't know."

"Why were you staying there?"

Since she couldn't see her fathers, she looked at Ryan, but Mr. Cory angled to block her vision and moved closer.

"You have this beautiful room, so why would you stay at Tom and Vince's?" Mr. Cory asked.

She could smell his toothpaste. "We moved there for a while."

"Who's 'we'?"

"Me and Dad."

"Not Michael?"

"No."

"Why not Michael?"

She leaned back away from Mr. Cory but still could not see around him. "They had a fight."

Mr. Cory smiled and straightened up. "Who had a fight?"

"Michael and my dad."

"How long is a while, would you say? A week? Two weeks? A month?"

"Six days, not even a week.." Brady said..

"Still a week within three months stay. Trouble happened awfully fast." Mr. Cory looked long and hard at Judge Robinson before turning back to Brady. "This must have been quite a fight. Do you know what it was about?"

Ryan stood up. "I object to the line questioning. She's a child and should not be asked to speculate on the subject matter of her parents' fight."

Brady was about to answer, *About me.*

"Sustained," Judge Robinson said.

Brady knew to stop talking.

"Okay, fine, how were things at Tom and Vince's?"

Brady shrugged, trying to remember past what happened in the basement to when she'd lived there. It really hadn't been bad.

"How did your dad handle the fight?"

Ryan objected again, and Mr. Cory changed tack. "Was your father still reading to you, helping with homework, and making lunches?"

Brady stared down at her hands and sighed heavily.

Mr. Cory leaned in again and said, "That was a heartfelt sigh. What are you thinking about?" His voice was gentle.

"It was a hard time for us."

"Why?"

"I missed my room and Michael."

"You missed your room and Michael," Mr. Cory said. "In that order?"

Ryan stood and said, "Objection, Your Honor. Mr. Cory's tone is completely inappropriate and unprofessional."

"Sustained, and please, Mr. Cory, remember that this is family court and you are speaking to a child," Judge Robinson said.

"Who made the decision for you to leave?"

"Michael."

"So what makes you say that your dad was having a hard time?"

"He was sad."

"How do you know?"

"He was quiet, and he didn't talk much."

"So were you taking care of yourself?"

"A little."

"Mrs. Patterson mentioned that your hair was dirty during that period. Do you remember that?"

Brady looked at Mr. Cory. Mrs. Patterson had noticed that?

Brady was shocked to see that Mr. Cory was trying to hide a smile. He's a bully, she thought and stole a look at Ryan, who mouthed, "Just tell the truth."

"I had trouble figuring out how the shower worked, so I didn't always wash my hair." Brady's head lowered, and she pushed her hands under her bottom in the seat of the chair.

"Couldn't you have asked your father?"

Brady looked toward her father.

Mr. Cory countered. "Did you hear the question?"

"I couldn't ask him because he was too sad," Brady said.

"That was thoughtful of you. Why was he so sad?"

"He missed Michael."

"So they had actually broken up during this period. Is that right, Brady?"

"For a little while, and then we all got back together." Brady shrugged, casting Mr. Cory a fleeting glance from the corner of her eye.

"What happened to cause you to still be at school at four thirty that one day?"

"My dad's car broke down."

"So what did you do?"

"I finally walked to Michael's house."

"You walked off the campus alone."

"I've always walked to and from school, except when we were at Tom and Vince's."

"Based on your attendance records, most of the tardies cropped up in late May. Does that sound like the time when you were staying at Tom and Vince's?"

"Yes," Brady said.

"So after only one month into the three months you had together, you and your dad were kicked out. The relationship doesn't appear to be as strong as one might hope, considering that it is Michael Elson who is paying the bills and he is the one who ordered both of them out of the house after the fight."

Mr. Cory was no longer talking to or even looking at Brady. He was talking to the judge. Brady wished she had never agreed to talk and felt she had made everything much worse for her Dad and Michael.

Over her head, Mr. Cory continued, "I just want us to pause before we place a minor in a house where decisions are made so swiftly that apparently no consideration is given to what is in the best interests of the child. Your witness."

Brady sat, head lowered, her arms limp and resting on the chair.

Ryan looked at Brady and asked from the table, "What made you go to Michael's on the day your dad's car broke down?"

Brady raised her head and pictured reading with Michael. The warmth of the memory made her feel brave. "I knew he would take care of me."

"But he and your dad had fought, and you were supposed to live somewhere else."

"Yes," Brady answered.

Brady looked up at him as he continued. "What made you think that he would take you in?"

"I knew he wouldn't want me to sit on the bench after dark."

"What happened when you got there?" Ryan asked.

"He made me dinner, I took a shower, and we read," Brady said.

Ryan looked at Judge Robinson and said, "So despite the difficulties between the parents, Brady knew she could go to Michael for help. And Michael overlooked the problems and saw to her needs. This shows a strong bond between a father and his daughter." Ryan sat down.

Brady walked back to Richard and Michael with her eyes trained on the floor, but instead of sitting between them as she had been doing, she sat closest to the aisle. Michael leaned toward her and put his arm on her shoulders, sliding her toward him. He leaned into her ear and whispered, "I should never have sent you two away. I would never let a fight break up our family again."

"I believe you." She paused. "I wonder if she does," she said, pointing at Judge Robinson.

MICHAEL TAKES THE STAND

Ryan called Michael to the stand and asked, "So what was the fight about?"

Brady sighed. *Oh not again.*

Michael stroked his chin and looked at the ceiling as he recollected the day. "It's actually hard to remember. We've come such a long way from that day, but it was mostly about setting limits with Brady, you know, knocking before you enter a room, eating at mealtime, that sort of thing. We've worked it out, and this will never happen again."

"How do you know it will never happen again?" Ryan asked.

"Problems are bound to come up, but our rules are established, so we know how to handle difficulties in the future," Michael said.

"When you arrived home that day that Brady walked to your house, how did you feel when you saw her?" Ryan asked.

Michael smiled. "Pleased, relieved just to see her. Later, I felt flattered that she came to me for help." He looked directly to her, and she smiled back.

"So you made dinner for Brady and read until Richard came home. Did you notice that she seemed unclean?"

"Yes," Michael said.

"Did you ask why?"

Michael nodded. "She couldn't figure out how to work the shower at Tom and Vince's," Michael said.

"How'd you feel about that?"

"Sad. She was obviously very embarrassed."

"So what did you do?"

Michael blinked and exhaled. "I started the shower for her and laid out pajamas."

"She was in her own home. Why didn't you just send her to her bathroom to shower?" Ryan asked.

"I wanted to help her get over the discomfort. I wanted her to feel better as fast as possible." He nodded. "This was a way to do that."

Ryan cocked his head and pursed his lips. "So, you were going out of your way to end an awkward moment?" he asked.

Michael nodded.

Ryan looked at Judge Robinson and said, "So an awkward moment put to rest by a sweet gesture. Considering the enormous changes these two men have been through in a short amount of time, some conflict is to be expected, and it sounds as though the safety net never failed. Your Honor, if this bond were not as strong, Brady would have continued to wait even in the dark. This was just a bump in the road for this family. In contrast to what Mr. Cory is trying to assert, it shows not weakness but strength in the family who can overlook personal conflict and see to the needs of their daughter."

Judge Robinson looked directly at Ryan and nodded.

* * *

Mr. Cory bounced up on his toes as he called Doctor Mary Carter to the witness stand. Michael thought Doctor Carter looked more like a real estate agent than a marriage and family therapist. She wore a red suit with a white blouse and low fire-engine red heels.

Her luxurious shoulder-length black hair stood out against the red jacket.

She hadn't even gotten through the basic introductions before Brady raised her left hand, and when she didn't get a response, she tugged at Richard's arm. Brady said she hadn't liked her when she'd met with her, but she had not told Michael why.

Richard rose without a word and, taking Brady by the hand, left the courtroom. Michael watched them go and saw Frank turn his head as they passed. When Frank turned forward, he glanced at Michael, giving him a slow nod.

Mr. Cory asked, "Why did you see Brady Lawson?"

"To assess whether she is best placed with her father and his partner or with her grandparents." Doctor Carter adjusted her glasses and smiled.

"And what was your professional opinion on this after talking to Brady?"

"I believe placement with the two men is misguided and in direct conflict with Brady's best interests."

Michael rolled his eyes, muttering under his breath, "Here we go."

"And why is that, Doctor Carter?" Mr. Cory asked.

"As you know, Mr. Lawson is gay, and statistics regarding the longevity of gay families are not good."

"In what way?" Mr. Cory asked.

Doctor Carter gave a wide and toothy smile as she tilted her head forward. "Homosexual couples are three times more likely to break up, and their children are more likely to abuse drugs or alcohol, drop out of school, become depressed, or consider suicide than are children in heterosexual families. This combined with other factors make staying with her grandparents the best setting for her."

Mr. Cory leaned toward her. "What other factors are those, Doctor Carter?"

"Brady's Christian faith is important to her sense of well-being. I think she will become confused by being nurtured by two men, and it will end in a crisis of faith that would be damaging to her personality."

Judge Robinson had been taking notes but stopped and turned toward Doctor Carter.

"Personality?" Mr. Cory asked.

"Yes, her father is engaging in a lifestyle that is considered immoral or contrary to the dictates of her faith. Her faith is integral to her sense of self. When I asked her who she was, she said, 'I am a Christian,' as the third answer after her name and that she was a girl."

Doctor Carter stopped talking, but her fingers twitched and she edged forward in her chair.

"I'm sure there are specific studies you can cite," Mr. Cory said.

Dr. Carter nodded. "In June of 2012 a huge study was published in *Social Science Research* that showed 63 percent of children from homosexual families were more likely to have low earnings and suffer from poor mental and physical health. They were more reserved, less likely to make friends, as well as hesitant to work in a team, which is a necessary skill for success in the business world."

"Did you observe any of this in Brady?" Mr. Cory asked.

"She had difficulty making and maintaining friends both in California and here in Oregon. She was involved in a fight in which she knocked over and punched a boy repeatedly, which resulted in her being suspended. She does not like to work in groups. She is afraid of being homosexual. So yes, Brady bears all of the hallmarks of a child at risk."

"And what are those risks specifically?" Mr. Cory asked.

"Dropping out of school and/or developing clinical depression, which makes her vulnerable for other more severe consequences, such as substance abuse or suicide."

"Thank you, Doctor Carter, that's all for now. Your witness," Mr. Cory said.

Ryan smiled as he walked toward Doctor Carter and shook her hand warmly, taking it in both of his hands.

"I checked out your website, Doctor Carter. Very impressive, I must say," Ryan said.

Doctor Carter smiled and ducked her head.

Ryan let go of her hand and reached for his notes. "All of those degrees, even in theology. You are a very accomplished professional."

Doctor Carter's smile faded.

"In fact, the doctorate that you hold is not in psychology or psychiatry, but in what, Doctor Carter?"

"I have a doctorate of divinity from Willamette University," Doctor Carter said.

Michael gasped.

Ryan nodded. "You were actually a minister in the Presbyterian Church. Isn't that true, Doctor Carter?"

"Oh my God," Michael whispered under his breath, wishing Richard was next to him to hear this.

"It is, until I retired fifteen years ago and got my master's in marriage and family counseling," Doctor Carter said.

"What prompted you to take on a second career, Doctor Carter?"

"I kept seeing people being diagnosed with clinical depression who were really suffering from a loss of faith. People were being put on antidepressants when all they really needed was spiritual searching and prayer."

"That'd save a lot of medical dollars. I wonder why HMOs don't cover it?"

Mr. Cory stood to say, "Objection, Your Honor."

"Sustained." Judge Robinson gave a warning look at Ryan over her glasses.

"And how would you use this with patients?" Ryan asked.

"Excuse me, Mr. Stephens? I'm not sure I'm following you," Doctor Carter said, eyebrows raised, her mouth a thin scarlet line.

"Really? You have *no* idea what I'm referring to?" Ryan placed his hand on his chest. "You did your master's thesis, which qualified you to sit here and advise families like Mr. Lawson's, on," Ryan read from a paper in his hand, "'The Pernicious and Systematic Misdiagnosis of Homosexuals in the 1980s.'"

"That was a long time ago. It was academic research, and it doesn't influence my day-to-day practice," Dr. Carter said, with one eyebrow arched.

"So the misdiagnosis was neither pernicious nor systematic? Your thesis is found to be unfounded?" Ryan asked, resting his elbows on the barrier and leaning toward Doctor Carter.

Doctor Carter moved back into the chair. "No, I believe that it was true. It just doesn't influence my practice," Dr. Carter said.

"Really? You'd have a gay man come in for counseling because he is clinically depressed, and it would never occur to you to ask him, 'Did you ever think you might be straight?'"

"I have a more spirit-based approach. People generally come to me because they already have strong faith and want their religion to be a factor in regaining their perspective," Dr. Carter said.

"In regaining their perspective, Doctor?" Ryan asked, leaning even closer.

Judge Robinson rested her chin on her hand and studied Doctor Carter.

Doctor Carter swallowed before she spoke. "Yes, I help patients to understand what makes their lives worth living so that they can get out of bed each morning and be productive. And for some of my patients, that means going back to church and praying."

"So you pray with your clients?" Ryan asked, squinting one eye in concentration.

"Not always, but many times, yes, that was exactly what they needed," Dr. Carter said, closing her eyes and nodding as she spoke.

"That's a bit of a gamble, isn't it? I mean, what if a patient really needed antidepressants, and you prayed with them and they went home and committed suicide?"

"I have to take it on a case-by-case basis. There are specific symptoms that trigger a referral to a psychiatrist or a hospital. I don't prescribe drugs."

"You don't? Or you can't because you didn't go to medical school?"

"It's not what I am trained to do. I do *talk* therapy."

Michael could see over Ryan's shoulder that Doctor Carter had straightened her back and was blinking rapidly.

"Or *prayer* therapy?" Ryan asked.

"I do talk therapy. Prayer is just a component of it. If the patient chooses to pray, I help with that."

"Help, Doctor Carter?" Ryan leaned close to her face.

She nodded. "I guide the prayers."

"Doesn't that put you in a position of enormous power, Doctor? I've read that the relationship between a counselor and patient is similar to that between a parent and a child."

"It can be," Doctor Carter said, nodding.

"When can a patient be like a child and a therapist like a parent, Dr. Carter?"

"When the patient is particularly needy, sees himself as incompetent or unhealthy. The therapist becomes a rescuer, and the patient imbues him with power similar to a parent's," Doctor Carter answered.

"So you're taking a person in crisis, and therefore dependent on you for well-being, and working not only as psychotherapist but also as an advocate between the patient and God. My catechism is weak, but I remember a quote about Jesus Christ: 'This is my son with whom I am well pleased. No one gets to me except through him.' So doesn't that put you up there with Jesus Christ himself? Since you're putting yourself between the patient and God?"

"You do need to study your catechism. We are praying to Jesus, who is our advocate to God. I have great credentials but not that kind, not in this world or the next."

Ryan took a step back and gently beat his chest. "You got me. Mea culpa."

Doctor Carter twitched her eyebrows and glanced over Ryan's left shoulder. Michael turned to see what she was looking at but couldn't find anything of interest.

Ryan smiled sheepishly and cocked his head. "Okay, but going back to our depressed gay man, who is in crisis and is willing to pray with you—do you kneel to pray, Doctor?"

"Generally no, but if the patient is accustomed to it, I will," she said.

"So, you're sitting and praying and . . . how long did you spend researching your thesis?"

"Over a year."

"So you're sitting and praying with this gay man, who is, say, thirty-seven, the age of Mr. Lawson, which would make him in his teens when he discovered that he was gay in 1987, the period on which you did your research—and you never think maybe he's one of the misdiagnosed gay guys? You never think to pray with him, 'Dear God, help Mr. Smith to figure out what is making him so sad. Maybe he needs to go back to his wife'?" Ryan ended with palms placed together in front of his chest, eyes heavenward.

"Objection, Your Honor," Mr. Cory said, "Mr. Stephens is mocking the witness."

"Sustained. Please cut the theatrics, Mr. Stephens," Judge Robinson said.

"No, Mr. Stephens, I have not done that," Dr. Carter said. Her smile was gone.

"Okay," Ryan said, "do you think that your years as a pastor coupled with your studies of the bible in any way affect how you read research on the health and success of same-sex families?"

"I am a clinician," she said slowly as though spelling it out. "I can evaluate the scientific methods that are used to measure data, which allows me to tell whether the research is meaningful or not."

"Really? I have read a lot of research on this topic lately, and I think it directly contradicts itself. You've quoted research that I recognize, and it's all negative, but the American Psychological Association—you've heard of them, right?"

"Objection . . ." Mr. Cory began.

Judge Robinson waved him off but said, "Sustained. Please show respect for the witness." She peered at Ryan over her glasses.

Ryan held out both palms. "I'm sorry," he said to Judge Robinson, and he turned to Doctor Carter. "You're familiar with the research?"

"Of course I am," Doctor Carter nodded, and Michael could tell Ryan was getting under her skin by the swiftness of the movement.

"*They* said that there was no difference between the kids of same-sex couples and heterosexual couples. Am I right?"

"That is what they said, and it has often been quoted, but I found some points for disagreement," Doctor Carter said.

"Who is going to be a better expert than the American Psychological Association?" Ryan asked.

Doctor Carter leaned forward. "I felt that they reached some broad conclusion that wasn't necessarily supported by their research."

"Can you be specific about that, Doctor?" Ryan asked.

"It's not just me questioning it. The sample was too small for real comparison. That's what prompted the research in 2012."

"Other professionals like yourself? Faith-based, spirit-driven professionals who aren't looking for scientific evidence but validation for their own beliefs? I believe that you are quite capable of leading very vulnerable families in crises right down the path to their own private hell."

Mr. Cory jumped to his feet. "Objection, Your Honor, he's attacking the witness for her personal beliefs, which she has stated she does not use in her practice."

Ryan spun around to face Mr. Cory, retorting, "Like hell, she doesn't! That's why you never mentioned that she used her religion in therapy. Were you hoping I wouldn't bring it up?" He gestured with arms and palms open. "If you didn't think it was going to look bad, you would have mentioned it before."

Judge Robinson was on her feet. "Mr. Stephens, you just earned yourself a $2,000 fine."

Michael watched the two lawyers swivel to face the judge. Ryan covered his mouth with both hands and said, "I am so sorry."

"So am I, Mr. Stephens. So am I. Never," she paused and looked down, "never have I seen such unprofessional, disrespectful behavior. Let's take a break, and *I pray* that cooler heads will prevail." Her chair was still moving when she disappeared through the door behind it.

Ryan's face went ashen as he sat silent and stared at the door the judge just shut. "My brother is gonna kill me," he said.

Michael reached over the partition to the lawyer's table and squeezed his shoulder. "I thought you were awesome," he said, and then shrugged. "Sorry about the fine. That's bad," he grimaced, "but damn! Wish Richard heard that." As he walked to the hall, he rubbed his hands together in anticipation.

* * *

Brady watched Michael offer Dad a robust high-five as he described the showdown between Ryan and Doctor Carter. They returned with renewed enthusiasm and watched Ryan, who seemed excited, call Janine Emerson to the stand.

Ms. Emerson was a psychotherapist Ryan had chosen to interview Brady. Her blue eyes and shoulder-length hair belied her forty-something years. Brady loved her even though she knew Michael thought she dressed weird. She wore a white blazer over an avocado-green scoop-neck knit top that topped a jeans skirt, and her shoes were Birkenstocks. Brady remembered that she smelled like incense and flowers.

She pulled at Michael's elbow.

"She's the one who taught me how to do the origami," Brady said, scratching her nose. "She's nice."

"That's good," Michael said, adding under his breath, "Something should make up for the lack of fashion sense."

Ms. Emerson waved to Brady from the stand.

Brady offered a tiny wave and giggled as others turned to see whom the woman was greeting.

Ryan walked up to her and asked, "How do you feel about a child being raised by same-sex parents?"

"Research has shown that there is no difference in the mental health of kids raised by same-sex parents and kids raised by heterosexual parents," Ms. Emerson said.

"How about Brady specifically? Is she going to be okay with two fathers?" Ryan asked.

"Brady is happy with her fathers in California and specifically feels safe and understood in their family," Ms. Emerson said, smiling.

"Safer than with her grandparents?" Ryan asked.

"Yes, because the men have been able, either due to their younger ages or openness in their personalities, to establish an effective rapport so that Brady confides in them and makes it possible for them to intervene on her behalf," Ms. Emerson said.

"Such as happened in the bullying incident in California?" Asked Ryan. "Exactly," Ms. Emerson nodded. "No matter how nurturing the grandparents are, if Brady does not feel free to communicate, she won't, and that makes it impossible to meet her needs emotionally and psychologically," Ms. Emerson said.

Brady heard something and turned to see her grandmother trying to get her grandfather to calm down.

"Well I don't care. It's ridiculous," Grandpa said.

Brady sank in her seat.

"So if she's placed long-term with her grandparents and visits her fathers, what effect will that have on her?"

"I think it could be destructive mainly because once a child has the kind of rapport Brady enjoys with her fathers, she expects it. If it is interrupted and replaced with a relationship that is not as close, it confuses the child and may cause her to withdraw. She may also feel that going for help—in this case, to the courts—backfires, since she is likely to feel that her expressed needs were overlooked and may make her feel hopeless. I need to stress this is no fault of the grandparents. It is a natural mindset of an adolescent," Ms. Emerson said.

"And the effect of hopelessness?" Ryan asked.

Ms. Emerson raised her eyebrows before answering, "Oh, further withdrawal, depression, and thoughts of suicide. Feeling hopeless is frequently sited as a primary motivation for substance abuse."

"Thank you, no further questions, Your Honor." Ryan smiled and walked back to the table, writing something as he went.

Mr. Cory approached Ms. Emerson, saying as he walked, "Okay, so Dr. Carter says it's going to rain, and you say it isn't. Where is the truth in all of this for the rest of us simple folk?"

Ms. Emerson studied Mr. Cory before answering. "Most professionals believe that being same-sex parents does not affect the mental health of the children the parents raise. What children need is to be raised by people who are crazy about them."

"Crazy about them?" Mr. Cory asked.

"Yes, kids are egocentric, and they are keenly aware of how people perceive them," she answered.

"Can you explain that?" Mr. Cory pursed his lips.

"They know when caregivers are going through the motions of loving and when they are genuinely loved, which for a child translates into being understood. A caregiver who treats a child as a source of joy and affection creates the ideal circumstances that nurture a child and bring her to her full potential."

"Are you saying that the Nordlands don't love Brady?" Mr. Cory asked.

"No, I am saying that Brady perceives that her father and his partner understand her better," Ms. Emerson said.

"And because of that perception, all that the grandparents have done for the past five years is negated by three months, right, Ms. Emerson?" Mr. Cory said.

Ms. Emerson shook her head, "None of this trivializes what Mr. and Mrs. Nordland did."

Richard watched Ms. Emerson look out into the court and direct her comments to the Nordlands.

"They overlooked their own needs and did what good, healthy families do in an emergency. They stepped up to take on the day-to-day responsibilities of caring for a child because at that time, the father could not do it. That was heroic and noble, but now Richard and Michael are ready to parent, and their home is the place Brady will be most nurtured. So the noble thing has become allowing her to go to the home that best suits her, as difficult as that may be for them."

Brady felt a twist of grief. She didn't want to lose her grandparents. What was this like for them? She looked over her shoulder.

Although they must have seen Brady move, they stared straight ahead.

"You are aware that during the three short months that Mr. Lawson had his daughter, his family dissolved and he and Brady were exiled to another home for a week? Do you know where they went, Ms. Emerson?" Mr. Cory asked.

"I know that Brady has told me that they stayed with family friends."

"Did she say any more than that, Ms. Emerson?"

Ms. Emerson's eyes drifted up and to the left. "I know it was a gay couple, two men, and they lived in a very large house in Palos Verdes Estates. And they had a dog. The presence of the dog soothed Brady."

"Did she mention any problems while they were there?"

"I am aware of the problems that have been mentioned before—that she had trouble running the showers and keeping clean."

"Did she mention that she was consistently tardy to school during this period?"

"I am aware of it, although she did not mention it."

"Does it strike you as odd that she didn't mention that her teacher kept her after school one day to talk to her about it?"

"Sometimes what seems important to adults isn't to kids."

"You really believe that having her teacher keeping her after school and calling home would not be a big deal for a sensitive child such as Brady?"

"She didn't mention it," Ms. Emerson said firmly.

"No more questions," Mr. Cory said.

BENEDICT ARNOLD WEARS ARMANI

———

Mr. Cory said, "I'd like to call Mr. Vincent Vilhard to the stand." Richard's stomach clenched and he tried to stifle a gasp but failed.

Ryan turned and pinned him with a silencing look.

"Okay, okay," Richard said.

Vince, clad in a well-tailored black suit, walked by the family, studiously avoiding all eye contact with them. He was sworn in and settled into his chair, lacing his fingers and resting his hands on the knees of his crossed legs. Mr. Cory asked his name and occupation.

"What's a golf pro?" Brady asked Richard.

He just shushed her.

Brady turned to Michael and hissed in his ear, "Why does he seem so straight?"

Michael pressed his index finger to his lips and took Brady's hand. "This is gonna get mean and nasty," he said as he led her around Richard, with whom he exchanged heavy eye contact.

Richard watched over his shoulder as they walked down the aisle, noting the grandparents' stare as they exited. He was relieved to have Brady out of the room for this but hated the idea of listening to Vince's testimony alone in front of the grandparents.

Mr. Cory asked Vince if Brady and Richard had stayed with him and Tom.

Mr. Cory asked if it was a pleasant visit.

Vince answered, "Yes, mostly."

"Mostly?" Mr. Cory prodded.

"Well, it's hard. Having people move in suddenly." Vincent shrugged one shoulder slightly and then raised his eyes to meet Mr. Cory's.

"So," Mr. Cory continued, "they invaded your house and it was disruptive, but they left in a week, right?"

"Yes," Vince said.

"Never to be seen again?" the lawyer persevered.

Vincent looked a little confused, as if he felt Mr. Cory must have forgotten some previous conversation. "Yes, until that one night when Richard, Michael, their daughter, and their dog came back for dinner."

Richard heard Ryan mutter under his breath, "I've got this. It's not a surprise. I have a plan."

It wasn't reassuring. Richard forced out a deep, slow breath.

"They brought their dog?" Mr. Cory asked.

"Yes, they brought their dog because Brady liked our dog and wanted to have it play with her new dog."

"So they came over for dinner, and how did that go?" the lawyer pressed on.

"Okay, fine, I guess, until the end."

"Until the end?" Mr. Cory asked, leaning forward.

"I was a little bit drunk, and at the end of the evening we wound up in the basement for, um, further festivities." Vince shifted in his seat as he spoke.

Richard stifled a moan, shook his head, and looked at Vince.

Vince's eyes were fixed on Mr. Cory.

Richard rested his elbow on his leg and his chin in his hand and tried to make himself as small as possible. He was keenly aware of the presence of the grandparents. This was like being nude in public. *Oh God, please let Ryan be able to pull us out of the fire.* Richard closed his eyes.

"Further festivities?" Mr. Cory asked, raising eyebrows to hairline, mouth open.

Vince put his shoulders back. "Tom sometimes entertains with a sort of cabaret act."

"A cabaret act?" Mr. Cory looked as though he'd like to jump in place.

Richard leaned forward with his elbows on his thighs and hands over his ears. He wished he could vaporize.

"Yes, Tom sings and dances."

"Sings and dances what?"

"Show tunes." Vince's eyebrows rose and fell.

"Sort of a top-hat-and-tux kind of thing?" Mr. Cory asked.

Richard covered his mouth with both hands.

"There are different characters."

"Come on, Mr. Vilhard, what was Tom dressed as that night?" Mr. Cory chuckled. He swayed slightly as he flopped his hand on the barrier in front of Vince.

What is this? Richard leaned forward, brows clenched. Was Mr. Cory hitting on Vince?

Vince smiled, raised his eyes, and held Mr. Cory's gaze for several seconds.

"Tom dressed as a fairy godmother and granted wishes," Vince said.

Judge Robinson began writing, and Richard wondered if it wasn't just to keep herself busy.

Richard stared at the back of Ryan and sank lower in his seat. He could hear Frank talking to Kathleen but could not bear to look at them. He wished he were outside with Brady and Michael.

"He wore a long satin dress, a wig, heels, and make-up. Is that right, Mr. Vilhard?" Mr. Cory asked.

"Yes," Vince answered.

"And what kind of wishes was he granting?" Mr. Cory's voice was hoarse, and he leaned toward Vince, who did not pull away.

"Sexual ones," Vince said, voice shaking with repressed laughter.

"You say that you were a little bit drunk. Had Richard or Michael been drinking?" Mr. Cory asked.

"No, they are seriously sober," Vince said. Vince looked at him, but Richard looked away.

"You're in a relationship with Tom, right?" Mr. Cory asked.

"Until very recently, we'd been together for over two years." Vince said.

"How old are you?" Mr. Cory asked.

"Twenty-nine."

"How old is Tom?"

"Forty-nine."

Mr. Cory looked up for a long time. "So Tom is twenty years older than you are? That's a lifetime. Did that ever cause trouble?"

"No, he understood that I needed to branch out sometimes," Vince said.

Richard pulled his arms around his chest and crossed his legs. *Not with us, never with us.*

"Branch out?" Mr. Cory asked, eyebrows shooting up.

"Yeah, you know, with other, younger men. He didn't want me to be frustrated. He was cool with it."

Mr. Cory's eyes narrowed slightly. "So did you have sex with both Michael and Richard? And I remind you that you are under oath."

Richard laced his fingers behind his head.

"No." Vince shook his head.

"Just one of them?" Cory asked.

"No, neither of them. They weren't completely into it." Vince shrugged and wagged his head.

"Objection, Your Honor. Mr. Cory knows they didn't have sex. He is simply trying to demoralize my clients."

"Sustained." Judge Robinson said.

Mr. Cory nodded at Vince, encouraging him to continue.

"And we were interrupted." Vince shifted in his seat and crossed his arms.

"Interrupted by what?"

"The girl, Brady, called down from the top of the stairs."

"Brady was in the room?" Mr. Cory leaned forward eagerly.

Richard's thoughts were no longer words, just waves of shame. His hands were palm-down under his legs, and his head hung low.

"Not exactly; she was at the top of the stairs."

"So you and Richard and Michael were about to engage in group sex with their ten-year-old daughter in the house?"

"Objection!" Ryan stood.

"Okay, I'll rephrase it. I do wonder though, Your Honor, if she hadn't interrupted, would Richard and Michael have engaged in group sex?"

"That's a hypothetical question," Ryan began, and he pointed at Cory but pivoted quickly to face Judge Robinson, who nodded.

"We're done with the line of questioning," she said. "And if you're thinking of asking any questions to Brady about this situation, Mr. Cory, let me tell you now, I will not allow it," Judge Robinson said.

Mr. Cory dropped his shoulders but nodded and turned back to Vince. "So you went downstairs for entertainment. What happened?"

"Well, Tom was singing, and things were warming up."

"Warming up?" Mr. Cory asked, drumming his fingers on the stand.

"We were having sexy fun. I like to end evenings with sex, don't you?" Vince asked, sweeping his deep brown eyes up to Mr. Cory's.

Mr. Cory backed up, and Richard could see he was blushing. Vince had a grin of victory lighting up his face.

Richard rested his elbow on his knee and covered his face. Whatever was going on between these two, he did not want to know.

Mr. Cory scrambled to recover and walked away from Vince as if escaping. "Why was Brady in the basement? What did she want?" Mr. Cory asked.

"I think she thought the dogs were having sex, and it woke her up."

"The *dogs* were having sex?" Mr. Cory turned to look at Vince.

Vince laughed, adding, "They couldn't because they were both male. But Tom's dog is a show dog and the center of his life. He didn't want anything to happen to him."

"What happened next?"

"Tom ran up the steps, and Michael and Richard followed him."

"Did Brady see Tom in a dress?"

"Maybe—I don't know. I couldn't see. They were ahead of me, so it blocked my view," Vince said, shrugging his shoulders.

"Can you describe the dress?"

"Objection, Your Honor, please, we know the man was in a costume. We do not need to know any more than that," Ryan said.

"Sustained," said Judge Robinson.

"I'm only pointing out that this must have been quite a sight for a ten-year-old girl," Mr. Cory said to Judge Robinson, his eyebrows arching like steeples.

RALLYING POINT

Ryan found it difficult to concentrate and pull them out of the hole Vince had dug. He wanted to quit, but he knew that if he did, this would be his last case.

Ryan called Vince to the stand. Ryan made it a point to smile at Vince, but in return Vince gave him the once-over with his eyes.

Ryan's thinking was derailed. He wished he'd worn his black suit, with its gravitas and solemnity. He cleared his throat and asked, "About how much alcohol did you consume that night, Mr. Vilhard?"

Vince looked upward. "Drinks before, wine with, champagne after, I don't know. I guess about six drinks." He shrugged.

"Is that typical for you?"

"No, Tom and I usually had wine with dinner but not the before and after stuff."

"What was the reason for the change?"

"It was kind of a celebration. Richard and Michael were back together, and it was good to have them back."

"But Richard and Michael didn't imbibe, you've said?"

"No."

"And remind us why not."

"They're reformed alcoholics. They met in treatment," Vince said.

"So you and Tom drank in front of them even though they are putting every effort into staying sober?" Judge Robinson looked at Vince and waited.

"I guess, yes." Vince shrugged.

"Did it ever occur to you to abstain for the comfort of your guests?" Ryan asked.

"They never asked us not to drink." Vince shrugged.

"Wow, that shows a lot of self-control," Ryan said. "On their parts, I mean."

Judge Robinson nodded to herself over her notes.

Confidence slowed Ryan's heart.

"Yeah, Richard told me when he was staying with us that he would never drink because he knew he would lose his kid and Michael, and without them, he would have no reason for living."

"That shows commitment, don't you think?" Ryan asked.

"Yes, we were surprised that Richard wound up with us after the fight. We couldn't imagine them away from one another."

"They are good together." Ryan looked at Richard, who shifted in his seat. "They are handsome, successful, and very much in love with one another." Ryan said. "You like them, Mr. Vilhard?" he asked.

"I do."

Ryan squinted one eye. "Both equally?"

Vince looked away.

"If you had to choose between the two, who'd it be?" Ryan smiled as he asked and moved closer to Vince.

"Objection, Your Honor," Mr. Cory said.

"Your point, Mr. Stephens?" Judge Robinson asked.

Ryan nodded, holding up his index finger. "Who, Vince?" he asked. His cheek muscles quivered from holding a grin so long.

"Richard." Vince shrugged.

"Makes sense. He's closer to your age and easy on the eye." Ryan leaned in and smiled.

"Objection, Your Honor. Mr. Stephens is telling Mr. Vilhard what he thinks," Mr. Cory said.

"Sustained. Mr. Stephens," Judge Robinson said.

Ryan nodded. "Tom did grant your wish to be with Richard. That's true, right?"

Vince nodded.

"Dream boyfriend, I gotta say."

"It worked for us," Vince said.

"One small problem," Ryan raised his finger. "I think you used the phrase, 'I couldn't imagine them apart,' in reference to Richard and Michael. Am I right?"

"Yes," Vince said.

"So how did you feel when your wish to be with this hand-some man could not be filled because he is committed to Michael, as you alluded to earlier?"

Vince shrugged. "I understood."

"Really? Richard said when he told you it wasn't going to happen, you forced a kiss on him." Ryan stepped back and stared at Vince.

Vince looked briefly at Richard and then away.

Ryan went on, "He quoted you as saying, 'You did want me. I know the truth.' Is that true?" Ryan asked.

"I did say that," Vince said.

Ryan leaned even closer, speaking gently. "It's understand-able, you know; you thought you were going to get Richard, but Richard rejected you. You were hurt, embarrassed, and then there's all that pent-up frustration."

"Objection—" Mr. Cory couldn't find the words fast enough, it seemed.

Judge Robinson gave a curt nod. "Make your point, or stop this line of questioning, Mr. Stephens," she said.

"My point is that Tom gave the go-ahead for Mr. Vilhard to be with Richard even though they both knew Richard and Michael were monogamous. As everyone expected, Richard turned Vince down. Vince was furious. So when Mr. Cory came looking for a witness to derail Richard and Michael's attempts to get custody,

Mr. Vilhard was happy to comply, in order to satisfy his need for revenge against Richard Lawson—not out of desire to tell the truth. Mr. Vilhard doesn't care about the truth; he just wants to get even with Richard. Mr. Vilhard is not a credible witness and should not be factored into your decision." Ryan looked at Judge Robinson.

"Duly noted," she said.

Ryan smiled and threw a glance at Vince. The fury on Vince's face made him look demonic. "Hit a nerve on that one," Ryan muttered under his breath before asking, "We know Brady woke up. Was the music loud?"

"Yes, Tom has a synthesizer, so it sounded like he had a whole orchestra backing him up: drums, horns, and everything." Vince smiled.

"Could she have been awakened by the music or the sound of Tom's singing?"

Vince shook his head. "It's a huge house, and the basement is insulated just for this reason. Tom didn't want music to bother anyone who wanted to sleep or work on other things. I don't see how she could have heard it."

"Did Brady ever enter the room?"

"No, Michael told her he'd come up."

Ryan stood back from Vince and said, "So, a nice dinner among friends, enjoying a little music, maybe a little burlesque, and some sexy fun, which my clients turned down, and all after having made sure that Brady was safely asleep. If not for the dogs' activities, Brady would have remained asleep, and we would not be having this discussion today. Would you agree with that, Mr. Vilhard?"

"Yes," Vince said, his eyes glaring and his tone angry.

"I have no more questions, Your Honor."

Judge Robinson nodded.

Vince left the witness stand, banging the half door behind him.

KATHLEEN'S TESTIMONY

"Your Honor, I would like to call Mrs. Kathleen Nordland," Ryan said, and Judge Robinson nodded.

Grandma walked forward straightening her shirt and then the pastel scarf at her neck. As she sat down, she adjusted the gold broach on the lapel of her light blue blazer.

The care she had taken with her clothes was unlike her, and it made Brady squirm to see how hard Grandma was trying. She loved her. So far no one had come off witnessing looking very good. Brady still wanted to live with Dad and Michael, but she didn't want anybody to be mean to Grandma.

"Can you tell us a little about Brady's mom?" Ryan asked.

"She was . . ." she paused and exhaled, "fine, I guess," Grandma said.

"You guess? This is your daughter, Kathleen. Seems like a mother would have more to say than 'fine,'" Ryan said, shaking his head.

Brady squeezed her eyes shut. *Don't, please don't.*

Grandma paused and smoothed her blouse. "She could be wonderful, loving, and loyal—to her friends. She was creative, very good at painting, and she played the piano really well." Grandma smiled and looked forward with unfocused eyes.

Brady sat straight up, mouth open, afraid to move lest she miss a word. She was hearing more about her mother than she had ever heard.

"But she was . . . hard to raise . . . defiant, you know—and hard to get along with. Some kids you say no to and that's the end of it. For Brenda, saying no just got her more interested." Grandma sighed and moved back in her seat. "She was colicky and stayed difficult even when she started preschool, and it never got better. She dropped out of high school, and that's when everything really started to fall apart."

"What do you mean by 'started to fall apart'?"

Grandma stared at Ryan warily before answering. "She got into trouble—got arrested."

"Arrested? What for?"

"DUIs, shoplifting, drugs."

"Describe how Brenda told you she was pregnant."

Grandma closed her eyes. "She came home out of the blue— we hadn't seen her for months—and she was all excited because she was pregnant and married to him." Grandma gestured at Richard. "She said she was off of drugs forever." Grandma frowned and rested her hand at the back of her neck, massaging it. "She didn't even have her own life under control, but she was happy to share it with an innocent life."

"That has to be hard for a parent to watch," Ryan said.

Grandma nodded her head, eyes round and soft. "You want to protect your children, but it's hard to protect them from themselves. She was an adult and we were so beaten down. There was nothing we could say that we hadn't already said. That she hadn't already disregarded." Grandma pressed her hand over her lips and lowered her head. As though becoming conscious that others were listening, she raised her head and straightened her shoulders. "I could see exactly what was going to happen," she said.

"And what was that?" Ryan asked.

Grandma looked to the side and said, "I could see that he was going to run off and that she would be raising the baby alone. Which is exactly what did happen." She stared evenly at Ryan.

Ryan nodded and turned as though about to sit down.

Grandma started to stand.

Ryan turned and asked, "Did you ever suggest that she have an abortion?" He leaned toward Grandma, who gasped and flicked a look at Brady and then over her head at Frank.

Ryan followed her gaze to Frank before turning back to her. "Kathleen, did you or your husband suggest that Brenda get an abortion?"

Grandma shook her head and looked at Ryan with wide eyes. "No," she said.

"No? Richard said that Frank did."

"It's not true," Grandma stated, eyes blinking rapidly. "He's lying."

"What did your daughter do for a living?"

Grandma shrugged. "She worked as a waitress and taught piano lessons."

"Where was Brady while she worked?"

Grandma stared at Ryan and then shrugged again. "I don't know," she said.

"Did you offer any money to your daughter?"

"She didn't ask for any."

"Where did she live, Mrs. Nordland?"

"Some little house in the middle of nowhere. She liked it there. Nobody bothered her. Seemed kind of isolated to me. It was her choice. I think it was free or nearly free."

"How far of a drive was it from your house to her house?"

"Twenty to thirty minutes."

"Did you ever visit or offer childcare for your grandchild?"

"No."

"It was a short drive, your daughter had a limited income, she was raising a child alone, and you never visited?" Ryan pursed his lips and flicked his eyebrows together.

"She didn't want us—me—there. We didn't get along. I've said that," Grandma said.

Brady squeezed her hands together and stared at the toes of her patent leather shoes. Did nobody want her to be born?

"Do you think she knew that you disapproved of her marriage?" Ryan asked.

"I told her how I felt, so, yes, she knew."

"So what did you want her to do? She was pregnant. Whether you approved or not, the baby was on its way," Ryan said.

"Your point, Mr. Stephens?" Judge Robinson asked.

"My point is that Frank and Kathleen didn't want to support Brady while their daughter was alive, but when she was not, they moved in fast and did little to notify the father. Is it your God-given right to shut Richard Lawson out of his daughter's life because you disapprove of the fact that he is gay?"

Grandma straightened up, and Brady recognized the anger on her face. "We are not trying to shut him out. We are protecting Brady. That's what good parents do," she said, punctuating each syllable by tapping her collar bone with her index finger.

Brady had never heard Grandma raise her voice. She stared at her openmouthed.

"Don't you feel that you could have gotten involved in Brady's life earlier if you'd laid aside your differences with Brenda?" Ryan asked.

Grandma rested her hand on her chest as though catching her breath. "Brenda would not have wanted us in her house, especially not to help her raise the baby."

"Did you love your daughter, Kathleen?"

She raised her eyes to Ryan's and stared at him before answering, her voice low. "Of course I loved my daughter, Mr. Stephens. I took care of her. Frank bailed her out of jail several times. We paid for treatment centers more than once."

Brady heard Grandma's voice shake and saw that her hands gripped the arms of the chair.

"Did you ever tell Brady you loved her?"

"Tell her? I'm sure I must have. Was I supposed to keep a tally sheet? I don't know. We gave her clothes and food, a roof over her head. If that isn't love, I don't know what love is."

"Did you do homework with Brady?"

"She didn't need help doing her homework. She was a straight-A student."

"Did it surprise you that her father and his partner were helping her with her homework?"

"Yes, she doesn't need it. I hope they don't give her sloppy habits." Grandma gestured at Richard and Michael.

"Sloppy habits, Kathleen?"

"Yes, you know how kids can be. 'This is hard. I'll get my dad to do it for me.' No wonder her grades are so good; she's got them doing her homework for her."

"She had straight As at Valley Christian, and no one was helping her, right? Why would you accuse her father of doing her homework for her?" Ryan asked.

"They've bragged about it, haven't they? It just isn't necessary. She didn't need it from us, and she doesn't need it now," Grandma said, hugging her body with her forearms.

Brady saw Grandma narrow her eyes.

"Do you have any kids, Mr. Stephens?" Grandma asked.

"No." He shook his head.

"I didn't think so. I don't know what kind of childhood your parents gave you, but it's more complicated than it looks," she said, and she swept her eyes forward.

Ryan said he had no more questions.

As Grandma reached Brady's row, she paused.

Brady stared up at her, trying to catch her eye but afraid to at the same time. She looked like she was going to stop and talk to her, but then she moved straight ahead. This was not the Grandma Brady knew. She seemed broken and lonely. The Grandma Brady knew was never afraid of anything.

MR. CORY'S CLOSING ARGUMENTS

B rady felt drained and was relieved to hear Mr. Cory say, "If you are ready, Your Honor, I am prepared to make my closing arguments."

Judge Robinson nodded and said, "Proceed, Mr. Cory."

Mr. Cory began, "Frank and Kathleen Nordland have been Brady's primary caregivers for the last five years because Richard was too busy coping with his own substance-abuse problems to be found. Once found, Richard was still unable to care for Brady, and at that point he allowed Brady's grandparents to be her parents.

"And now, Richard has suddenly developed the whim to raise his daughter after all of these years and wants not only to take full custody but also to move her some seven hundred miles away, which will make any joint-custody arrangement prohibitively expensive. Richard is financially dependent on Michael in order to support his daughter, but their relationship is unstable. In the short time that Richard has had custody of her, he and Brady were cast out after a fight with Michael. What will happen to Brady if the two men do break up? Richard can't afford to raise a child himself; he can barely afford to support himself.

"Brady has clung to her Christian faith through the death of her mother. Mr. Lawson's choice to lead a gay lifestyle will conflict with what Brady has been taught and could cause a crisis of faith, putting her at risk for drug abuse, dropping out of school, or suicide, according to the testimony of Dr. Carter. Mr. Stephens has tried to say that Brady was better understood by her father and his partner in California and so they were able to intervene more effectively. But the truth is if she weren't with her gay father and his lover, she wouldn't be bullied. And the bullying wasn't only in Oregon but also in California where Brady, an otherwise gentle child, was moved to the point of beating up a classmate. Indeed, she was suspended for it. So the father failed to understand the severity of Brady's anger at the injustice of the bullying to the point that she had to defend herself in an aggressive manner. It was not his intervention but her outrage that resulted in getting help. Surely, this is not the gold standard of parenting Mr. Lawson was hoping to create."

Mr. Cory pointed to Brady and softened his voice. "Your Honor, with Brady in the house, the two men chose to engage in group sex with a transvestite directing the show. The fact that Brady saw this man in a dress does represent current circumstances that are damaging. We have a chance to protect her. Please, Your Honor, I urge you to allow Brady to stay with her grandparents so they can love and support her as they have been doing successfully for the last five years."

Mr. Cory bowed to the judge, pivoted, and returned to his seat, where he folded his hands as if in prayer.

"Thank you, Mr. Cory." Judge Robinson nodded. "Mr. Stephens, you may close."

Dad was leaning forward with his elbows on his legs, and his fingers were entwined in his hair at the back of his head.

Brady closed her mouth and swallowed, blinking back tears. Their family wasn't the way Mr. Cory was making it look. She felt safe in their house. Brady wished she could have some more time with the judge. This was her life. She was the one who was going to have to pack up her clothes and books and move back to Oregon.

There would be no Fiona, or Mrs. Patterson, and what would happen to Cyrano? Brady pictured the moment in her mind. She would have to put Cyrano in Dad's arms and turn away from all of them. She gave in and sobbed, hugging her arms around her body as if to hold in the pain.

"Whatever happens, we're going to be okay," Michael whispered. "We're a family, and they can't take that away."

RYAN'S CLOSING ARGUMENTS

All eyes turned to Ryan, and Brady watched him ruffling his papers, straightening his tie, and pushing it down, like it was choking him. His hands were shaking, and the papers in his hands made it look worse. *Oh no, he's scared.*

Ryan began, "When people set out to have children, they do so with the best of intentions. They hope to be the best parents possible, to emulate their own parents if they were a good example, or to not make the same mistakes if they were not. Most of us fail a little, but we do not harm our children. Richard Lawson is no different. He went a step further and tried to change himself. Despite the fact that he was gay, he married Brady's mother, Brenda, but was so alienated by living a lie that he couldn't be present at the baby's birth. He felt even worse when Brenda died and he still couldn't parent Brady. He has never denied that he was an alcoholic and for that reason would not have been a good father at the time. But he never said that he was unwilling or unable to raise his child. He was never asked. The grandparents made the judgment on their own that he would be unstable, and without ending his rights, they took Brady as their own.

"But then Mr. Lawson did something truly heroic. He quit drinking, came out as a gay man, and found a loving partner who shared his sobriety. And then he did the bravest thing of all—he called his child's grandparents, knowing that they were going to confront him with all the irresponsible choices he had made. Mr. Lawson could have walked away. In addition, he and Michael Elson have agreed to take on a large amount of financial debt by agreeing to pay past child support.

"Not that all of it has been easy—no, far from it. In Oregon Brady experienced such cruel harassment and was unable to confide in the grandparents for fear that they would take the side of the bullies and blame her father for being the cause of the bullying. There were harassment issues for Brady at school in California as there had been in Oregon and while Mr. Cory points out that Brady ended up defending herself. She at least felt confident enough to stand up for herself rather than take her own life. She felt secure enough in herself to fight back against bullies and that comes from a healthy family. There were the domestic difficulties that have been dissected and explored by Mr. Cory that led to Brady's moving temporarily to a friend's house with her father. But when she really needed help, she, by herself, felt comfortable enough to go back to Michael's, where he took care of her. I've worked closely with this family, and I can tell you, this is a happier, healthier, stronger little kid than I met at the beginning of the case. This is a loving family, destined to become even stronger and healthier.

"It's true that Mr. Lawson wasn't available when his wife died, but he is now, and he is so ready to parent. His work makes him available to go to the park, attend field trips, and host play dates, all of which he has done. More than anything, he isn't stepping up to the plate duty-bound and resentful; he is choosing to be there because he loves Brady and wants to help her grow.

"Mr. Cory has argued that Brady's being present in a house when a party was going on, even though she never actually entered the room, constitutes circumstances detrimental to her. I have a confession to make: I walked in on my parents when they were having sex when I was eight years old. It was embarrassing; obviously I still remember it. Was I hurt by it? No. Traumatized by it? Grossed-out, more like, but not traumatized.

"My parents hadn't even locked the door, but Richard made sure Brady was asleep one story up in an insulated house. He went further than my parents went. No one threatened to take me away." Ryan fixed Mr. Cory with his eyes and continued, "I think that some members of the court have transposed their homophobic values onto Brady and feel that she *should* be traumatized. That this *should* wreck her faith. But she's a better Christian than you, Mr. Cory, more acceptant and loving. And her love for her father has done what it's supposed to do. Richard's gone to church with her, and they've prayed together. The daughter's love has strengthened the father's faith. Brady has told the court this is where she wants to live. Aren't these all classic elements of a fully functional, thriving family?" Ryan stood gazing at Judge Robinson, both arms extended above his shoulders, palms out.

"I argue further, Your Honor, that the love and acceptance that Brady has come to understand cannot be duplicated by the grandparents. According to the social worker, in her fathers' house, Brady fits in and is understood. Her grandparents can certainly meet her needs, but being understood made it possible for Brady to go to her fathers for help when she was being bullied at school. I remind the court that Brady was not able to go to her grandparents for help in Oregon, and the result brought her close to self-destruction. Imagine what her teenage years will be like. Your Honor, I have asked Brady what she wants you to decide, and this is what she said: 'Let me stay at home with my dads and be the center of their universe.' Please, Your Honor, do what is in Brady's best interests."

Ryan turned and walked back to his seat, but before he sat down, he winked at Brady, who gave him a thumbs-up and a big smile, despite the tears that lay wet on her cheeks.

Judge Robinson said, "Thank you, Mr. Stephens. I would like to take a break for lunch. The court will reconvene in two hours."

Brady sat silently between the two motionless families and stared at the door that had closed behind the judge. She wanted to run after her and shout, but what was left to say? It was all in the hands of the judge.

PEACE TALKS

B rady reached for Dad's hand as the group walked out of the court.

"So now what?" Dad asked Ryan.

"Now we wait," Ryan said.

"But what do you think might happen?" he asked.

Ryan exhaled and cocked his head to one side as he considered the options. "Vince's testimony didn't help," he said.

Brady looked back at Dad, who shot a look at Michael.

Ryan stopped walking. "Now we have a more immediate problem."

Richard ground to a halt beside him and asked, "What?"

The emotion in Dad's voice made Brady stop and stare at him.

Ryan looked at him intently before responding, "Where're we going for lunch? I am starving."

Brady pictured soggy vegetables from the cafeteria and then bumpy raw ones from the vegan restaurant Michael liked. "There's a McDonald's just across the street," she suggested, smiling in what she hoped was a winning way.

The three men stared at her for a heartbeat. "I'm thinking that little Italian place," Ryan said.

Brady jumped in place and watched them smile. "Yes, I want that cheesy macaroni thing. That was so good last time."

"It's walking distance," Michael commented.

Brady remembered he hated parking the car so would walk long distances to avoid moving it. She found it hard to keep up with three men.

"And risk being late for the judge's decision?" Ryan shook his head. They piled into Ryan's car and squealed out of the garage, around the corner, up seven blocks, and into the restaurant parking lot. The restaurant was tiny, with ten tables mostly set for two. They settled in the front at the only table big enough for four. Brady looked in the direction of the bathroom, and there were her grandparents. She sighed and sat down, wishing she had gone to the bathroom before she left the courthouse. This was so weird. They had been like parents to her, and now she felt awkward talking to them.

From behind the menu she listened to Ryan say, "The fact that Nordland found you but didn't have you sign the papers ending your parental rights makes him look dishonest—like he's trying to get an adoption without going through the courts. That has to rankle the judge. Did you notice how she looked at Nordland when the story came out? Total score for us."

Brady looked up at Ryan. He was talking about her grandparents like they were thieves. It sounded mean. She felt her back stiffen. "They're right there," she whispered through gritted teeth, nodding her head at her grandparents.

Brady watched Ryan look at the elderly couple and touch his mouth and frown before looking down at his menu.

The tension made Brady thirsty. She drank an entire goblet of water, and since it was instantly refilled by the busboy, she took another sip. She was aware of mounting pressure in her bladder and looked at the sign for the restrooms that was directly above her grandparents' heads. She pictured herself trying to make conversation with them and chose to stay put. By the time the salad arrived that Michael insisted she share with him, she was holding onto the arms of her chair to ease the pressure. She shoveled a large leaf of Parmesan-encrusted romaine into her mouth.

"Cut the lettuce up before you eat it. You're going to choke yourself," Michael said.

"Sorry," Brady said, while simultaneously squeezing her knees together. She jiggled in her chair, sending a seismic wave across the table.

"Do you have to go to the bathroom?" Dad asked.

She nodded.

"Then go," he said, pointing at the sign.

She threw both her fork and napkin into the salad, pushed back her chair, and sped toward the welcoming sign. Passing her grandparents' table turned out not to be a problem, since she was sprinting.

She burst through the bathroom door and into the stall, ramming the latch through. A split second later the relief made her smile.

She sighed noisily as she washed her hands with the lavender-scented soap and considered her options. It wasn't that she didn't want to talk to her grandparents. She did, desperately. She just didn't know what to say. What should she say? *It's not that I don't like you. I just want to live with my dad.* That was it. It wasn't that there was anything wrong with them. What kid doesn't want to live with her own dad? Why did this have to be so hard?

When she returned to the noisy restaurant, her grandparents' table was empty. She saw them walking to the exit and ran after them. They were almost to the door and in a minute would be gone. She reached out to close the space and touched Grandpa's elbow.

"Brady?" he asked, turning toward her.

"I'm sorry, it's just . . . I wanted to talk to you," Brady said.

Her grandparents looked at her two fathers in the corner, who had continued to talk and eat.

"Go ahead," Grandpa said.

"I don't hate you," Brady said.

"That's good to hear, after all that's been said," Grandpa said, and Grandma smiled. Still Brady could see tears in her eyes.

Brady continued, "There's nothing wrong with you. I love you. I just need to live with my dad." Brady felt silly and trailed off.

"Do you really feel safe in that . . . in your father's house?" Grandpa asked, and Brady recognized his serious expression.

"Yes, I do," Brady said, nodding.

"I don't know," he continued, shaking his head. "They did have a fight, and they—Michael—made you leave." His face hardened.

"But it wasn't the way that lawyer guy made it sound. I mean, there was that one time, and we did move out, but it's been great ever since. Really great."

Grandpa tilted his head and looked away, but then he said, "I watched them take you out of the court when you needed to get away. It says something that they were watching you that carefully."

"They're like that, Grandpa, careful," Brady said.

Grandma interrupted, "I couldn't bear it if something happened to you. We love you so much."

Brady raised her arms and hugged her, saying, "And I love you. But I'm okay." Brady pointed at her father and Michael. "Maybe it's their turn to be with me. I think they need me. We are a family because we want to be," she said, shrugging.

Grandma said, "You've changed since you've been with them." She stroked Brady's hair and studied her face. "You're tan, and your hair is shiny. You look healthy, but there's something else." Grandma looked away. "I've watched you handle things that would scare most adults. You've gotten brave." Her voice broke, and she pressed her fingers against her mouth. "You used to be afraid of things, shy. I always thought it was because of your mother's death—thought you'd grow out of it, but you didn't." Grandma gestured at Richard and Michael. "You got better with them."

Grandpa added, "You seem happier."

Brady wanted to speak, but her throat was clogged. She nodded deeply.

The three stood without speaking. Finally Grandma cleared her throat, and Brady noticed her eyes were shiny. "I never thought I'd say this, but you probably do belong with them."

"Can you tell the judge that?" Brady asked. But Grandpa interrupted.

"It's not up to us." He gave Grandma an angry look. "We have to see what the judge says." And he guided Grandma out of the restaurant. "Bye, Sweetheart." He kissed her on the tip of her nose the way she remembered him doing.

Brady turned back to her table.

"Feel better?" Richard asked, pushing back her chair.

Brady looked at the four-cheese ravioli and realized she had no appetite.

"Not hungry?" Michael asked.

Brady shook her head. "I was hungry when I ordered. I'm not now. Can we get it to go?" Brady said.

"And let it sit in the hot car all afternoon?" Michael asked. "You'll wind up with food poisoning. Just let it go."

"I'll carry it with me," Brady insisted.

Time was running out, and no one wanted to be late for the judge's ruling. It took time to flag the waiter, time to pack the food, time to get and pay the bill, and all of this led to a frantic, tension-filled ride back to the parking lot and into the courthouse. For this reason there was no time for Brady to tell them about her conversation with her grandparents. To top it off, they were in the elevator when Brady realized she'd left the food in the car.

Michael closed his eyes and leaned his head back with the resignation of a condemned man. "Just forget it. Oh God, it's going to stink up Ryan's car. Goddamnit, Brady, I told you not to forget it. I knew this was going to happen." He raised his hands in frustration over his head just as the doors of the elevator opened and the judge walked by. Michael's hands dropped so rapidly and the look on his face was so guilty that the judge actually stopped and looked at him curiously.

Brady wanted to say, "We're okay," but she stopped herself.

He covered his mouth and then reached out and touched her shoulder, whispering, "I'm sorry, Brady, it really doesn't matter."

THE JUDGE'S DECISION

As Brady came before the judge, she stood and looked up at her, a woman who was as short as her teacher and could have been anybody's mom, except for the black robe with the lace collar. Judge Robinson was settling into her seat, arranging her notes, and talking to the bailiff. On Brady's right sat Mr. Cory with her grandparents, and to her left Ryan sat with Richard and Michael. All of the adults were talking to each other, and no one seemed to notice that she was there. The bailiff called them to order, and everyone stood.

Brady stared at Judge Robinson for a sign, a smile, or eye contact, something to show what she had decided. Judge Robinson began, "These matters are emotional, and using the law to outline my decision will be helpful in minimizing some of that emotion. The most basic question is, who is operating in the best interests of the child? The grandparents who stepped in when their daughter died and the father could not be found, or the father who has been raising her for the last three months? The grandparents"—Judge Robinson gestured at Frank and Kathleen—"became the primary caregivers of their granddaughter. This period lasted five years. They reached the father and could have adopted the child, which would have ended any question of custody for the child, but they did not."

Brady looked sideways at Grandma and Grandpa, who stared at the judge.

"It is unclear, however, whether the father would have had appropriate mental competency to make a decision about the daughter he never met."

Grandpa nodded.

Judge Robinson continued, "We do not feel that the father showed himself as being unwilling or unable to provide for the needs of the child because he was never asked. Therefore the pre-sumption holds that since he is her father, he is working in the best interests of Brady."

Brady looked at Dad, arms tight across his chest, as he sighed and smiled.

Judge Robinson continued without response. "However, the grandparents have functioned as the parents of Brady, providing tuition and housing and attending piano and play recitals as well as church with her, and these experiences far outweigh the time she has lived with her father.

"The grandparents claim that granting full custody of the child to the father would be detrimental to Brady because she would suf-fer the loss of being in their family and they would lose her."

No they don't, Brady thought.,

Judge Robinson continued, "They also claim that Richard is not a good risk for complying with a custody agreement between the two states because he has already kept her from flying back to Oregon, but he says that he was not denying contact but protecting Brady from harassment from classmates in Oregon. The fact that Brady was able to confide in her father and not her grandparents about her problems at school is evidence that the father is func-tioning more effectively as the parent. Richard's move to intervene and protect Brady supersedes compliance with the court order, which was issued in ignorance of the harassment issue. Keeping her in California did not disrupt her life because she was able to continue at school there."

Ryan squeezed his fists in front of him in a tiny display of victory.

"There is evidence that Richard was not working in the best interests of Brady when there were admitted indiscretions to which Brady could have been exposed. Also there are conflicts between Brady's faith and her fathers' lifestyle, and these factors could show that Richard is not working in the best interests of Brady."

All of the faces turned and looked at the judge. The room was silent.

"The question then becomes, is granting custody of the child to the grandparents in the best interests of the child? Since most of the evidence shows the grandparents have effectively functioned as Brady's parents for the last five years, it is sufficient to conclude that granting custody to the grandparents is in the child's best interests."

Dad leaned forward as though translating Judge Robinson's words.

"Because an important bond has been formed between father and child over a significantly less amount of time than she has had with her grandparents, I suggest that a visitation schedule be worked out. The fact that neither of the parties involved recognized the importance of one another in the child's life indicates a certain myopia that may need to be addressed at a later date. So with the power vested in me by the state of Oregon, I grant custody of the child, Brady Lawson, to her grandparents, with visitation rights by her father."

There was a pause as everyone in the room thought through Judge Robinson's words.

Brady spoke first. "What did she say? Where am I going?" she asked Dad.

"You're going to your grandparents," he said.

"And you're visiting us," Michael added.

"What? No." Brady whipped her head to look at her grandparents. They looked the way she felt—openmouthed and shocked.

Only Mr. Cory looked jubilant. He held his hand high for a big high-five, but the Nordlands just stared at him. Mr. Cory lowered his hand to the back of his head and smoothed his hair as though that had been his intention all along.

Ryan sat back in his seat. He turned to Dad first. "I'm sorry. I thought I had it nailed. But you started out wanting a visit, and you got it. It's a start. We can try again." Dad stared at him.

"You will come and visit—regularly," Michael said, smoothing Brady's hair and offering her his handkerchief.

Her grandparents walked over to her.

"I don't want this." The words appeared in Brady's mind before they catapulted out of her mouth. "Can't you see? Look at us; everyone is sad. Please, you can't do this."

But Judge Robinson was gone.

Her grandparents walked to her side, and Grandpa took her hand. "We'll work it out," he said. Brady looked up at him and noticed that his face was flushed and his voice was hard to hear.

Brady looked around him to Grandma, who said, "We need to go now, Brady."

"Is this what you want?" Brady asked her.

"Let's go." Grandpa began to move and held her hand while keeping one hand on her shoulder.

She moved with the group out of the court and to the parking lot. Her eyes blurred with tears, and she wiped them off on her sleeve. She could see Michael's Acura across from Grandpa's truck, and for a minute she stood between them, unable to move. She felt the pressure of Grandpa's hand on her shoulder increase. "All right, I'm coming." She just needed a moment to sort out the anger, frustration, and sadness of it all. That was when she heard Grandma call out.

"Help, somebody, help!"

Brady felt herself shoved aside. She looked down to see Grandpa lying on the ground. His face was red and squished up like he was crying. His hands clutched at his throat, and his body jerked all of the way down his legs. Brady covered her mouth and cried. Someone walked her to the curb and sat her down. She watched the backs of a thicket of people and spied Grandpa's shoe lying on its side, only partly untied. It looked abandoned. She remembered talking to him while he polished his shoes with such care, the smell of the polish and the pleasure of making the dirty leather shine. She rushed to get it and brought it back with her to the curb. She sat with Grandpa's shoe in her lap, running her fingers over the worn places where his toes had pressed from the inside. She stroked it as though soothing it, and somehow this made her feel better. The ambulance pulled in with lights and sirens at full blast. The noise jarred her, and she pulled her shoulders up. She squeezed the shoe tightly and prayed, "Help!"

HEALING

When Frank came to, he thought he was caught in a whiteout. He thought he might have gone to glory until the beep of a heart monitor brought him back to earth. Gradually he realized the white came from walls and the ceiling. He groaned and tried to move his body in the bed, but there were so many wires taped to him and so many tubes running through him that he gave up.

"Frank, welcome back," he heard Kathleen say to his right, and he tried to open his eyes and focus but fell back asleep. The next time he opened his eyes, they focused on Richard at the end of the bed.

"Hey." He waved at Frank and smiled.

Frank had paragraphs of thoughts forming, but words were hard to find. When they came, they weren't what he meant to say. "Guess you win," Frank seemed to snicker. He was embarrassed.

Richard's smile fell into a frown.

"Aren't you going to take her?" Frank asked hoarsely.

Richard shrugged. "No, actually, we're all working pretty hard to bring you back into our lives." He raised his eyebrows.

There was a movement at the window to Frank's left. Brady and Kathleen were holding a sign that read, "Grandpa, Get Well," in a rainbow of large letters. Brady blew him a kiss.

Frank smiled and winced at the feel of the tape catching.

Kathleen rushed to his side and kissed him on the cheek, taking care to avoid the tube taped into his nose. "Brady can't come in because of fear of contagion. We have been staying at the ranch and driving in every day to visit you. It's fun to have company." She leaned in again. "Really, Frank, I wouldn't have wanted to go through this alone. Do you want anything?" Frank was exhausted by the exuberance with which his otherwise taciturn wife was speaking. He asked for water, and she rushed out to see if that was possible.

Frank looked at Richard. "Are you going to use this to take her from me?" he said, his voice stronger this time.

"No, right now she wouldn't go with me if I could take her. She loves you, and you are all she's thinking about. Kathleen needs her—all of us."

Frank felt chastened. He could hear Brady in the hall talking with great excitement. He looked out of the window and noticed she was talking to Michael. Life had moved on in spite of him. How could he consider himself anymore fit to parent than Richard and Michael? How many years would Frank be alive? How did he want to spend them?

"I was wrong about you," Frank said. Richard started to cut him off, but Frank forced his voice louder and then coughed. "Let me speak. I thought you were still that dumb punk who took up with Brenda. Calling me must have been hard, and I'm sure I didn't make it any easier."

Richard shook his head. "No, you did not make it any easier."

Frank waited to summon the energy to reach out his hand before he said,. "Okay, let's try this again. Hi, I'm Frank, I'm an alcoholic."

"Ho-ly shit!" Richard blurted out and then covered his mouth. "Sorry."

Frank nodded. "I have been sober thirty-eight years now."

AFTERCARE

"Okay, people, we wanted to be on the road by now in order to beat the lines."

Brady heard the testiness in Michael's voice and took one last look at her Alivia Simone floral sundress with matching sandals before tearing herself away from the mirror and pounding down the stairs. She looked down at Michael sitting on his couch with *The New York Times* abandoned on his lap. He was fingering his watch.

Cyrano the Dachshund, as he had come to be known, stood at the top of the stairs and barked. It was the dog's pattern to follow Brady everywhere, including up the stairs. Unfortunately, since most of his weight was behind him, the trip down put him at risk for falling, slinky-like, butt over head. Brady ran up to get him. With Cyrano secured like a football, she shot back down the stairs and then set him down next to the couch.

"Poor Michael," she commented, "when are people going to appreciate your punctuality?"

Michael shook his head wryly. "I know what you mean. Even your grandparents can't follow a schedule." He glanced at the clock. "They were supposed to be here—" The doorbell rang.

"Right now," Brady said, sprinting for the door with Cyrano following.

Brady flung open the door with such force that it hit the wall. She winced at the sound and then again when she caught sight of Grandma and Grandpa.

Grandma wore a yellow-and-pink floral sundress, and Grandpa had on . . . shorts? Colored tangerine?

"Grandpa!" Brady said. "Nice shorts." She shook her head in amazement.

They took turns hugging Brady, who asked. "Did you sleep well?"

"Yes, once we figured out how the crazy shower worked. Why can't they make them all the same?" Grandpa asked.

"You know, I've thought that too," Brady said.

Her grandmother whispered, "I have never seen your grandfather pay so much attention to his clothes before. I think California is affecting his brain."

Brady shot a look at her glad-to-be-alive Grandpa. His soft white Ralph Lauren polo shirt worked with the tangerine shorts . . . until you got to the socks. The socks were white cotton, and he had them pulled up to mid-calf and stuffed his feet into black leather gym shoes.

"Where did you get those socks?" Michael asked.

Brady could see he was struggling not to laugh.

"Costco, I have whole bag of them. Want some?"

"I'm good, but thanks," Michael said.

"Brady, go get your dad so we can get this show on the road," Grandpa said. He ran his finger along a schedule. "We're going to miss the breakfast with Minnie and Mickey." Brady giggled and started up the stairs, dog on her heels.

"Who is this character breakfast for anyway?" Brady turned and asked. "You all seem very excited about it."

"Oh, it's totally for us," Dad said, coming down the stairs. "You're our designated child, which allows us many liberties, of which the character breakfast is just one. Don't forget eating large tubs of overpriced popcorn at movies. Today, I plan on eating cotton candy with impunity."

"Who's impunity?" Brady asked, smiling, and she added, "Pink or blue?"

"Haven't decided, maybe both—yeah, it'll form a purple blend of ambiguous sexual orientation in my gut. Seriously, can't wait." Richard smiled.

"Stop talking and get in the car," Michael said.

Grandpa pulled out a tour book of Disneyland, a map, and what appeared to be an itinerary.

Michael squinted at it.

"I hope you don't mind. I didn't want to miss anything, so I've drawn up a schedule so that we'll be in a good place for the parade and still be able to see the World of Color light show," Grandpa said.

"Excellent planning," Michael said. "Richard, you don't mind sitting in the back with the women, right?" Michael gestured at Grandpa and said, "He can navigate."

"Absolutely not a problem," Dad said.

Brady knew he'd rather be in the back and unaware of Michael's aggressive driving.

Brady felt Dad's phone buzz in his pocket just as Michael's did. The two men exchanged glances and pulled their phones out. This surprised Brady; the family rule was family first—so no phones on family trips. Dad was smiling openmouthed at Michael, who was slow to return his gaze but smiling at his phone.

"You said that if it became legal, you would marry me," Dad said.

Brady held her breath. She knew the Supreme Court was going to decide on making it illegal to stop marriages for people like her dads. But here? When her grandparents were in the car?

"Hm," Grandpa snorted out of his nose.

Don't ruin this day, Brady prayed silently.

"You're raising his daughter. Might as well make an honest man of him," Grandpa said with a weird little smile. What had gotten into Grandpa?

Michael turned to face Dad between the front seats. "Richard, if you'll have me, I will absolutely marry you."

"I'm a witness," Grandma raised her hand.

"I can't believe this is happening this way. It's all so surreal,"

Dad said. "We're already two generations of a family, and now we're really legal."

Grandpa stared at Dad over the seat. "Well, what's the answer?"

"Yes, yes, yes, oh my God, yes." Dad thrust his head between the front seats and pulled Michael's face to his, planting a big, huge kiss on him. Right next to Grandpa and in front of Grandma.

Brady snapped her focus to the buildings far beyond the car window.

"Well," Grandma said, "you get to be a flower girl after all."

Brady felt her heart uptick and her eyes widen. "Oh yes, I already have the dress picked out. Oh yes!" And then, overwhelmed by her own life, Brady nestled safely between her grandmother and her father. She stroked Grandma's hand, which was soft, wrinkly, and smelled like soap. There was so much to look forward to!

DISCUSSION QUESTIONS

1. Is Richard being responsible or selfish when he decides to contact Brady? If he doesn't make amends for not being present in her life, especially at the time of her mother's death, isn't he still being a deadbeat dad? Or is he just assuaging his own guilt? She is okay with her grandparents and without him.

2. Is Richard using Michael and his acquired solvency to make himself appear more secure so he stands a better chance of gaining custody, or does he really love Michael?

3. The characters of Richard and Michael are sometimes unsympathetic. Richard is selfish and impulsive; Michael is inflexible. I wanted them to be flawed, authentic, and lovable, the way the people in my life are. I took great pains not to make them stereotypes. Were they sympathetic enough to carry the book?

4. The scenes of shopping and hair cutting were almost deleted because there was so little conflict in them. Ultimately I left them in because they showed that Richard and Michael knew

how to help Brady fit in, while her grandparents could not. Did those scenes add to the story or bog it down?

5. Was Brady trying to break Richard and Michael up when she told Michael she blamed him for Richard's being gay, or was she just being a naïve kid?

6. When Richard and Michael are fighting about whether or not it is a good time to contact Brady, Richard asks, "If not now, when? She's going to be a teenager soon and emotionally shut down." When would have been a better time to contact Brady? Did it have to be right when they had just moved in together?

7. In both California and Oregon, state law presumes that biological parents are always acting "in the best interests of the child." Who is the more meaningful parent to a child, the one who raised her or the biological parent?

8. Are the grandparents homophobic or just people of faith? If you are brought up in the church and taught that homosexuality is an abomination, is excluding gay people still bigotry?

9. The scene where Tom is in drag caused one friend not to write a blurb for my book. I put this scene in to show how lack of understanding can lead to prejudicial interpretation of the law. It almost destroyed this family. Did the scene in the basement go too far?

10. In a conversation between Richard and Brady's California principal, Richard uses a slew of racial slurs. Was this good to include for realism or does it keep damaging insults in circulation? Should or would Richard have used a euphemism instead?

11. The court mantra is to operate "in the best interests of the child." But children don't hire lawyers. I wanted to show how a custody case looks to a child. People tend to think joint cus-

tody is the best solution in the case of divorce—and for the parents, it is. The kid, however, just wants the family to stay intact. Brady loved all four of the people who were fighting each other for her, but it was painful for her too. Did this give you a different perspective on child custody battles?

12. The ending has been criticized for having "too much sunshine" or going the way of "and they lived happily ever after." I felt that my characters had suffered enough, particularly Brady, and I wanted her to be happy. Was the ending too sentimental? What would have been better?

ACKNOWLEDGEMENTS

To American Family's first book club holders, JoAnn Freda and Donna Emerson, we met during the Summer Institute 2006 of the Writing Project at San Jose State University under the leadership of Jonathan Lovell and Laura Brown. Without the Writing Project and your encouragement this book would not exist. Thank you.

To Lynne Formigli who ran next to me through all the ups and downs of rejections and revisions, and never let me give up, or slow down. Thank you.

To my sisters, Joyce and Frances, and sisters-in-law Charlotte and Ginny, and all my early readers who read cringe worthy rough drafts and never said, "Don't quit your day job."

Thank you.

ABOUT THE AUTHOR

Catherine Marshall-Smith teaches writing and history to 6th graders, runs long distance, is married to the love of her life, mother to three adult children, has two grand dogs and one dachshund with a very straight nose. In the process of writing *American Family*, she observed in Family Court, interviewed lawyers and a judge and read the Supreme Court ruling on grandparents' rights with a lawyer. She has her bachelor's degree in English from University of California at Berkeley and earned a Creative Writing Certificate from the Writing Program at UCLA where she was short listed for the James Kirkwood Award for Fiction 2012.

Author photo © Marc Bennington

SELECTED TITLES FROM SHE WRITES PRESS

She Writes Press is an independent publishing company
founded to serve women writers everywhere.
Visit us at www.shewritespress.com.

Appetite by Sheila Grinell. $16.95, 978-1-63152-022-8. When twenty-five-year-old Jenn Adler brings home a guru fiancé from Bangalore, her parents must come to grips with the impending marriage—and its effect on their own relationship.

Eden by Jeanne Blasberg. $16.95, 978-1-63152-188-1. As her children and grandchildren assemble for Fourth of July weekend at Eden, the Meister family's grand summer cottage on the Rhode Island shore, Becca decides it's time to introduce the daughter she gave up for adoption fifty years ago.

The Rooms Are Filled by Jessica Null Vealitzek. $16.95, 978-1-938314-58-2. The coming-of-age story of two outcasts—a nine-year-old boy who just lost his father, and a closeted young woman—brought together by circumstance.

Fire & Water by Betsy Graziani Fasbinder. $16.95, 978-1-938314-14-8. Kate Murphy has always played by the rules—but when she meets charismatic artist Jake Bloom, she's forced to navigate the treacherous territory of passionate love, friendship, and family devotion.

A Cup of Redemption by Carole Bumpus. $16.95, 978-1-938314-90-2. Three women, each with their own secrets and shames, seek to make peace with their pasts and carve out new identities for themselves.

Keep Her by Leora Krygier. $16.95, 978-1-63152-143-0. When a water main bursts in rain-starved Los Angeles, seventeen-year-old artist Maddie and filmmaker Aiden's worlds collide in a whirlpool of love and loss. Is it meant to be?